— Orchids —

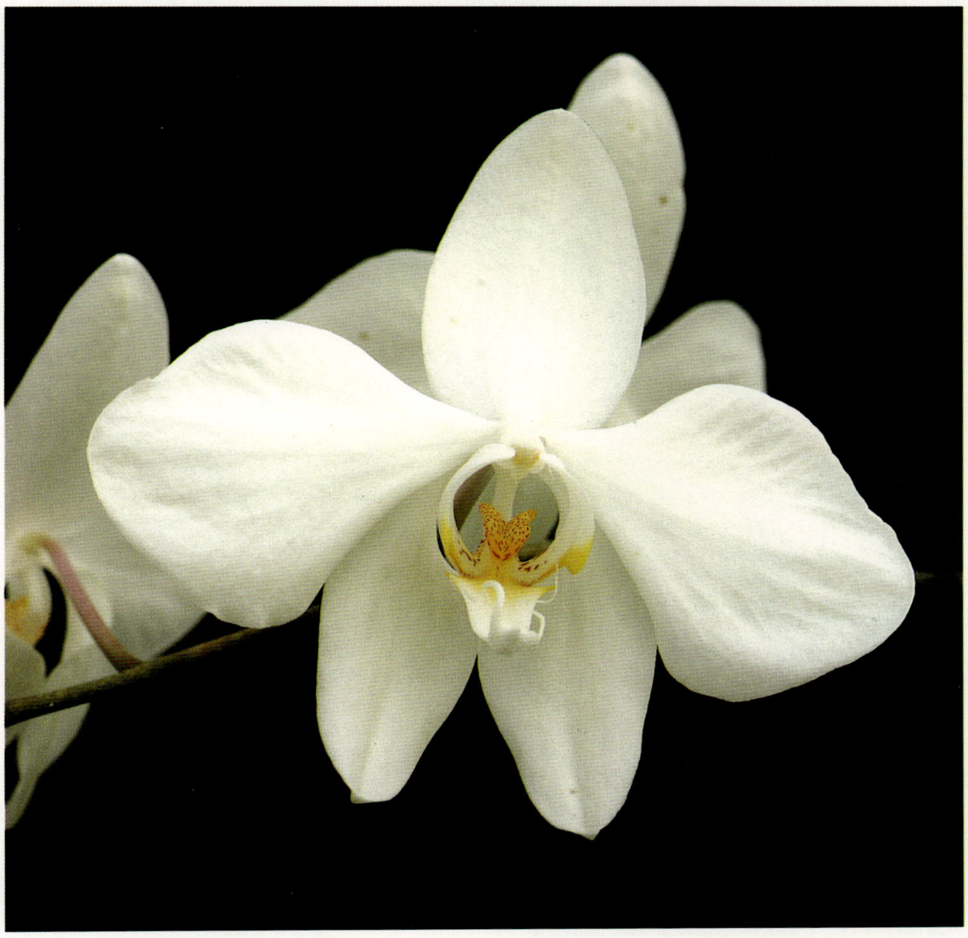

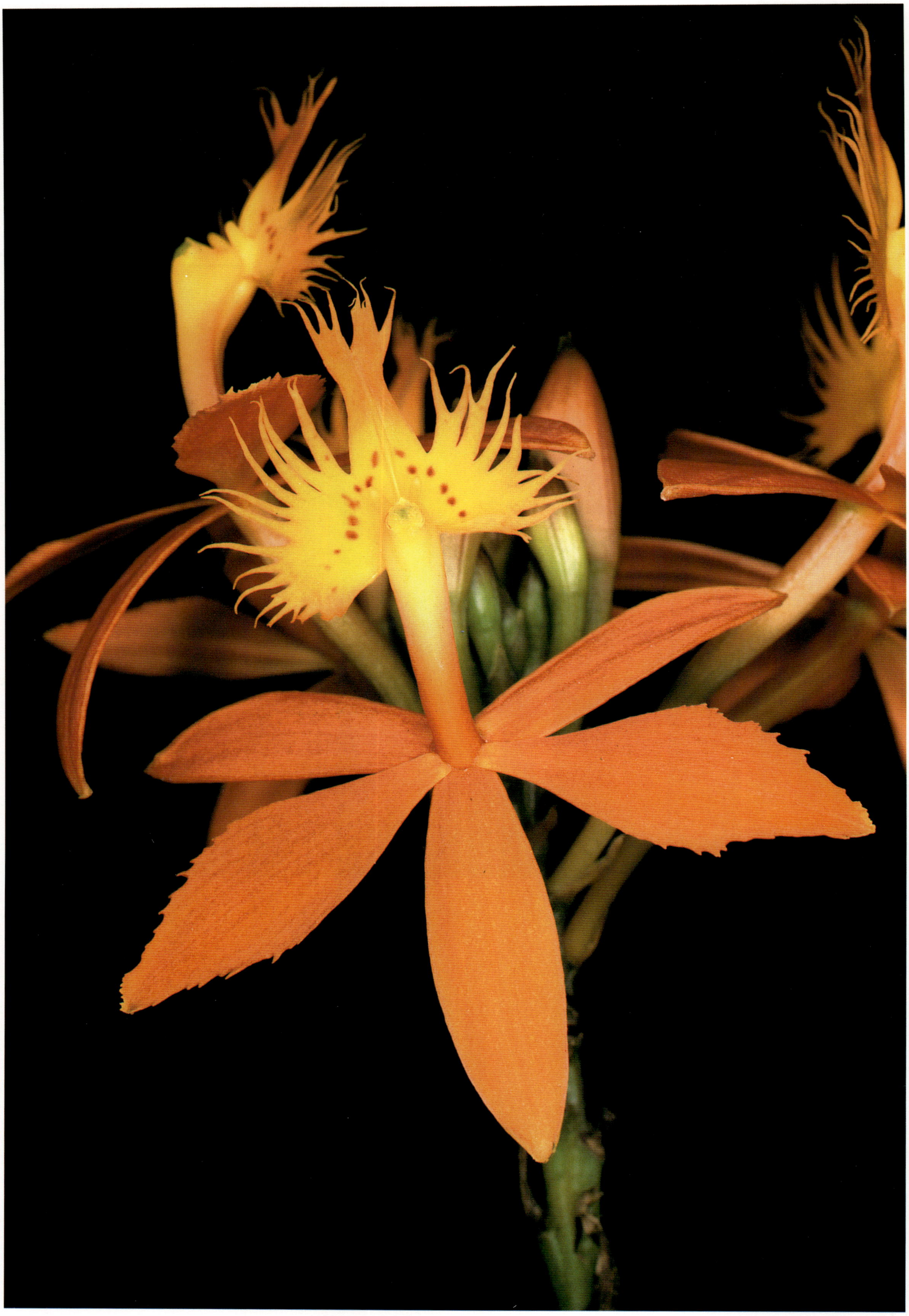

Orchids

– DAVID MENZIES –

MALLARD
PRESS

First published in the United States of America in 1991
by The Mallard Press
Mallard Press and its accompanying design and logo are
trademarks of BDD Promotional Book Company, Inc.

ISBN 0-7924-5508-8

Printed in Hong Kong

PAGE 1: *Phalaenopsis amabilis var papuana*

The classic white *Phalaenopsis* hybrids originated from wild forms such as this one, collected in Papua NewGuinea, but found also in tropical Queensland, Australia. A very similar variety occurs in Indonesia. *Phalaenopsis amabilis*, with its thick fleshy leaves, needs warm humid conditions, so it usually grows as an epiphyte in sheltered lowland areas. The large flowers are long lasting and are displayed on an arching inflorescence.

PAGE 2: *Epidendrum cinnabarinum*

Allied to the Central American species *Epidendrum radicans* but with much larger flowers which are presented with the lip uppermost, *Epidendrum cinnabarinum* is native to northern Brazil. The plants form dense clumps of leafy stems up to a meter (3 feet) or more in height, growing terrestrially in scrub. Each stem produces a tall inflorescence from its apex with the flowers opening in succession over a long period.

Contents

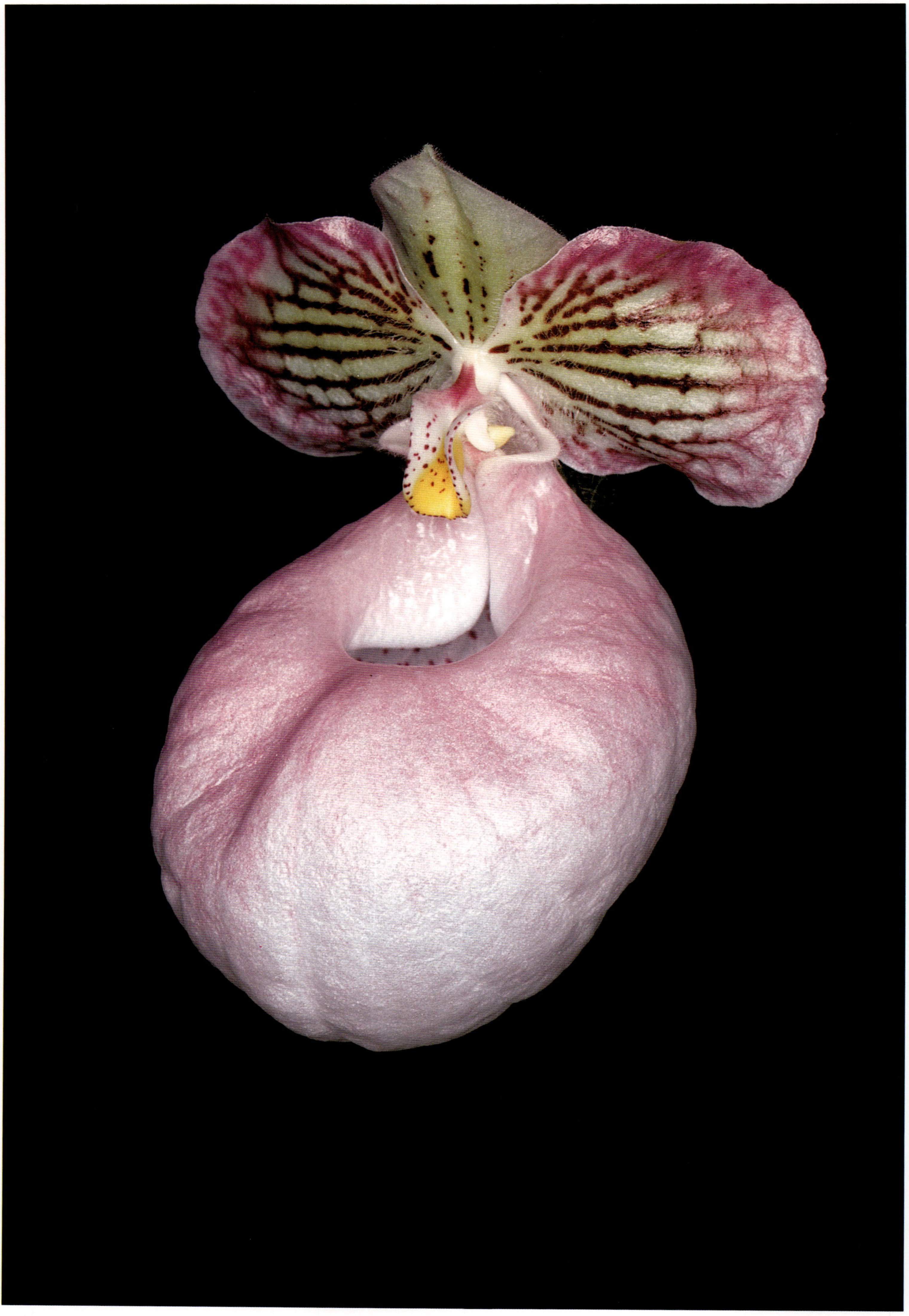

— 1 —
Introduction to the Orchid Family

Paphiopedilum micranthum

With its striking inflated labellum or lip, *Paphiopedilum micranthum* from south-east Yunnan in China, near the Vietnamese border, is differently proportioned from most other slipper orchids, but the basic structure is clear enough. The dorsal or upper sepal appears between the two striped and rounded petals, while the joined lower sepals are hidden behind the lip. In the center of the flower is the staminode and the other parts of the reproductive structure.

GEOGRAPHY Orchids are everywhere. They grow naturally in the north as far as Sweden, Greenland and northern Russia, and in the south to Tierra del Fuego at the tip of South America, New Zealand and Macquarie Island on the way to Antarctica. The only significant areas where they are not found, are the great deserts of the world. The orchid family is considered to be the largest group of flowering plants, with about 20,000 different species known. These are by no means evenly distributed, since temperate regions are poorly endowed compared to the tropics. The commonly held belief that orchids thrive in hot humid places is, however, very misleading, as the richest tropical areas are above 1000m (3300 feet) in the mountains, where rainfall is high and well-distributed through the year. Drier forests may have an abundance of plants, but these will represent a lesser variety of species.

In the absence of a fossil record, it is difficult to trace the evolution of the orchid family, but since each continent has its own distinct orchid flora, with few overlaps, it is assumed that rapid evolution took place after they had moved well apart. There are however, a few relatively primitive genera such as *Vanilla*, which are spread through the tropics, and this probably occurred at least 50 million years ago, when the continents were much closer together. Since that time, there have been many upheavals to plant life as climates have changed, and so migrations of both plants and their pollinators have taken place. This has led to many anomalies in distribution, and a typical one would be the close correlation between plant species, including trees and shrubs, of remote parts of China and Japan, and eastern North America. On a smaller scale, during the last million years, plants natural to the conifer forests of Northern Canada migrated southwards in advance of the ice sheets, but on their retreat, some remained high up on the Appalachian Mountains, well to the south.

Since most orchid seed is fine and dust-like, the normal means of dispersal is by air movement. In many cases, this means a distance of only a few meters, but on occasion, seed may successfully travel tens or even thousands of kilometers. The volcanic island of Krakatoa exploded in 1883, destroying all life on it, but within fifty years, 35 orchid species were found there. They must have arrived on winds blowing from other islands like Java, about 40km (25 miles) away. The North Island of New Zealand is around 2000km (1243 miles) from the east coast of Australia, but a number of Australian terrestrial orchids have been found as isolated examples in the far north of the country, where they may never establish and naturalize. It is assumed that their seeds came across on the prevailing winds which are very strong at times.

Paphiopedilum micranthum

A feature which distinguishes slipper orchids from almost all other orchids is the presence of two fertile anthers or pollen bearing structures on the flowers instead of one. They are seen here as pale yellow objects on either side of the central staminode. The stigma, to which the pollen is transferred for fertilization, is hidden behind. Pollinating insects escape from the slipper by pushing past the pollen, which is then fastened to their bodies, ready for the next flower.

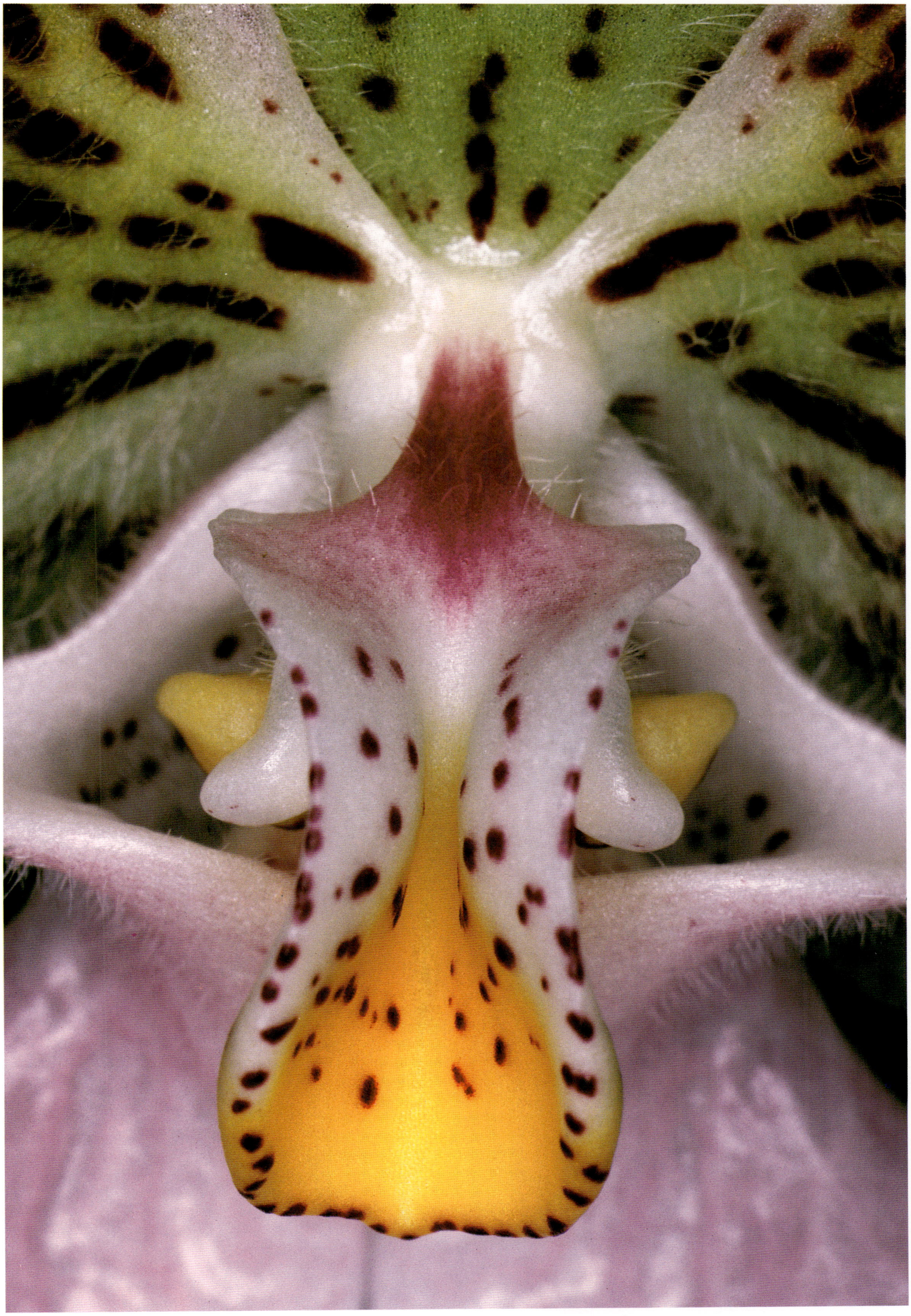

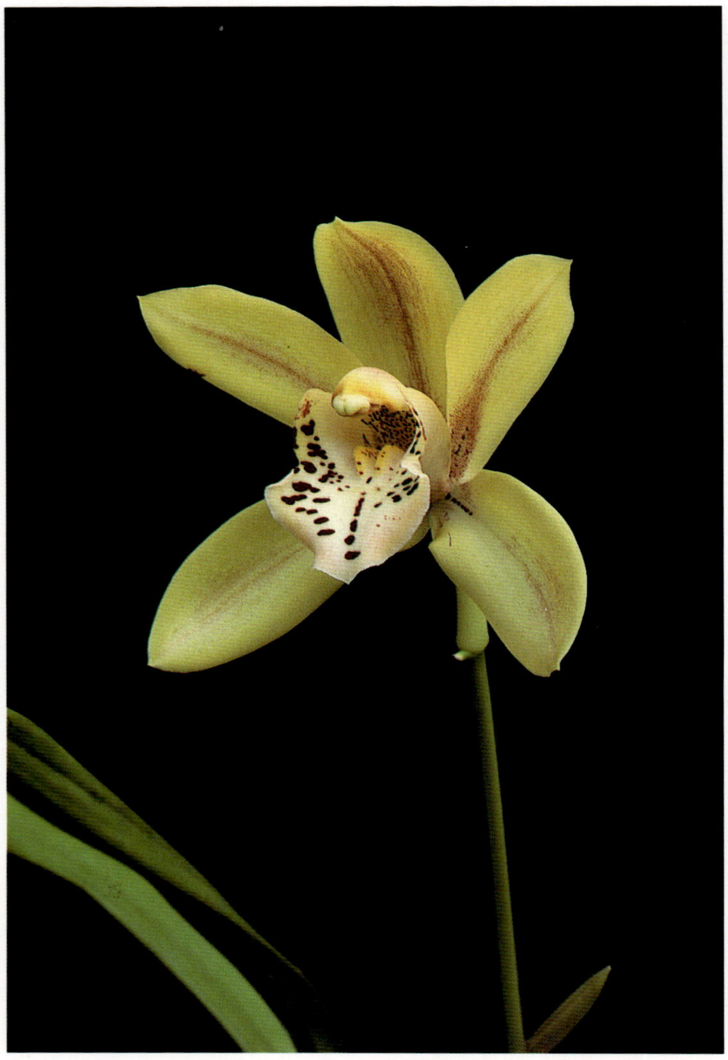

Cymbidium Tiger Meadow

The dorsal and two lateral sepals show clearly here on a typical orchid flower. It is these which form the covering parts in the bud stage. Between them are the two petals which in this case look very similar, and then in the center, the decorated lip with the column arching above it. Forming the upper part of the flower stem is the immature ovary which will swell to form a seed capsule after pollination.

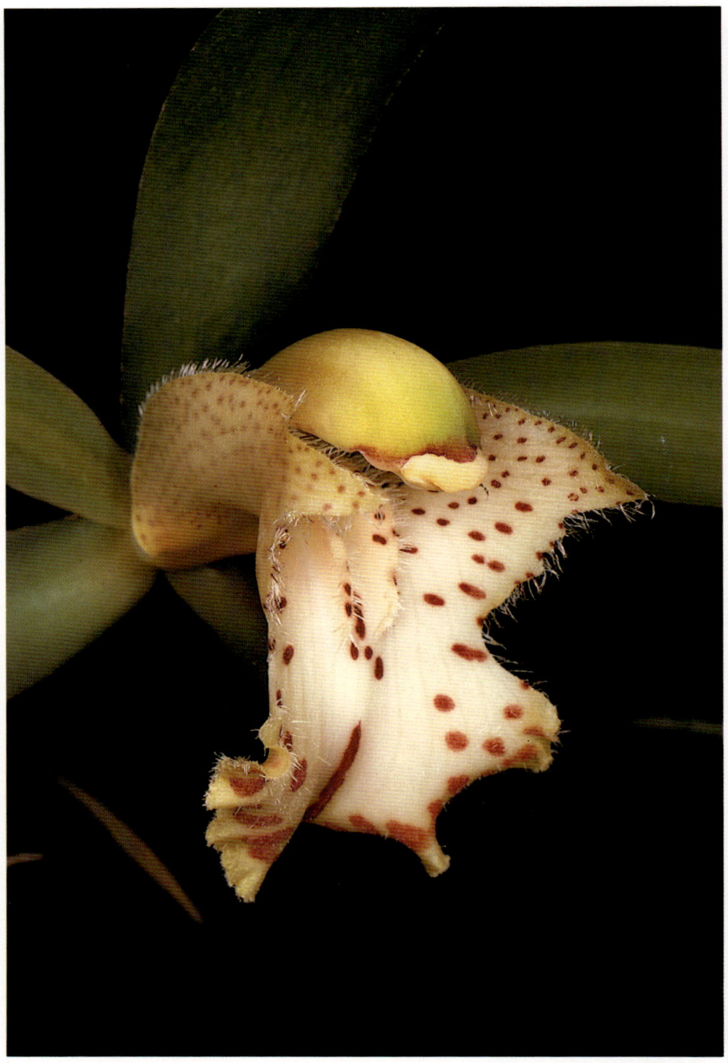

Cymbidium hookerianum

This closer view of the lip and column of *Cymbidium hookerianum*, native to North India and China, shows how the lip of many orchid flowers, through resupination, forms a landing platform for pollinating insects; in this case, large bees. At the column tip is the anther in which is found the two pollinia or pollen masses. The stigma is hidden further beneath.

The numbers of orchid species native to each region are by no means certain, but it is interesting to compare the figures which are available. In the whole of Europe there are about 150 species, and about the same number in North America north of Florida. Australasia, which includes Australia, New Zealand and numerous small tropical islands, has about 600, whereas the whole of Tropical Africa has over 3000. The richest areas however, are Tropical Asia, with nearly 7000, and Tropical America, including Central America, with over 8000 species.

STRUCTURE What makes a plant an orchid, and what are its nearest relatives? The orchid family is part of a great division of the plant kingdom known collectively as the monocotyledons, which also include the grasses, palms and all bulbous plants. Although orchids have certain features in common with lilies, they are much more specialized and therefore stand alone without close connections to other families. Flower parts of the monocotyledons generally occur in multiples of three, and orchids are no exception. A typical lily flower has three colored sepals and three petals of the same color, inside which are six stamens covered with yellow pollen, and a central sticky stigma. The stalk above the flower is also the ovary, which will contain the seeds after fertilization. The basic orchid flower has the same number of colored sepals and petals, but one of the petals is nearly always modified in shape to become the lip or labellum. The flower stalk is still the ovary, but the other reproductive parts in the center are, with a few exceptions, fused together into a single structure, the column, which usually has the pollen at its apex, and the sticky stigma as a shallow depression on the underside. Although these elements are present in all orchid flowers, they are sometimes obscured by being joined together or hidden

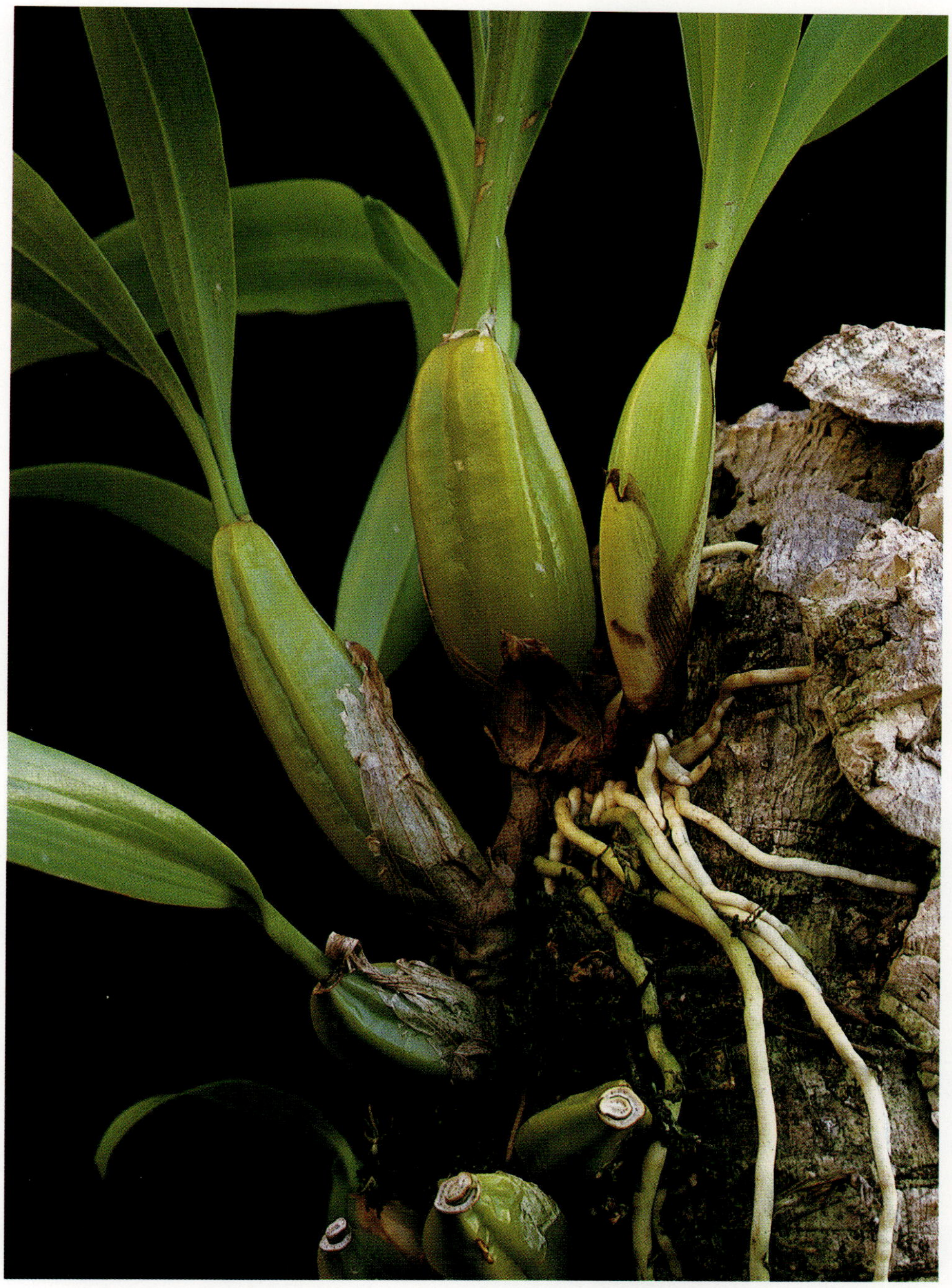

Coelogyne lentiginosa

A healthy plant of the Thai species, *Coelogyne lentiginosa*, established in cultivation on a piece of cork bark. It clearly shows the swollen pseudobulbs connected at the base by a tough rhizome, and the white spongy roots which are gripping the cork. Such a plant would initially be tied on to the cork with nylon fishing line and hung up in a humid glasshouse until the roots had grown.

by their small size. When looking at flowers it is important to remember that the plant produces them for a vital purpose, namely to attract pollinators, which in the case of orchids, are invariably animals of some kind. An obvious modification to aid pollination is the position of the lip in relation to the rest of the flower. In the bud stage it is uppermost, but in many cases, as the flower develops, it becomes lowermost to act as a landing platform. This is known as the resupinate position, and is reached by various means, including the twisting of the ovary through 180 degrees, and the bending forward of the flower.

Unlike plants such as grasses, which produce masses of powdery pollen grains, orchid pollen is present as discrete clumps or hard particles called pollinia, so that thousands of grains are transferred in a single operation. After pollination, when pollen is placed on a stigma, tubes grow down into the ovary so that fertilization can take place, and in due course, the ovary swells to form a seed capsule. After a few weeks, or up to a year later for some epiphytes, the capsule splits and the tiny seeds float out. It has been estimated that the capsule from a large tropical epiphyte could contain more than a million seeds, so it is as well that they do not all germinate.

Coelogyne species

A number of species which normally would grow as epiphytes, may establish as seedlings on suitable rock surfaces. This *Coelogyne* species in northern Thailand is successfully growing on a large boulder in the middle of a permanent stream. Even in the long dry season, there is running water nearby, and surrounding trees provide partial shade. The plant's pseudobulbs are obviously shrivelled, but the maturing seed capsules are healthy, and when ripe, the seed will be blown over quite an extensive area.

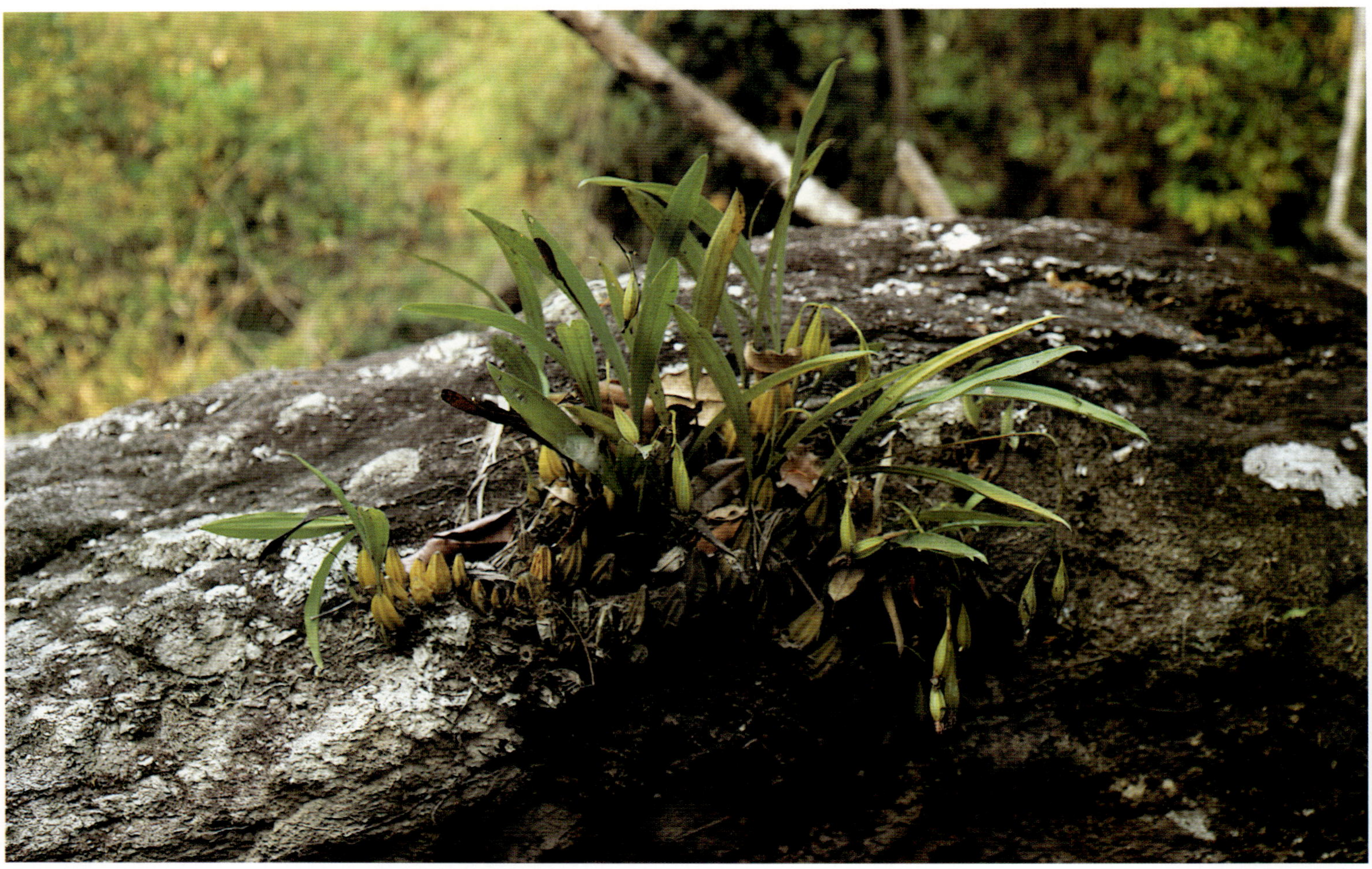

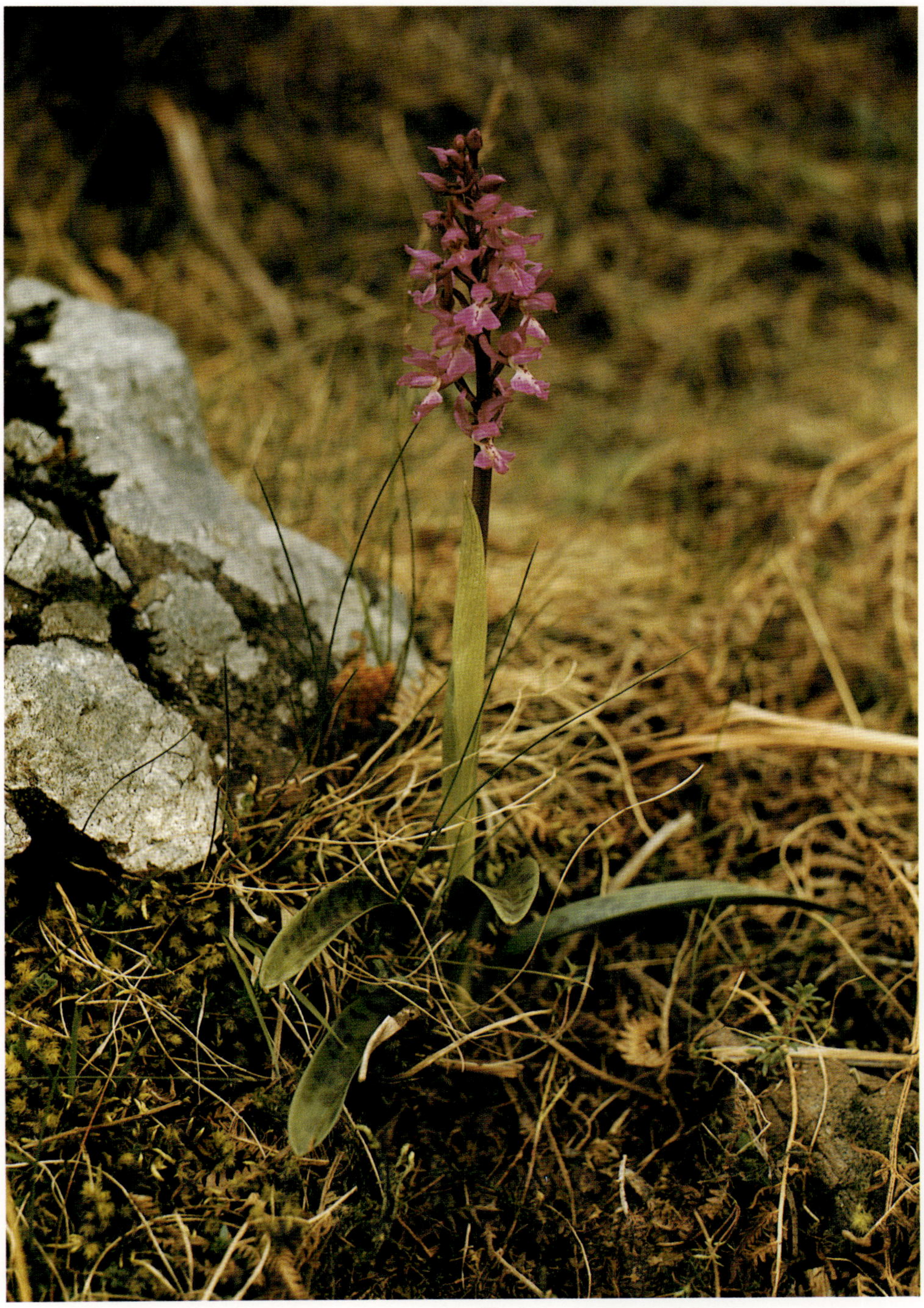

Orchis mascula

Orchis mascula, the Early Purple Orchid, growing and flowering on a Scottish hillside in early summer. The habitat here is typically thin rock-strewn soil covered with short grasses which will grow up after the orchid has set seed and died down. Other species, such as the marsh orchids, require more moisture to thrive and so would be found mostly in hollows or on level sites.

One of the attractions of orchids is their infinite variety of color, with only blue being uncommon, and true black non-existent. In terms of size, genera such as the African and Asian *Oberonia*, often has flowers a millimeter across, whereas *Cattleya warscewiczii* from Colombia may reach 20cm (8 inches) and the petals of the Asian *Paphiopedilum sanderianum* can be up to 90cm (35 inches) long. Except in the smallest plants, there is little correlation between flower and plant sizes. The giants of the family, like *Grammatophyllum speciosum* from Tropical Asia, which forms enormous clumps of fleshy stems up to 4m (13 feet) long, produces quite modest flowers only 10cm (4 inches) in diameter. Another very tall species is *Dendrobium discolor*, native to tropical

Australia and New Guinea, whose tough stems may measure up to 5m (16 feet), but are more slender. For sheer length, there are the climbing vanillas, which may be more than 20m (66 feet) long, and the Australian leafless straggler and climber, *Galeola foliata*, up to 15m (49 feet) tall, with a spectacular display of golden yellow flowers. At the other end of the scale, are a few of the tiny moss-like *Pleurothallis* and *Platystele* species from Tropical America, and some of the Australasian bulbophyllums like *Bulbophyllum globiferum* and *B.minutissimum* from Australia, and *B.pygmaeum* from New Zealand, which form mats only a few millimeters thick on tree trunks and branches.

Orchid plants follow two basic growth habits, of which the sympodial one is the more widespread and common. In this case, each shoot is of limited growth, often annual, to be followed by a similar shoot arising from a bud on the stem. Such plants tend to progress horizontally or to form clumps. Plants with a monopodial habit extend indefinitely from the shoot apex, growing taller over many years. Obvious features of many epiphytic orchid plants, are the swollen stems or pseudobulbs, which sustain them during dry periods. Pseudobulbs take many forms, and may be smooth plumlike objects, wrinkled or ridged, flattened or rounded, short or tall. They always have one or more leaves on top, and in some cases, at the base or at nodes in between, as in many dendrobiums. Terrestrial orchids use different storage organs in order to survive periods of dormancy. Some have corms, much as a *Gladiolus* does, while many temperate species have special tuberous structures which combine the functions of storage roots and stems, and which are renewed each year. Most orchid roots are covered by a spongy layer called velamen which protects them and is especially obvious in epiphytes where the growing tips are often green, or in some case, orange or purple.

Examination of orchid leaves gives clear information about natural growing conditions so that most terrestrials have relatively soft thin leaves which need shade, whereas many epiphyte leaves are thick and leathery to withstand much harder conditions, and may even be succulent or terete, that is, circular in cross-section, like a rat tail. Leaf color is usually shades of green as expected, but a number of species, collectively known as jewel orchids, have leaves beautifully veined in contrasting colors.

Inflorescences carrying anything from a single flower to hundreds, arise from various parts of the plant. The simplest come from the top or base of the stem, but others appear at nodes along its length or from the center of new shoots. In the case of monopodial orchids, they are always from the side of the stem, often between leaves. Not all inflorescences die off after flowering, as in some species, they may persist and produce flowers over several years.

POLLINATION In 1862, Charles Darwin published a book entitled *The Various Contrivances by which Orchids are Fertilised by Insects*, in which he recorded his detailed observations and conclusions for much of the orchid family. In so doing, he laid the foundation for our present understanding of the subject. Orchids are pollinated by animals, especially insects, but also birds, and the whole process depends on the principle of reward. The animal concerned must be expecting some benefit for it to repeatedly visit flowers of the same kind. About two thirds of orchid species secrete nectar, sometimes openly available, but in other cases concealed in long tubes or spurs. The other third relies on devices such as imitation pollen which is present on the lips of many species; color and shape; secretions of other useful substances such as waxes and resins; and of course odor, which covers a vast range in orchids and is not always apparent to us.

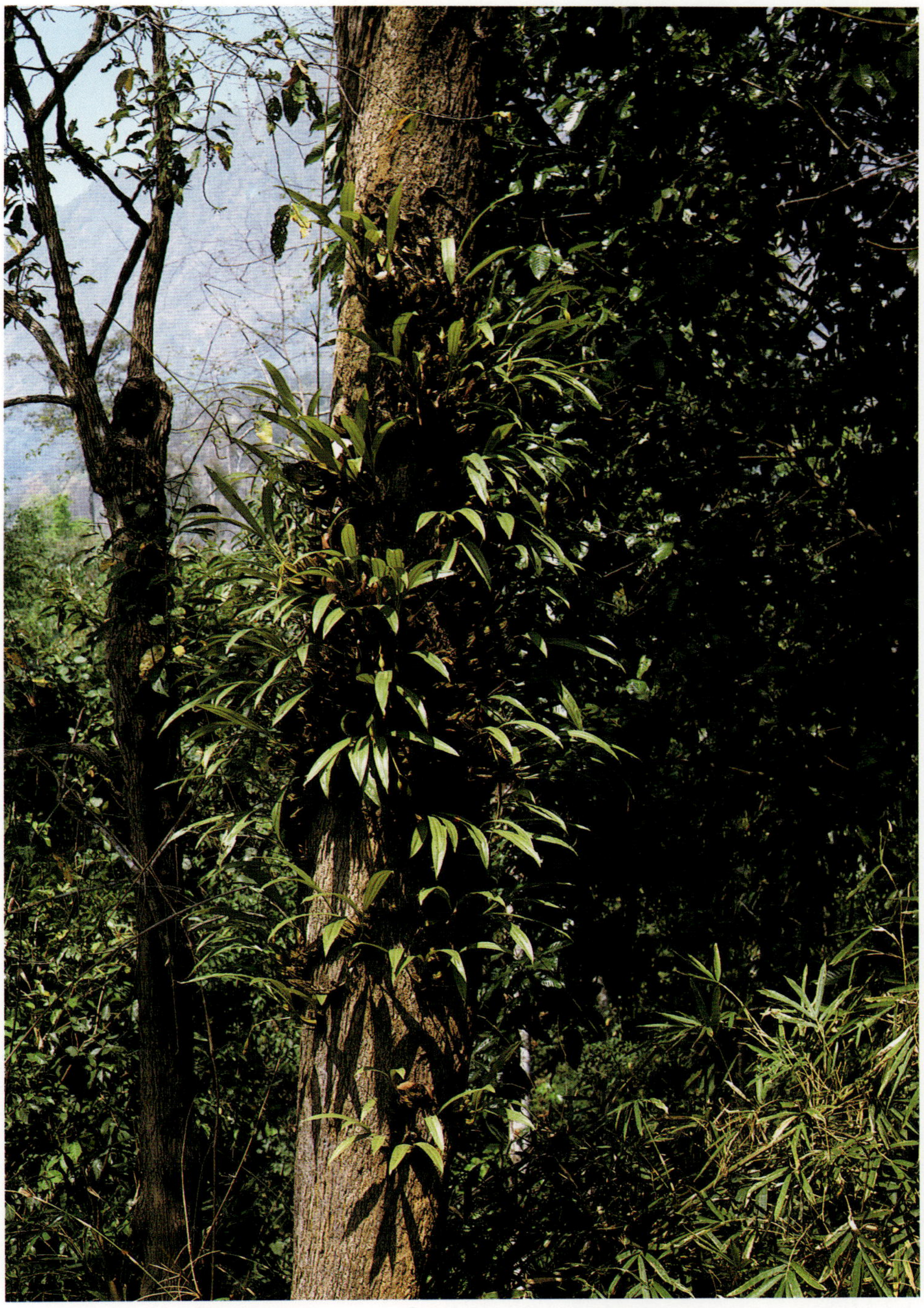

Coelogyne species

Another *Coelogyne* species established on the bare trunk of a roadside tree in northern Thailand. In this case, the dusty road winds over mountain foothills, where at night, the temperature falls sufficiently for dew to form, so providing moisture for the plants. In more favorable situations, a greater variety would be growing together in communities.

The animal having been attracted to the flower, it is vital that its subsequent behavior should not only result in the pollen being collected, but also that for the next flower visited, the pollen should be deposited on the stigma, and orchid flowers are particularly adapted for such precision. The different types of pollinators are simply divided into four: bees and wasps, moths and butterflies, flies and birds.

Bees have excellent senses of smell and taste, while their vision extends towards the blue end of the spectrum into the ultra-violet. Flowers which attract them are therefore brightly colored but not red, and pleasantly scented. They also have a prominent landing platform with nectar guides in the form of lines or ridges, which may be visible to bees but not to us. A number of mechanisms are involved in bee pollination, depending on the size and behavior patterns of the bees concerned. Commonly, the bee lands on the lip and then crawls between it and the column. In backing out, the pollen is stuck to its back so that on entering another flower of the same type, transfer to the stigma takes place. The most elaborate mechanisms involve the genera *Catasetum, Cycnoches, Stanhopea, Gongora* and *Coryanthes*. These all have strong fragrances which attract male bees only, and the flowers produce an intoxicating liquid when the insect scratches part of the lip. In the case of *Catasetum*, there are separate male flowers in which the pollen is under tension, so that when the bee moves into the flower, the tension is released, and the pollen fired on to the bee's legs where it sticks. Over several minutes, the pollen straightens out so as to be in the correct position for the next female flower.

Butterflies and moths are equipped to feed on nectar through a hollow proboscis or tongue, and so flowers attracting them have nectar in a long spur. Since butterflies are active during the day, and need a landing space, flowers using them have vivid colors including red, a horizontal part for landing, and if present, a pleasant scent. Moths on the other hand, fly at night, so that their flowers tend to be white or green and heavily night-scented.

The flies are very diverse group of insects, whose behavior is much more erratic than that of bees. Flowers using them have therefore to guide them in some devious way in order for pollination to be effective. Attraction may be by smell, either sweet or revolting; by color, usually dull; by various fine hairs and other appendages which move in the wind, and sometimes translucent windows which confuse the insects. Many fly-pollinated genera have balanced lips which move suddenly to throw the fly exactly on to the column, and examples are *Bulbophyllum* and *Pterostylis*.

Birds are attracted to bright colors like reds, yellows and oranges, but in addition, have little sense of smell. Flowers pollinated by them, both in Asia, and in Tropical America, provide plenty of nectar, and are tubular in construction so that the beak is thrust well in without damaging the flower.

The ultimate form of pollinator deception by orchids brings about the process of pseudocopulation. This occurs through the flowers resembling in shape and scent, the females of certain bees, wasps and flies, so that the males of the species think that they are on to a good thing and behave accordingly. Well known examples are the *Ophrys* of Europe, and *Cryptostylis* and *Drakaea* in Australia.

ECOLOGY Unlike the seeds which we eat, orchid seeds are mostly too tiny to contain food reserves, and so can germinate and develop only by forming an association with a fungus. This is termed a mycorrhiza, and is a common relationship for many plants. The fungus is present in the roots, and part of it is digested by the orchid to provide nutrients. While terrestrial orchids may

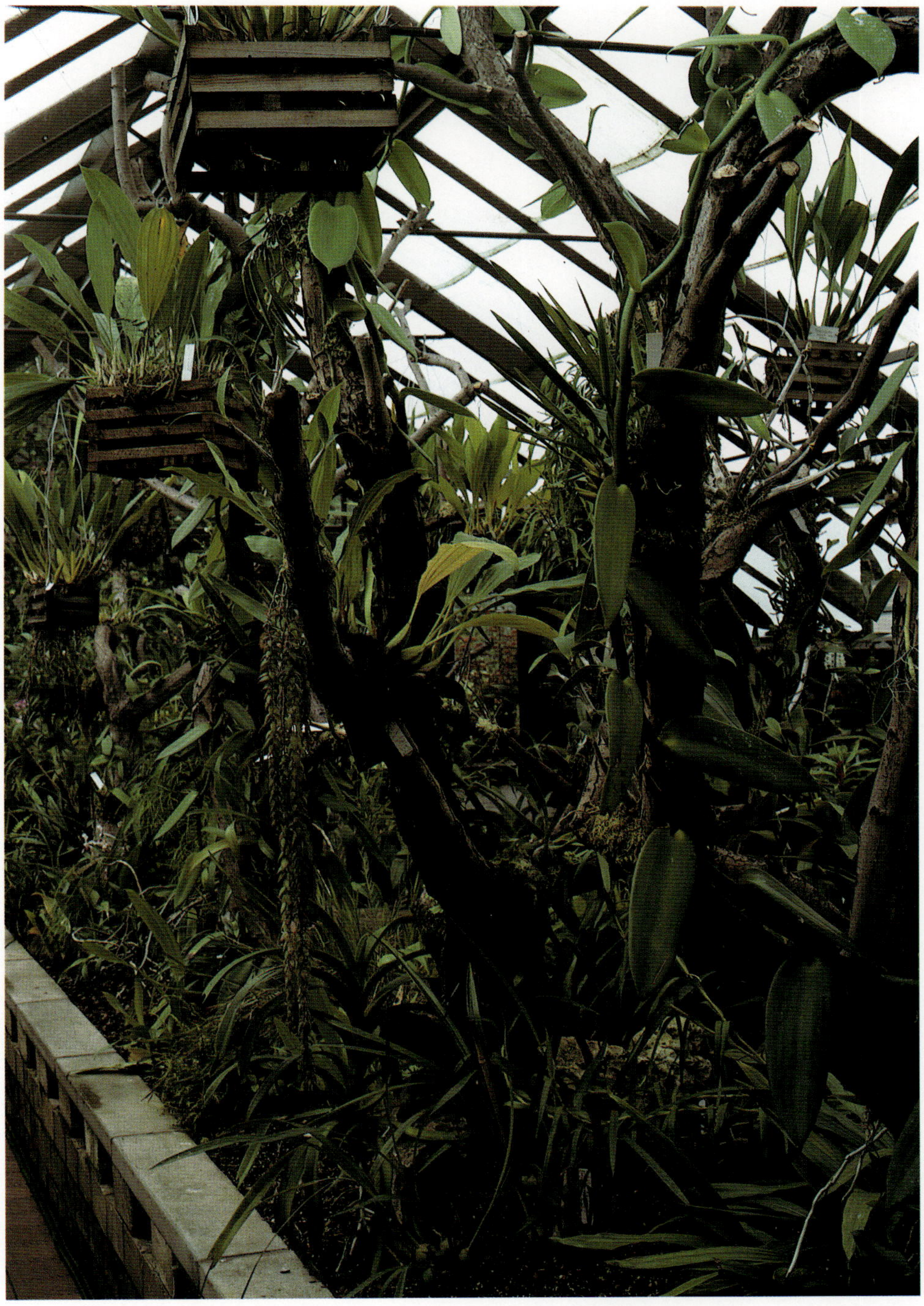

Glasgow Botanic Gardens

For the purposes of public exhibition and display, orchid plants need to be grown in a variety of ways. This is part of the orchid showhouse at Glasgow Botanic Gardens, and it clearly shows a raised bed containing many plants growing terrestrially, as well as tree trunks and branches on which are growing a wide range of epiphytes including a vanilla vine. Hanging from the roof in wooden baskets are epiphytes which naturally display their flowers in a pendent fashion.

remain dependent on the mycorrhiza all their lives, many epiphytes under favorable conditions grow very well without it. All plants need air, water nutrients, and in most cases, light, for healthy growth.

Orchids are slow growing and therefore have low nutritional needs so that they survive as terrestrials in poor soils, on rocks or rock crevices as lithophytes, and on trees and shrubs as epiphytes. A great many different plants, including ferns and mosses, grow epiphytically in the tropical and sub-tropical regions of the world, often as mixed communities. They have been sorted into three simply types; those which require a soil layer on the bark; those which prefer bare bark on trunks and branches; and twig epiphytes which grow mostly in the air on very small branches. Certain kinds of trees are much more suitable for epiphytes than others, so that even related tree species may prove inhospitable, probably through the presence of chemical substances in their bark. Within a single tree, conditions vary considerably, from the moister shady lower trunk, to the lighter large branches and the dry, light branches under the upper canopy. It is one of the paradoxes of epiphytic growth, that even in apparently wet forest, the plants high on the tree are subject to drought, and so need storage organs. It is only in higher altitude cloud forest that moisture is constant, and so many small epiphytes can thrive there without pseudobulbs. In such habitats, there is also less distinction between epiphyte and terrestrial since both may grow in wet mosses on trees or on the ground. Even the creation of road cuttings and limited forest clearance may encourage rapid colonization by some orchids. Unfortunately, their survival depends on reduced competition from other plants, and as soon as new trees and scrub grow up, the orchids will disappear.

A number of tropical orchids associate with ants, either growing in their nests, or providing homes for them. In both cases, the ants protect the plants from predators, including plant collectors, and bring nutrients. Two tropical American genera, *Caularthron* and *Myrmecophila*, go so far as to have hollow pseudobulbs, with an opening in the base so that ants are encouraged to enter. Another adaptation to increase food supplies, is the collection of forest debris by special stiff vertical roots produced by a number of genera, including *Grammatophyllum, Ansellia, Cyrtopodium* and *Catasetum* species.

Plants without chlorophyll, and which therefore cannot manufacture their own food, are called saprophytes. Amongst the orchids are a number of species both temperate and tropical, which come into this category. They tend to spend most of their life below ground, sending up flower stems only when conditions are favorable. These stems are nearly always white or dull brown, but sometimes purple, so are difficult to see against surrounding vegetation. Saprophytic orchids depend entirely on their mycorrhizal fungi, which in turn feed on rotting vegetation including wood, but in some cases, living trees are attacked by the same fungi, thus making the orchids indirect parasites. Common examples of saprophytes include the European Bird's Nest Orchid, *Neottia nidus-avis, Limodorum abortivum* of the Mediterranean region, *Corallorhiza trifida* of Europe and North America, *Galeola* of Australia and Asia, and *Gastrodia* of Australasia. The ultimate orchid saprophytes must be the two Australian species which carry out their entire life-cycles underground. *Rhizanthella gardneri* was discovered accidentally by a Western Australian farmer in 1928, and has since been found a number of times, growing under bushes of *Melaleuca uncinata*. Its companion species, *Rhizanthella slateri*, comes from the other side of the continent, in New South Wales, where it grows in *Eucalyptus* forest. Both species grow as branching fleshy stems from which the flower heads rise almost to the surface.

When do orchids flower? This question is frequently asked of botanists and growers, and is rarely answered to the satisfaction of the enquirer. The truth is that they flower through the year, but at differing times depending on the season. Each species tends to flower at the same time even if over a month or more, so that pollinators can move between individuals. However, some species with short-lived flowers, such as the Asian *Dendrobium crumenatum*, are synchronized by a fall in temperature, so that all plants open their blooms on the same day. In South Africa and Australia, a number of orchids flower profusely after fires which occur naturally in these areas.

Glasgow Botanic Gardens

From looking at the previous illustration it would be reasonable to ask, 'But where are the flowers?' Unfortunately, most orchids usually flower only once a year, and never at the same time, so to provide color it is necessary to have plants in containers to be moved as they come into bloom. This is a late summer display in the same showhouse, and it involves both hybrids and species from many parts of the world, including cattleyas from South America, dendrobiums from Australia and phalaenopsis from Asia.

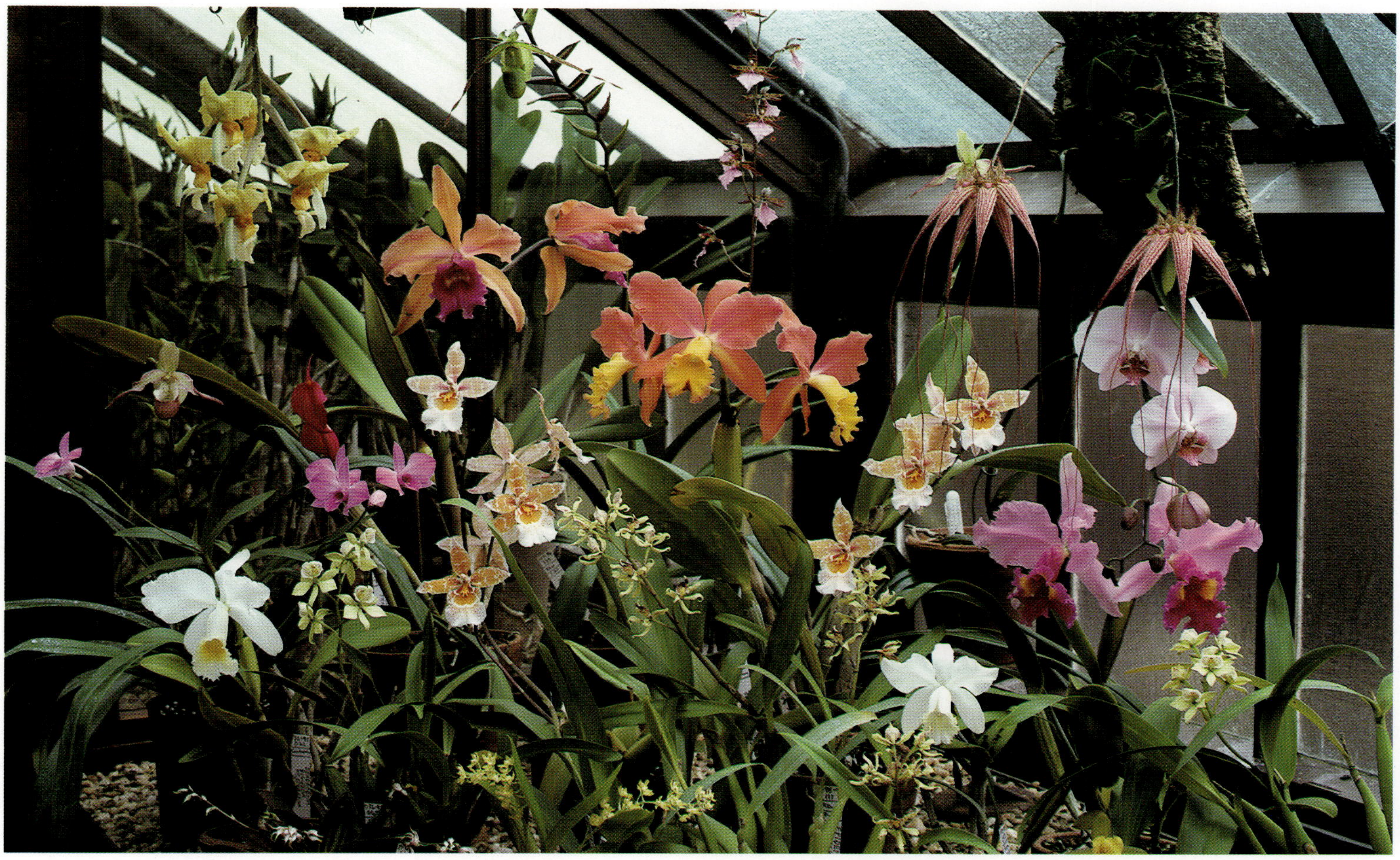

NAMES The naming of plants is intimately involved in their classification, and our present understanding goes back to the publication, in 1753, of *Species Plantarum* by the Swedish botanist Carl von Linné, better known by his academic name, Linnaeus. In his classification of all the plants then known, he promoted the binomial system, where each species has two names; the first, the generic name, always written with a capital, and the second, the species name. Since Latin was the language of scholarship, all names are written in a latinized form, and the original descriptions of species are all published in Latin. By this means, they are universally understood throughout the world, and today they are further standardized by two International Codes of Nomenclature covering wild and cultivated plants. A genus groups together species which have a number of features in common. In the orchid family, there are perhaps 750 genera in accepted use, each containing from one to more than a thousand species. Classification is always subject to opinion, but so long as these opinions are clearly set out and published for all to consider, there is room for differences.

Plant names are derived from many sources, but the main ones are references to prominent anatomical features, usually derived from Greek; figures from classical mythology; names based on geographical areas, and commemorative names. Thus the genera *Cypripedium* and *Paphiopedilum* come from Greek words meaning slipper of Venus, an obvious reference to the slipper-shaped lip; *Laelia* is probably named for one of the Vestal Virgins of that name, and *Cattleya* was named after the Englishman, William Cattley, an enthusiastic orchid grower of the early nineteenth century.

To most of those interested in plants, name changes give cause for annoyance but in many cases, they are a necessary part of stabilizing names for the future. Changes come about for a number of reasons. In the past, there was less communication between botanists of different nationalities, so that the same species might be given a number of different names. This also happened when a species has a wide distribution through several countries, and in both cases, it is the earliest published name which is the valid one. Sometimes, plants in cultivation were wrongly identified when they were introduced, and only later was the confusion resolved. For many large genera, species have in the past, been assigned to them for convenience but in the light of more recent understanding, it becomes necessary to separate groups into new genera, as has happened with *Dracula, Trisetella* and *Dryadella* being removed from *Masdevallia*.

The naming of orchid hybrids also follows an International Code, and is best explained by example. When two species of the same genus, such as *Cymbidium suave* and *Cymbidium devonianum* are crossed together, the resulting hybrid plants are given a grex or collective name, in this case, *Cymbidium* Sweet Devon. Sweet Devon is then the name used for any hybrids using the same two parents. Since orchid seedlings from the same cross may vary considerably, those which are selected for superior qualities, may be given a third cultivar name which is always written inside inverted commas. Thus a plant might be labelled, *Cymbidium* Sweet Devon 'Perfection'. When two different genera are crossed, such as *Ascocentrum* and *Vanda*, the resulting hybrids are given a hybrid generic name, *Ascocenda*. Prior to 1959 grex names were often latinized in the manner of species, for example, *Cymbidium* Coningsbyanum, but they are always written with a capital and in normal type rather than italics.

CULTIVATION A history of orchid cultivation begins not in Europe, but in China and Japan, where native orchids, particularly fragrant ones, have been appreciated for at least 2500 years. Between the tenth and seventeenth centuries, a number of treatises are known to have been published in China, while the first such work appeared in Japan in 1728. The first tropical orchid to be cultivated in England was a terrestrial *Bletia* species from the Bahamas, which flowered in 1732. Later eighteenth century introductions came from China and the West Indies, so that by 1794, there were 17 species of epiphytic orchids cultivated at Kew Gardens. Due to ignorance of their natural habitats, these early importations were subjected to hot and wet conditions which must have killed them quite quickly. By the 1830s, enlightened growers were beginning to heed travelers who had reported the much cooler and fresher

Singapore Botanic Gardens

At the famous Singapore Botanic Gardens, there is a long history of orchid growing and this outdoor bed of hybrid vandas is tall enough to form a constantly flowering hedge. Under such conditions of consistent light, warmth and humidity, some plants will thrive. However, in order to grow and display plants from cooler or more seasonal areas, the Gardens have had to construct a special air-conditioned growing house.

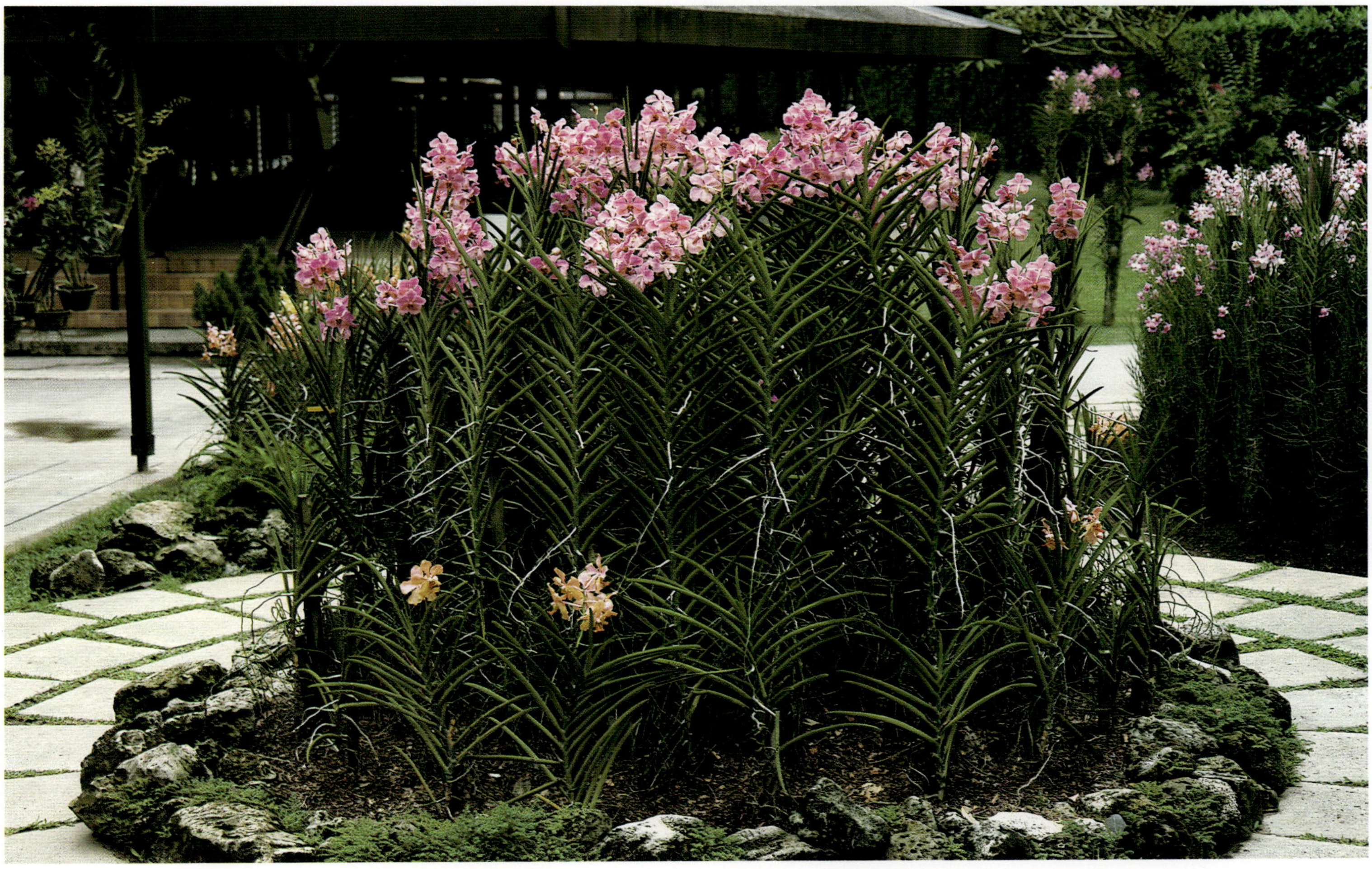

conditions which they had encountered. The leader among them was Joseph Paxton, gardener to the Sixth Duke of Devonshire, who established separate houses for species from different climates, and further improved their growth by allowing more ventilation and careful control of watering and humidity. As more and more plants were collected and sent to Europe, books on cultivation began to appear, and even today, the advice they give is generally sound. Of course, vast numbers of orchids perished during the long sea voyages from the tropics, but it says a lot for their toughness, that many survived to be sold and successfully grown in climates far removed from those they came from.

The cultivation of orchid plants is an absorbing pastime throughout the world, and is encouraged both by a widespread network of active societies, and by specialist orchid nurseries. In addition, there are many Botanic Gardens and other public institutions where orchids may be seen. Cultivation in tropical countries is not as straight forward as it might seem at first sight. Apart from heat, everything else has to be provided for plants removed from their immediate environment, and there are numerous pests and diseases which are never seen in more temperate places. A few plants will thrive unprotected in full sun, either tied to hardwood posts, or planted in beds or containers, but the majority need shelter of some kind, which is easily provided by a framework covered with wood laths or cloth. A clear roof may be necessary for rain protection, and it is then important to keep temperatures down by shading and good air circulation. For many species, living trees make satisfactory hosts, and have the advantage of providing natural shade. Clay pots and pans, preferably with drainage holes in the sides, make durable containers for most plants, whereas hardwood baskets are more suitable for species which prefer their roots to be completely exposed. Conventional organic potting materials have a very short life in the tropics and are replaced by inert charcoal and broken brick, which need regular applications of weak fertilizer. At higher altitudes, a much wider range of plants may be grown in a similar manner, although night temperatures would fall too low for lowland plants.

In sub-tropical regions, cool-growing plants are accommodated in a shade house with a clear roof and cloth sides which reduce wind, but still allow free air movement. An unheated greenhouse could provide higher humidity for those plants like odontoglossums and masdevallias which need it, although shade would be required in summer. Once heating is essential, then control of humidity becomes very important for the health of the plants, and a balance has to be achieved between the elements of temperature, light and humidity. This is particularly difficult in areas which have hot dry summers where it is often necessary to use evaporative cooling with wet pads covering greenhouse ends, and large fans drawing air through them. This has the double effect of cooling the air and increasing humidity. Even in northern latitudes, where winters are very cold, insulated houses, sometimes built partially underground, allow the successful cultivation of all but the most light-loving of tropical orchids.

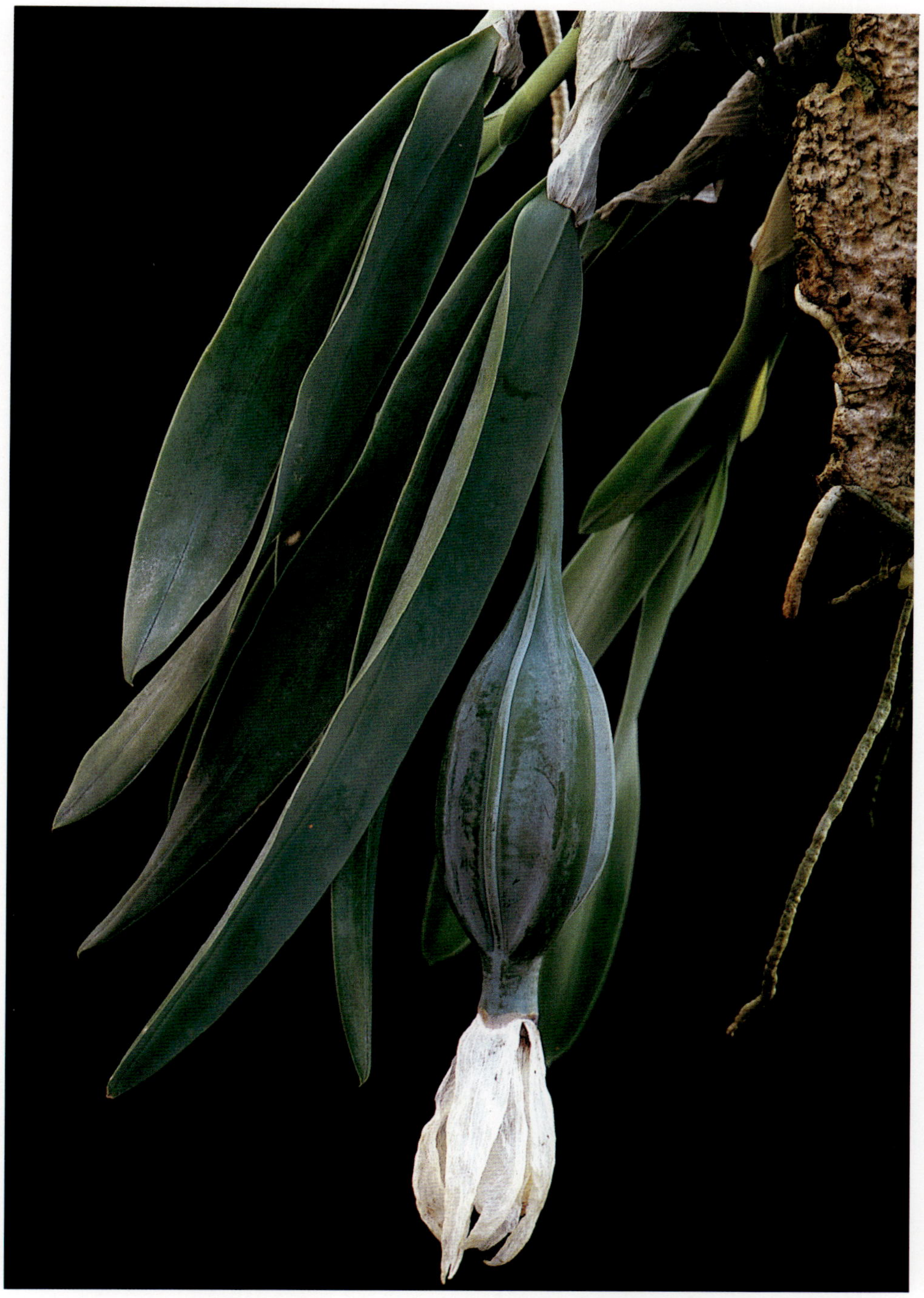

Encyclia citrina

Whilst terrestrial orchids tend to ripen and distribute their seeds within a few weeks, many epiphytes may take up to a year to do the same. This capsule, on a plant of the beautiful Mexican species, *Encyclia citrina*, is already six months old, and would probably take another three to ripen. On the end of the capsule are the dried remains of the flower and also visible is one of the ribs which will split to release seed.

Away from the tropics, orchid containers are much more varied, from clay pots and pans, the equivalent shapes moulded in plastic, and a wide range of net pots and wooden baskets. All are successfully used, but allowance has to be made for the slower drying of plants in plastic containers. A number of species grow better tied to cork or wooden slabs where their roots are constantly exposed to the air, and these can be hung in large numbers on frames within a greenhouse. Potting materials ultimately depend on availability, so that the fern fiber which was widely used in the past, has now gone and has largely been replaced by graded pine bark for epiphytes with the more recent inert rockwool showing considerable promise.

For those without greenhouses, it is still possible to grow good plants on a well-lit windowsill, away from direct sunlight, so long as humidity is increased by standing the containers on damp gravel trays or pans. A stage further is to rely entirely on artificial light in a basement or glass case, and ingenious growers, particularly in the United States, have shown the possibilities.

Although the principles of orchid cultivation were well understood in the nineteenth century, seed germination was not. Early efforts relied on sowing fresh seed on the compost surface of the parent plants, but the results were erratic and few seedlings survived to flowering. It was the great French scientist, Noël Bernard, who in 1909, published the results of ten years work which explained the relationship between orchids and mycorrhizal fungi, and how this allowed germination in the wild. The German, Hans Burgeff continued these studies, and established a workable method of using fungal cultures to germinate seed. This was used commercially by several firms but was eventually superseded by the asymbiotic method published by the American, Lewis Knudson in 1922. He used a sterile gel containing mineral salts and sugars, on which epiphyte seed germinated readily, forming the basis for the mass production of seedlings. Other formulae have been developed which are more effective for the germination of terrestrial and slipper orchids, but Knudson's is still used. Another French scientist, Georges Morel, working on virus elimination, discovered a means for propagating thousands of identical plants from a single tiny piece of *Cymbidium* shoot using tissue cultures.

USES For such a large and diverse family of plants, orchids have comparatively little to offer us when compared to other groups such as the grasses, or the potato or pea families. Their exotic, colorful and long-lasting flowers appeal to many people, so that production and marketing of them takes place all over the world. In the tropics, Singapore, Thailand and Hawaii are major producers of cut-flowers, especially dendrobiums and hybrids of the vanda type. Because of the climate, they are available during all months of the year, and of course, there are no heating costs, since the plants may be grown either in the open, or under simple shade structures. Strangely enough, far more orchid flowers and plants are produced in sub-tropical and temperate countries, where artificial heating may be required, and some form of covering definitely will, if only to keep off the rain. In the Southern Hemisphere, in Australia, New Zealand and South Africa, cymbidiums grow to perfection with only rain and wind protection, using a clear covering on top with cloth sides. These are plants which delight in cool nights and warm days, flowering mainly in the fall, winter and spring months. Their long-lasting flowers, in a range of sizes and colors, form an excellent export crop. While cymbidiums are also grown on the west coast of the United States, it is the large-flowered cattleyas which have traditionally been popular throughout the country. In Northern Europe, and in Germany and the Netherlands in particular, a wide range of orchids are grown

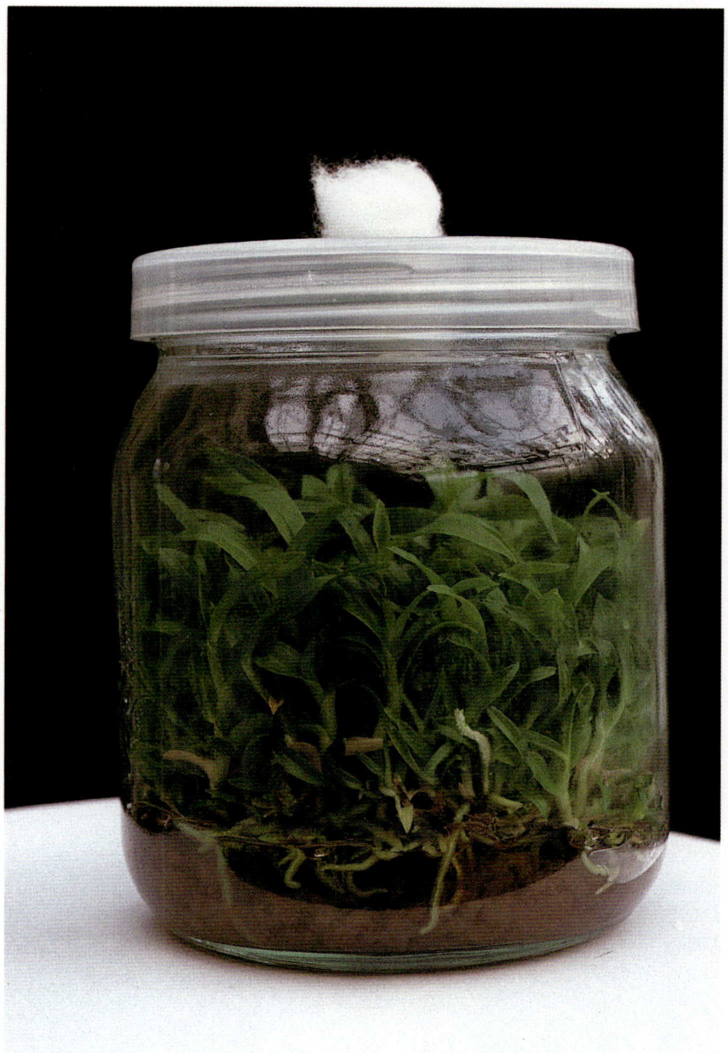

Sterile seedling culture

The beginning of it all; a jar of sterile orchid seedlings, in this case, *Dendrobium miyakei* from Taiwan. Any number of different containers have been used for the purpose, from old medicine bottles to laboratory flasks and custom made plastic disposables. These seedlings, after nine months growth, are ready to face the outside world. Their home is a common honey jar, capped with polypropylene and capable of being sterilized and reused many times. The cotton wool in the cap allows the sterile movement of air for the young plants.

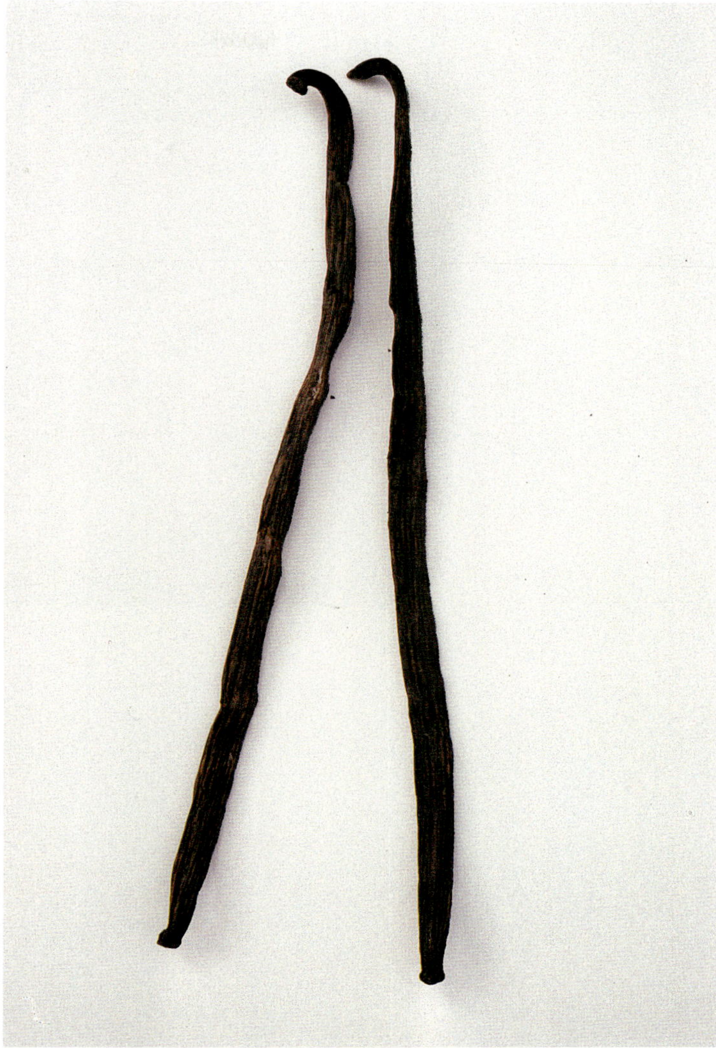

Vanilla pods

At first sight, vanilla pods do not look very promising and certainly do little to betray their exotic origins. When fresh off the vine, they are plump and green, without any sign of the delicious fragrance to come. It is only after months of the curing treatment that the full and familiar aroma is developed.

under glass for mainly local consumption as flowers and house plants. Tropical phalaenopsis and paphiopedilums are popular, as well as cooler growing miltonias, vuylstekearas and of course, cymbidiums.

Without doubt, the best-known orchid product is vanilla flavoring, which comes from the seed pods of a tropical vine. It was cultivated and used by the Mayas and Aztecs, and introduced to Europe, along with chocolate, by Spanish explorers in the early sixteenth century. By the latter part of the nineteenth century, the principal ingredient, vanillin, had been identified and synthesized, and synthetic vanilla is widely used today. However, the natural product is a complex combination of many substances, and for some purposes, icecream flavoring in particular, it is superior. Of the three species used for commercial production, *Vanilla planifolia*, native to Central and northern South America, and the West Indies, is by far the most important. It grows best under partial shade as a fleshy vine, and the flowers, which appear in succession,

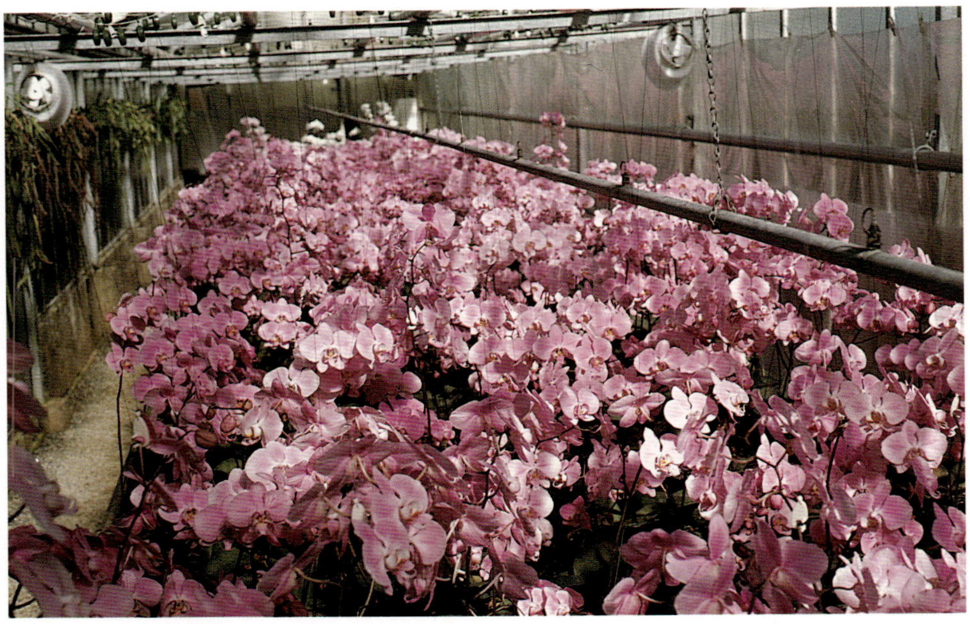

Phalaenopsis in Germany

The growing of tropical orchids for their flowers is a well developed industry in northern Europe. Here in Germany, 20,000 pink phalaenopsis blooms await cutting for the market. Each is about 10cm (4 inches) across, and each plant carries a spray of ten or more. While the main flowering season is in the summer months, there are some flowers available throughout the year. In order to recover the cost of heating the glasshouses to a minimum temperature of 18°C as many plants as possible are grown together.

last only a few hours. Vanilla cultivation has been introduced to many tropical countries, but the most important are Madagascar and Mexico. In the absence of effective pollinators, the flowers are artificially pollinated, after which the long green seed capsules slowly mature over many months, before being harvested. Processing to bring out the characteristic aroma, involves a lot of handling, from initial heating and drying to the final conditioning in closed boxes. The resulting black sticks are the vanilla beans of commerce, usually pliable if kept wrapped, but soon becoming brittle when exposed to the air.

A great many orchid species around the world are known to provide items of food and medicine, and even claimed to offer aphrodisiac properties, but only one substance apart from vanilla has ever been widespread in its use. Salep was known to the Greeks in the third century BC, and its use in Asia Minor spread both to India and China, and to Europe, where it was popular in the Middle Ages. It was prepared from the dried tubers of many terrestrial orchids, but especially those of *Orchis* and *Ophrys* species. Numerous claims have been made for its medical properties through the ages, but they could be summed up as restorative and nutritional. The production and use of salep in present-day Turkey is still an active business. During the flowering season, tubers of *Orchis* and *Ophrys* species are dug up, washed, boiled, and dried in the sun to aid preservation. They are then sold as tubers or as milled flour, which is the usual form in which salep is used. Common preparations include a sweet, hot milk drink, a stiff icecream and as an ingredient of sticky confectionery.

An unexpected use is found in the Philippines, Indonesia, Papua New Guinea and other Pacific Islands, for the dried stems of various *Dendro-*

bium and *Diplocaulobium* species. These dry to a bright yellow, and thin strips are variously woven and used in bindings to create utilitarian and decorative articles of great delicacy and beauty.

CONSERVATION Conservation of the world's natural resources has become a major issue only in recent years, and although the extinction of hundreds of orchid species is unlikely to provoke an international outcry, their continuing existence is proof that their habitats are healthy. It is ultimately the survival of habitats on a large scale, which will determine whether orchids will remain a signficant part of the Earth's flora in the future. National Parks and Nature Reserves obviously have an important part to play, so long as they are large enough, and are given the resources and funding in the long term. Unfortunately, it is in the tropics that the most plants are in need of conserving, and it is here too, that there is the greatest pressure for human needs of land, fuel and food. The most likely habitats to survive, are those mountainous areas which are unsuitable for habitation or agriculture. These are also rich in plant life, which in turn, can support a diversity of animals.

Trade in wild orchid plants has been greatly curtailed by regulation, but there are relatively few species which are threatened by collection, and far more by destruction of tropical forests. An increasing number of horticulturally desirable species is being grown from seed and made available by nurseries, so that pressure on natural populations is reduced. Reintroduction into the wild is sometimes advocated, but is fraught with difficulties. However, there are several successful examples of young plants establishing, both in temperate and tropical habitats.

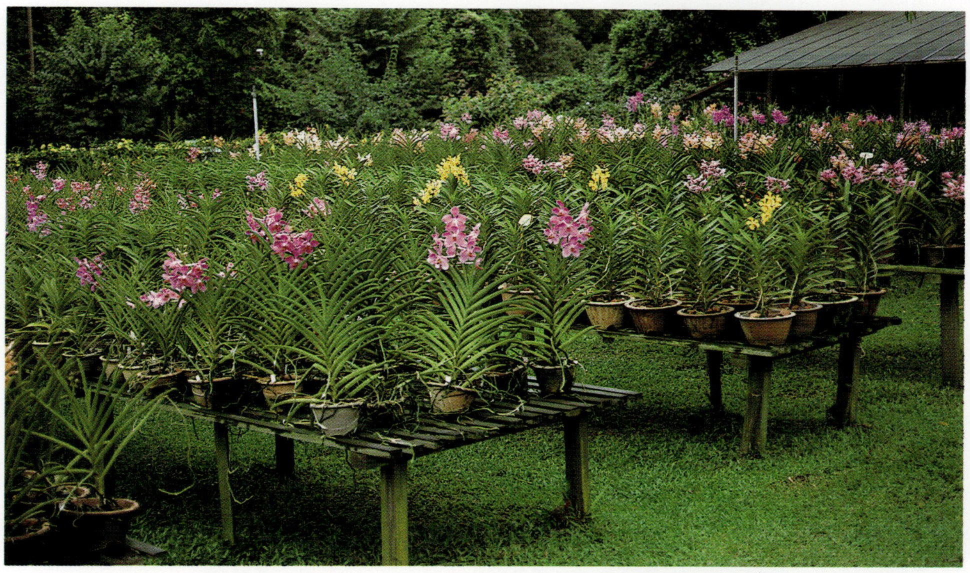

Vandas in Singapore

By way of a contrast; orchids grown by the acre for their flowers at the Mandai Orchid Gardens in Singapore. No problems with heating here, and plenty of water from above. These hybrid vandas are grown in pots containing only charcoal or broken brick. The wooden benches ensure free drainage of water, and just as importantly, plenty of air movement around the plants. While vandas need full light to flower well, other orchids such as dendrobiums are grown here under the shade of wooden laths.

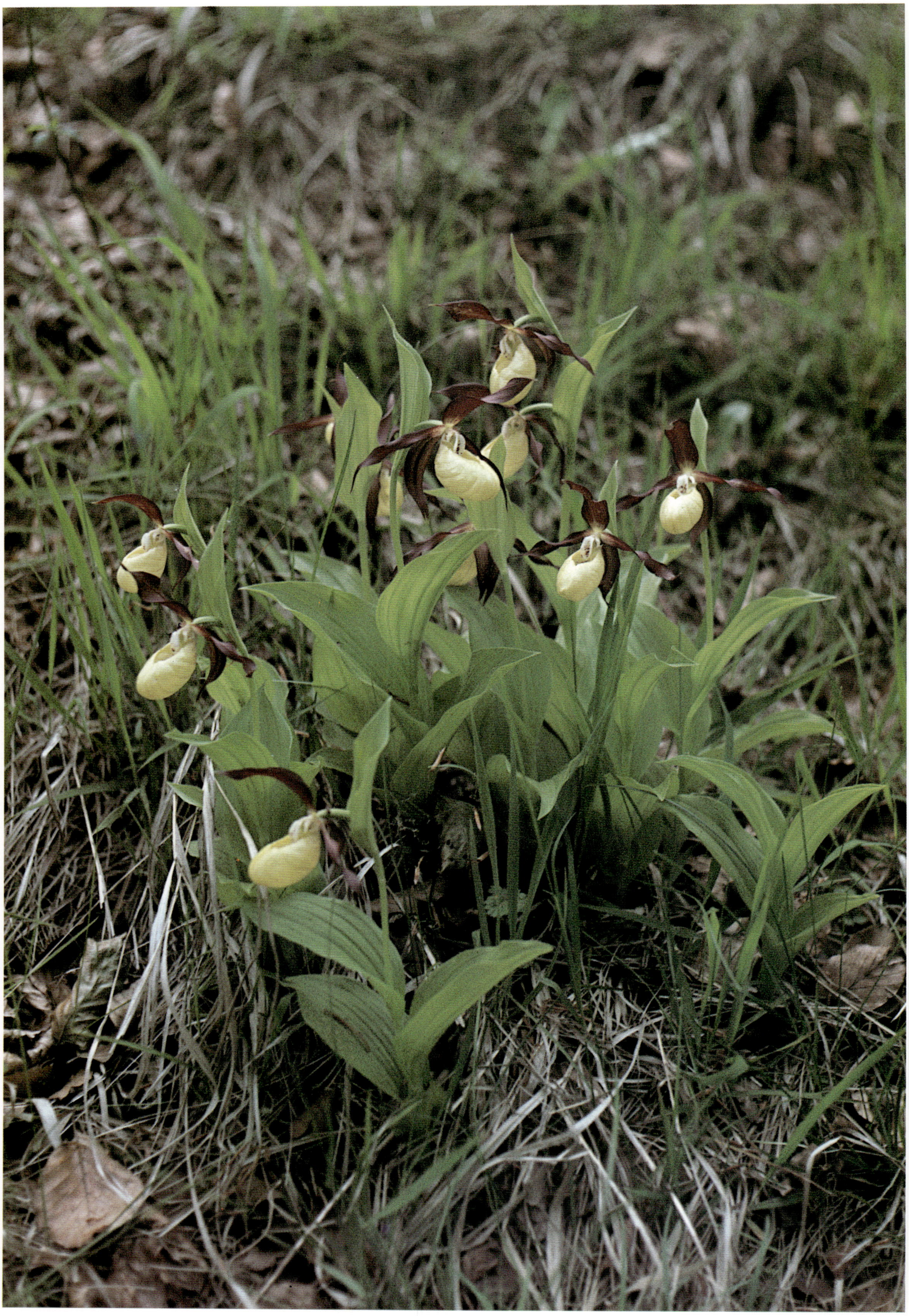

– 2 –
Climates and Habitats of Europe and the Americas

Cypripedium calceolus

The Lady's Slipper, having the largest flowers of any European orchid species, has always been admired and therefore heavily collected. In Britain it has been reduced to a single small colony. These plants were growing in Germany on a typical site of a steep limestone hillside scattered with grass and low bushes. *Cypripedium calceolus* is widespread in Europe, being found as far east as Siberia, and a close relative occurs in North America.

The orchids of Europe are, without exception, terrestrial in habit, so that suitable habitats depend largely on soil types and their associated vegetation. Climate has less effect than might be expected, since all species spend part of the year underground, avoiding either hot dry summer conditions or cold winter ones. At higher altitudes or in more northerly areas, the growing season is short compared to that of southern lowland regions. Although some orchids are found in almost every habitat, most favor calcareous soils, and common examples of these are the chalk downlands of southern Britain, and sloping grassland through the rest of Europe. So long as such areas remain uncultivated, then orchids will thrive, even if controlled grazing takes place later in the summer, when they have died down. Similar habitats are roadside verges and embankments, disused vineyards and other places which have been cleared of competing scrub. Around the Mediterranean are large expanses of taller evergreen scrub and smaller low-growing bushes on poor, stoney soils. These provide a rich habitat for orchids in the early spring, but are soon dried up in the summer. Open woodland, whether conifer or beech, is widespread in Europe, and on calcareous soils, this is home to other species. More specialized habitats are sphagnum bogs and various fens and marshy areas. Such places have their own restricted species, but are often threatened by draining for agriculture. On higher ground, alpine meadows are important habitats from France across to Italy, but even above the tree-line, a few orchids are to be found.

Apart from the subtropical and tropical plants of southern Florida, the orchids of North America are related to those in Europe, and are all terrestrial. In general terms, orchid habitats of significance may be divided into the eastern deciduous forests, with their good rainfall and limestone areas; the northern coniferous forests, extending from Alaska to Newfoundland, with sphagnum bogs and constant moisture; and the western mountain forests which have less rain than the east and therefore offer less suitable habitats for orchids except along streams, especially in the more southern parts. Two enormous areas which are almost devoid of orchids are the prairie grasslands of the center, and the southern deserts. An altogether different habitat exists on the Florida peninsula where numbers of tropical orchids, including many epiphytes, grow on forest trees amidst the swamps of the Everglades which sadly, are a declining remnant as draining and clearing continue to take place.

The countries of Central America, from Mexico south to Panama, have an extensive range of tropical habitats for orchids, from sea level up to at least 4000m (13000 feet). The greatest variety of epiphytes occur in the rain forests which are found on both Atlantic and Pacific sides, especially on mountain slopes between 1000 and 2300m (3300 – 7550 feet). These areas enjoy abundant rainfall all year round, in contrast to other regions, both higher and lower down, which have distinct wet and dry seasons, thus limiting the range of plants found there. Above 3000m (9840 feet), most orchids grow as terrestrials in a relatively dry climate.

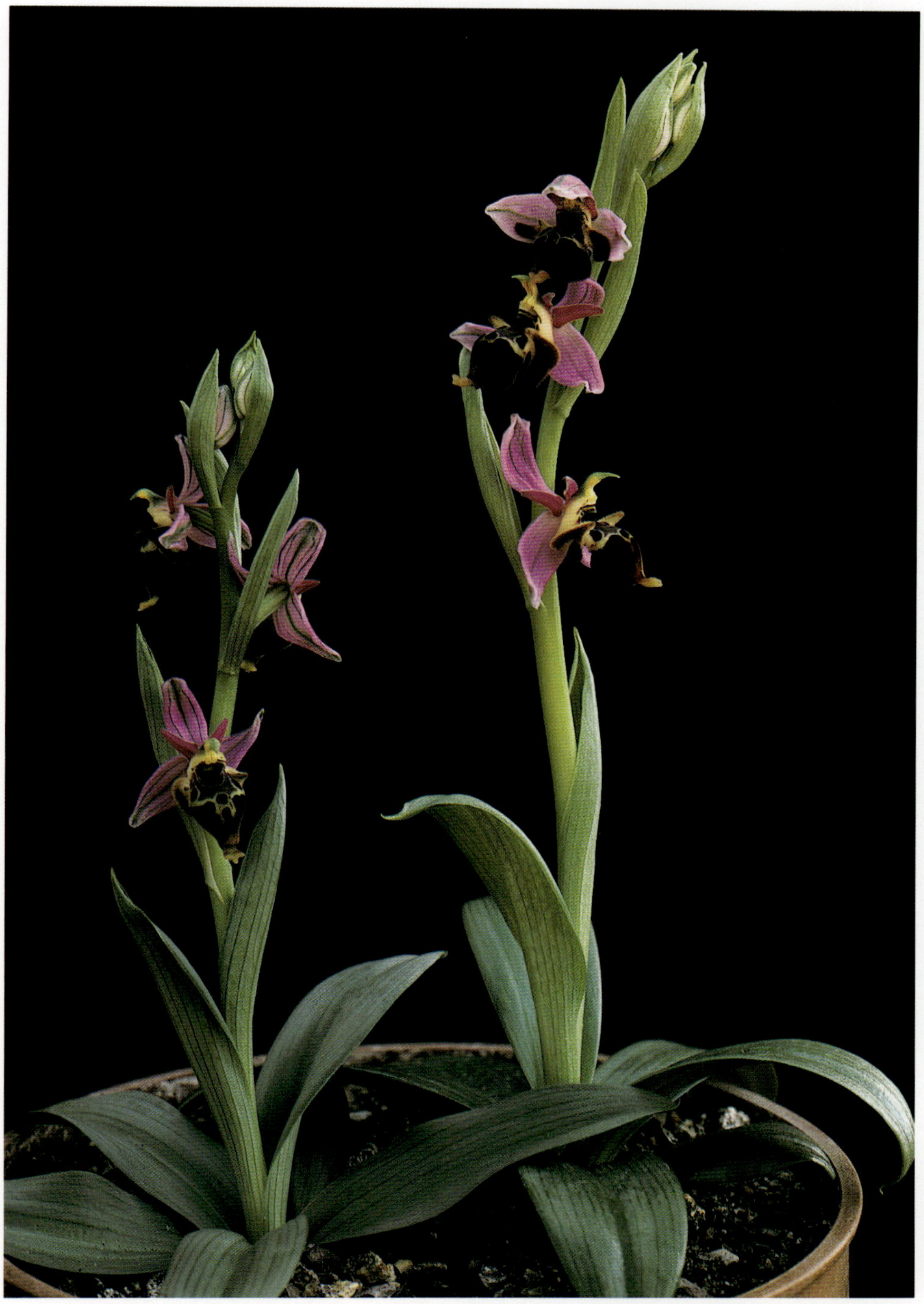

Ophrys scolopax ssp heldreichii

As part of a major conservation program at the Royal Botanic Gardens Kew, an extensive collection of European orchids is maintained in cultivation. These plants are growing strongly in their third year of captivity, and will provide not only fresh seed but also the root fungus which will aid germination. In order to protect them from the cold and wet, they are grown in a special glasshouse.

The islands of the Caribbean have similar habitats on a much smaller scale, so that, for example, the mountains of Jamaica are home to many typical rain forest epiphytes. As a less conventional habitat, abandoned citrus or coffee plantations are popular with certain species.

The western side of South America is dominated by the Andes mountain chain which stretches from Venezuela in the north to the south of Chile. As in Central America, tall rain forest still clothes some slopes, and while the hot lower forest up to perhaps 600m (1970 feet) contains some orchids, a far greater variety is found in forests up to 3000m (9840 feet). These are in areas of high rainfall, but even in dry periods, humidity is maintained. At the upper levels, the trees are shorter, and when daily mists and cloud cover the area, this is cloud forest where temperatures are moderate and moisture always available. Above the tree line, between 3000 and 4000m (9840 – 13000 feet) a number of terrestrial orchids are found growing among grasses and rocks. Savanna grassland has few species, but there is often gallery forest along rivers and streams, and epiphytes are common here. Venezuela, Colombia, Ecuador and Peru, all have extensive orchid floras, concentrated particularly in wet forests, but on the other side of the Andes, in Brazil, there is another range of rich habitats, associated with mountains which run parallel to the coast. These attract rain throughout the year and so are covered by dense forest, at least where it has not been cleared. Further inland are drier mountains where numbers of orchid species have adapted to growing on rocks under quite hard conditions with seasonal rain and cool nights. The far south of the continent is too cold for epiphytes to grow, so only terrestrial orchids are found.

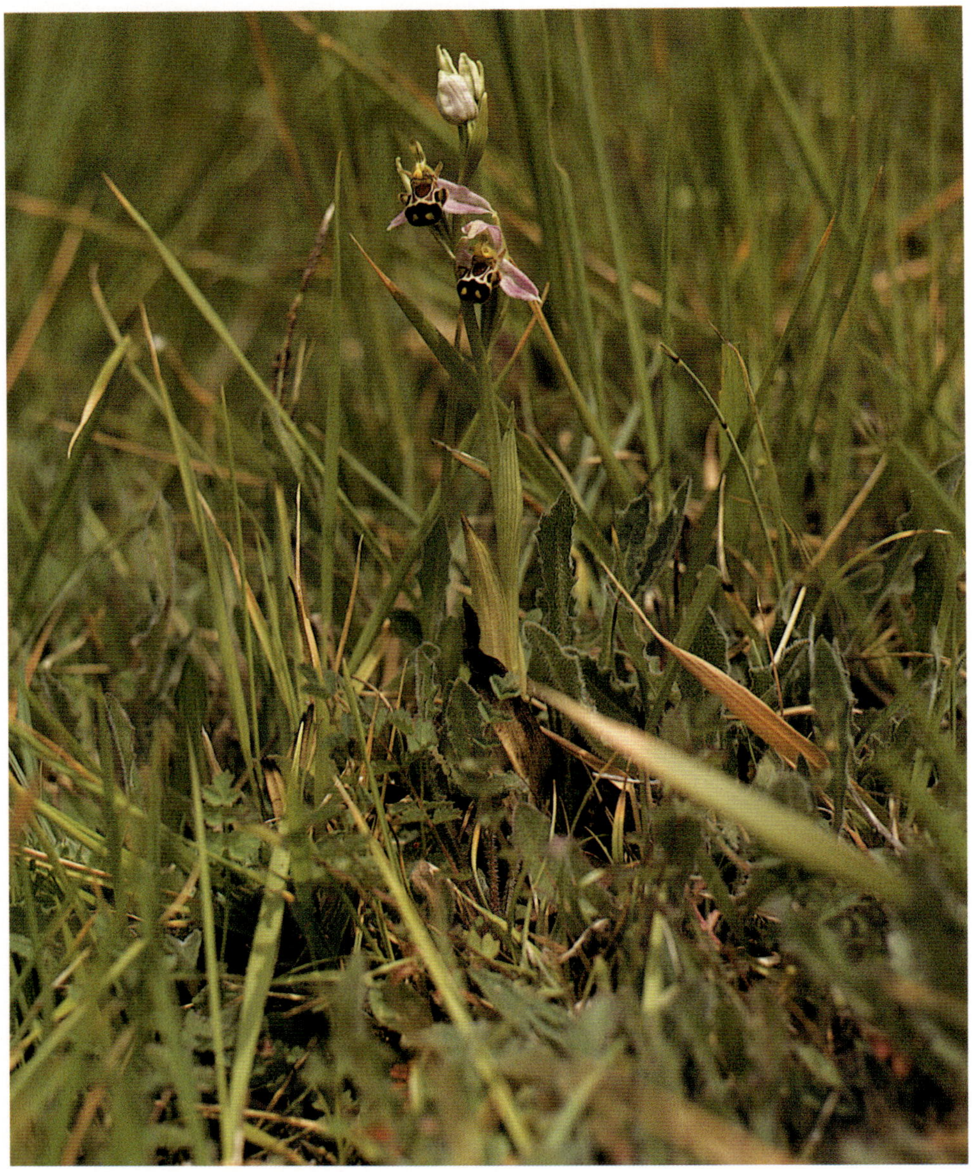

Ophrys apifera

The Bee Orchid is certainly a plant to capture the imagination, with its complex flowers and sporadic appearances. Seen here, growing among short grasses on chalk downland, it is only about 15cm (6 inches) tall and easily overlooked. In addition, the flowers are soon over and like all European orchids, part of the year is spent underground. Of the 30 or so *Ophrys* species, only four occur in Britain, with the greatest variety being found around the Mediterranean.

Ophrys apifera

Looked at more closely, the flower has a typical orchid structure, with the three pink sepals more or less identical, the prominent lip, and in this case, the remaining two petals greatly reduced in size. It is no accident that the lip resembles an insect, for it smells and feels like the female of the pollinator so that in attempting to mate with the flower, pollen is transferred. *Ophrys apifera* is probably unique in the genus as it relies on self-pollination whereas the other species attract the males of various wasps and bees.

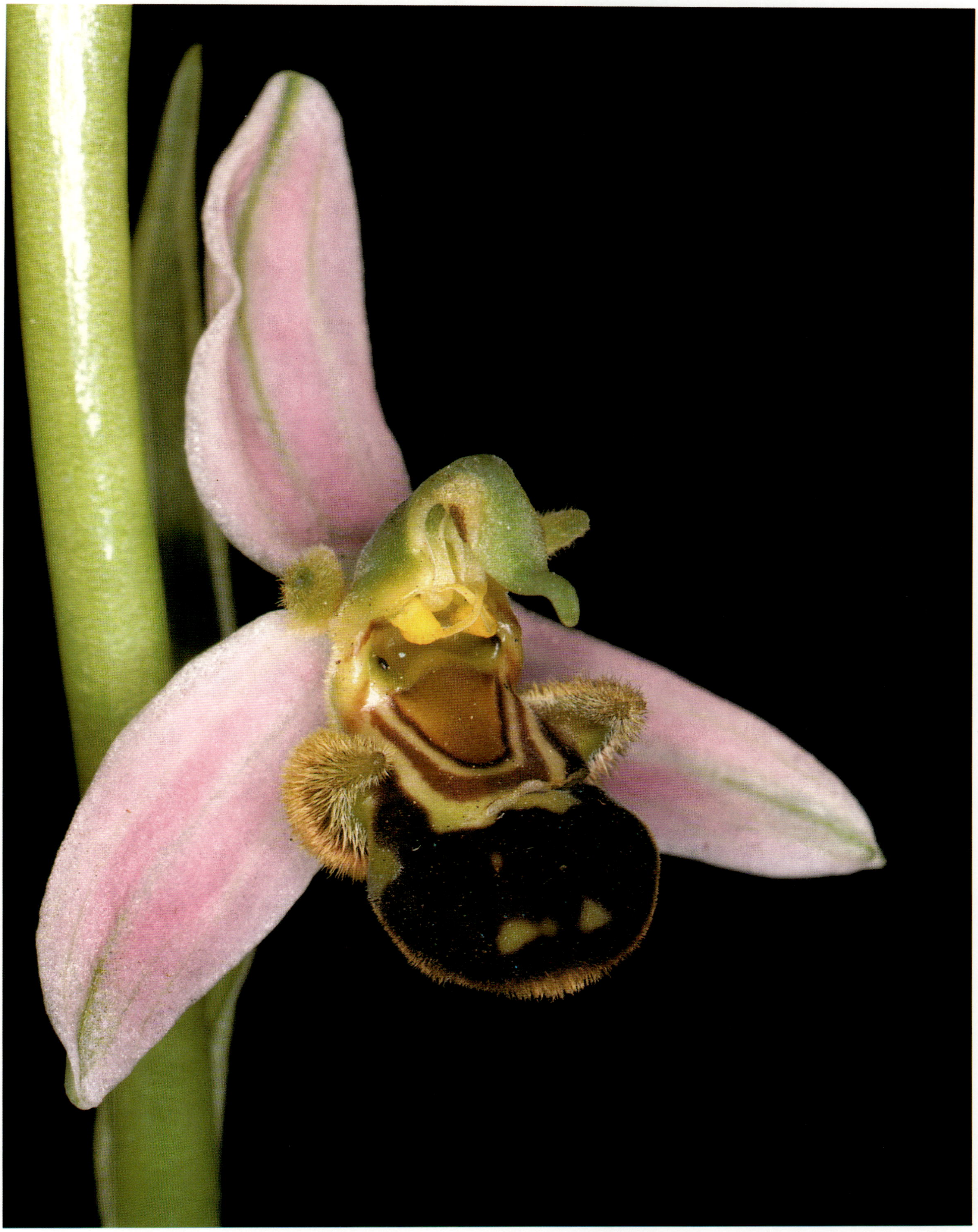

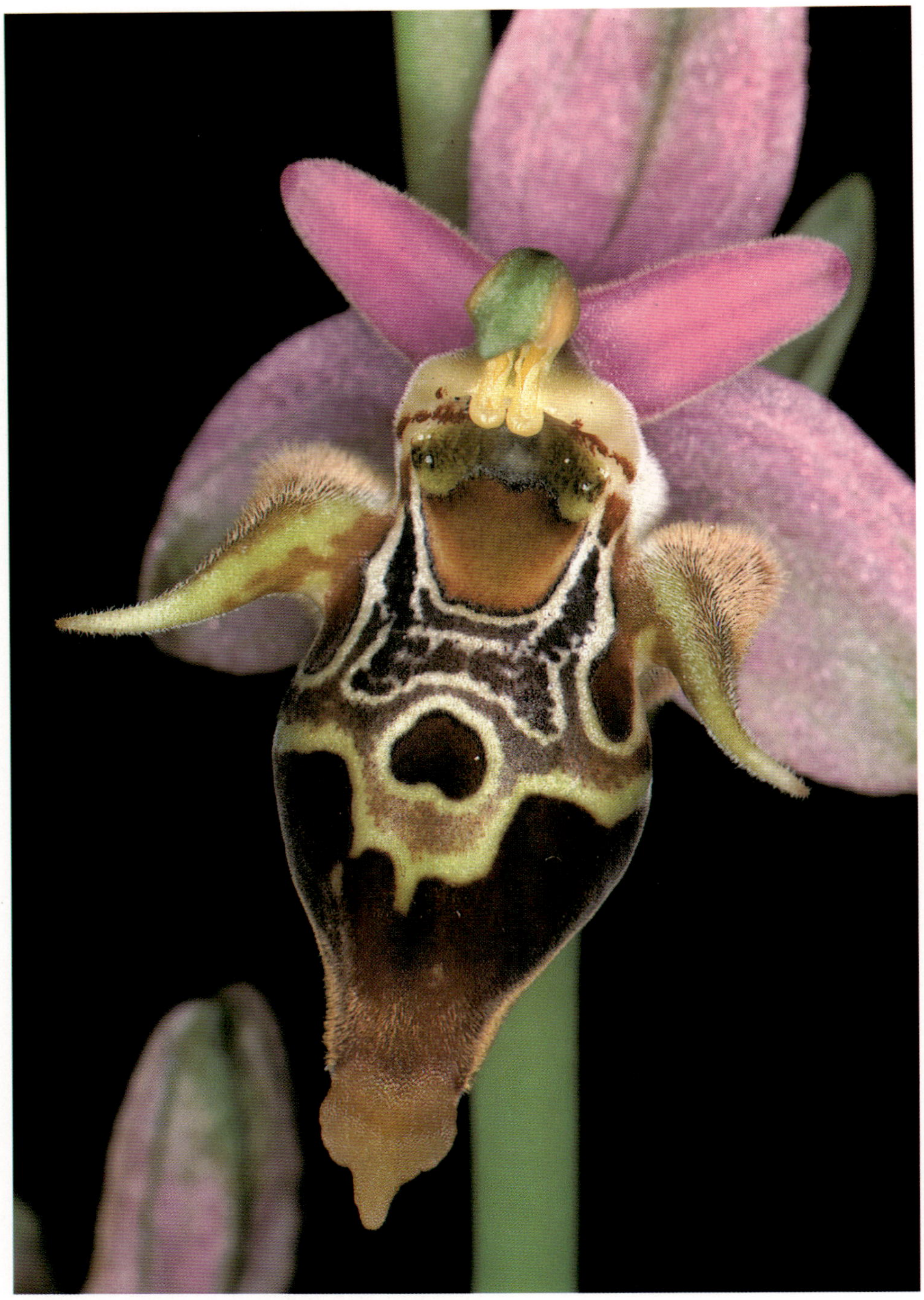

Ophrys scolopax ssp heldreichii

Orchids of the Mediterranean region have adapted to growing in poor soils under harsh conditions. Their growth cycle begins with the winter rains and flowering is early to avoid the summer heat. By the time drought sets in, the plants are dormant underground, having ripened and distributed their seed. This species is found in south-western Turkey and on some of the adjacent Greek islands.

Orchis simia

It has never been claimed that the Monkey Orchid is pollinated by monkeys, but the lip bears an extraordinary resemblance. Now very rare in England, *Orchis simia* is widespread in Europe, growing in open grassland, scrub or woodland. Unusually, the upper flowers open first, and as can be seen here, seed capsules are developing while the lower flowers have only recently opened.

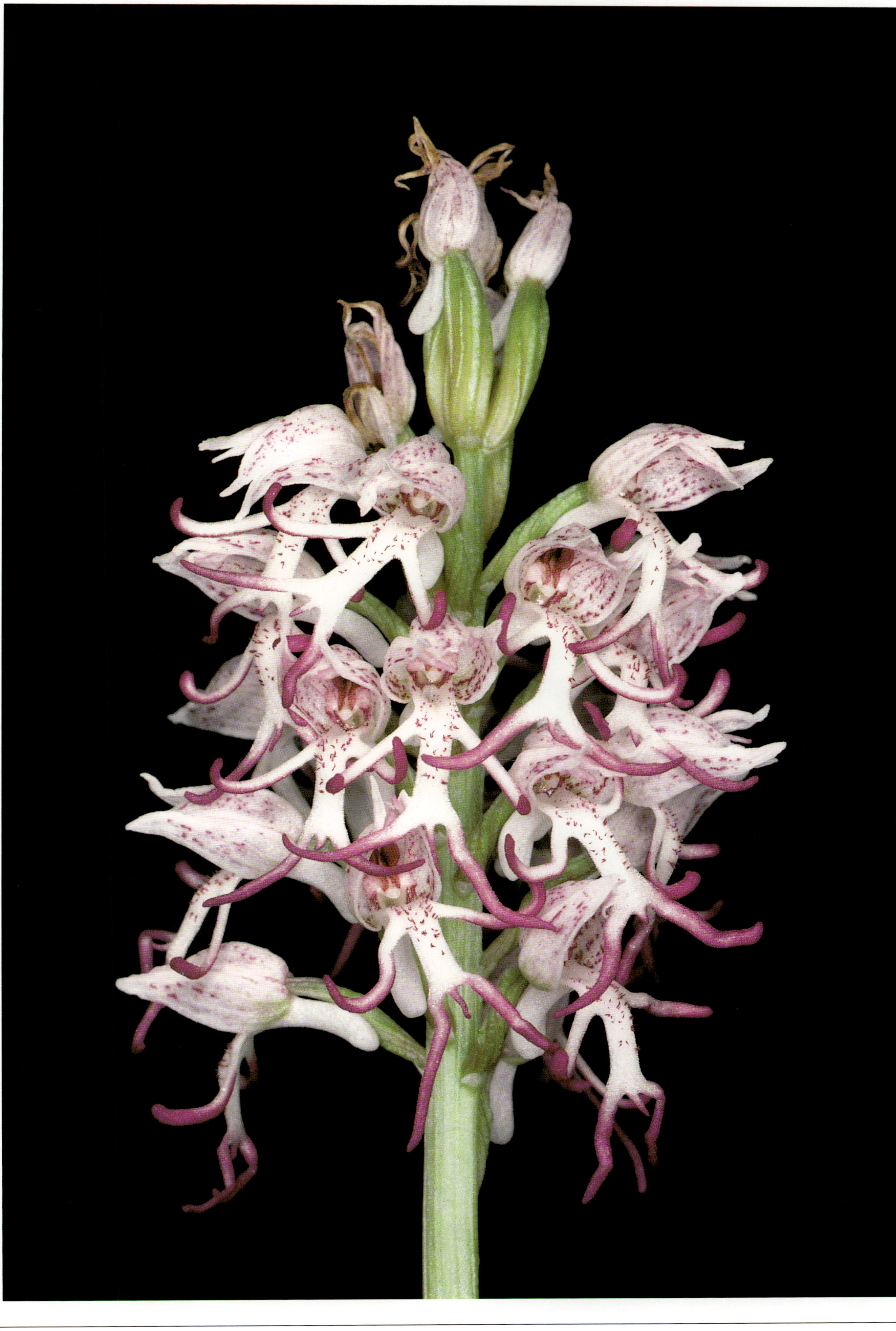

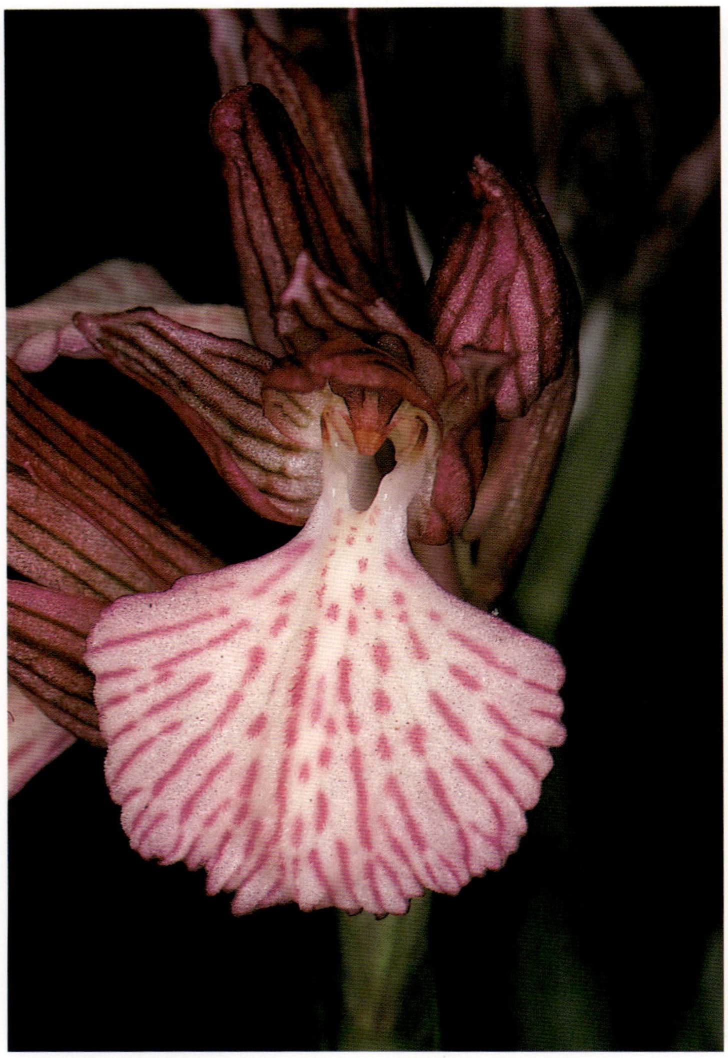

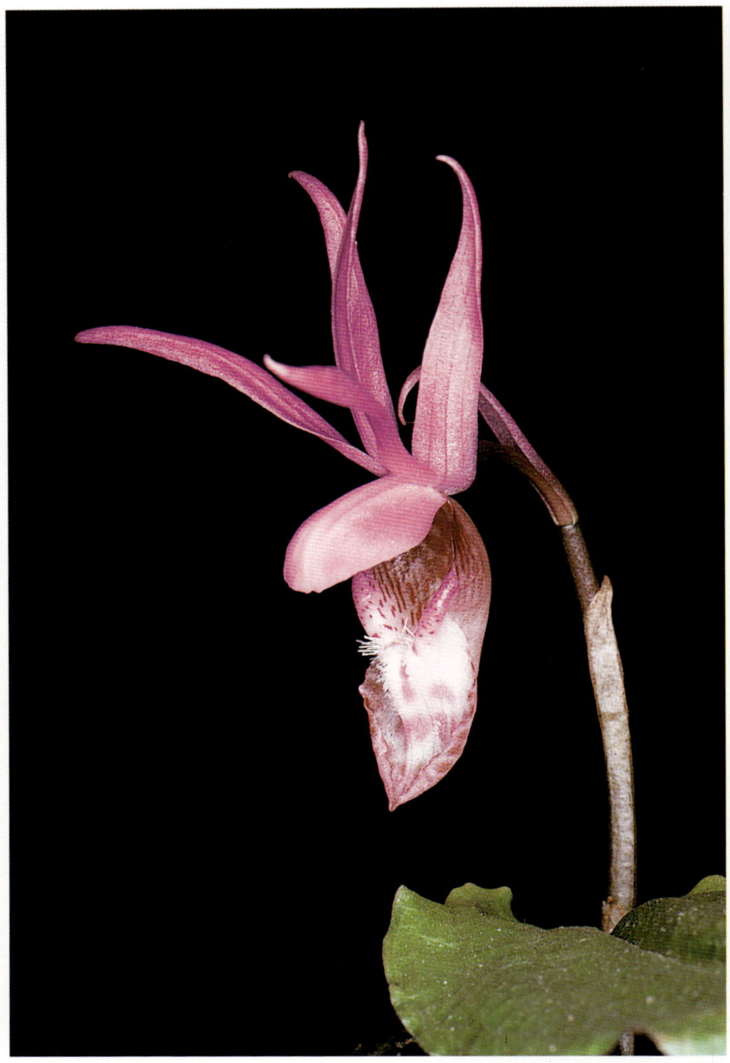

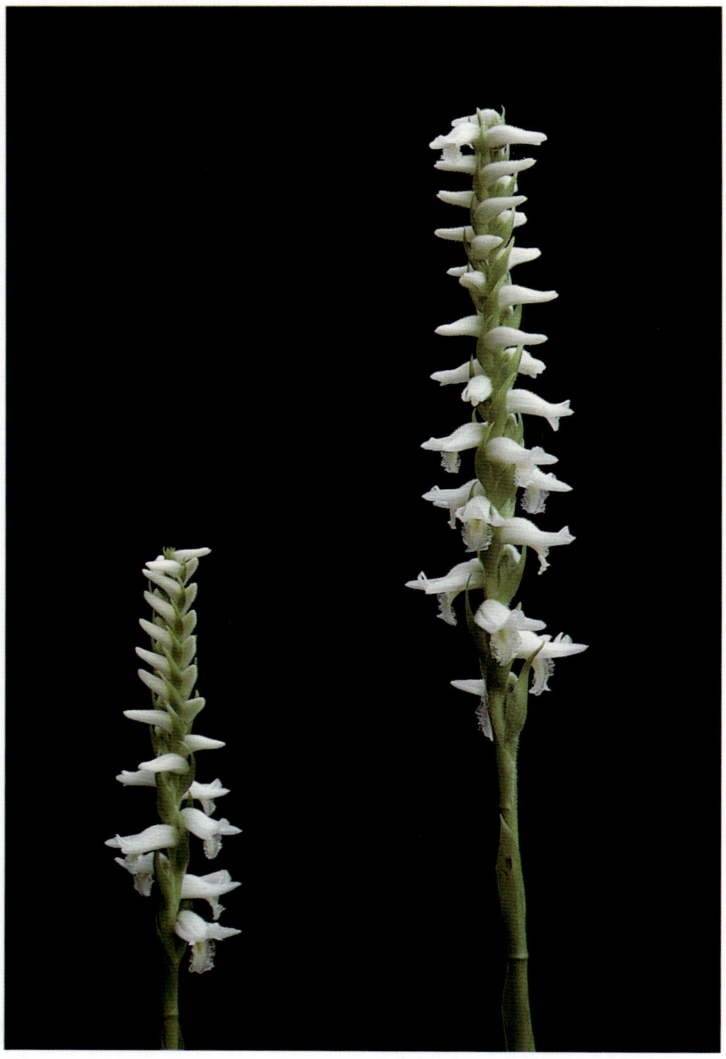

ABOVE LEFT: *Orchis papilionacea*

Sometimes called the Butterfly Orchid, the flower is dominated by the beautiful striped lip, while the sepals and petals form a hood over the column. *Orchis papilionacea* favors dry areas in the open, such as olive groves, scrubland and roadsides, and is found around the Mediterranean including North Africa. In common with other orchids of this region, it survives the hot dry summers by means of underground tubers.

ABOVE: *Calypso bulbosa var occidentalis*

The genus *Calypso* contains only one variable species which is found in a broad area from Scandinavia through to Siberia, Korea and Japan, and in North America, where there are two varieties. The one illustrated occurs only in the Pacific Northwest from California to British Columbia at fairly high altitudes under coniferous forest. The plants arise from fleshy corms buried in moss and the beautiful flowers open in the spring or early summer, often in extensive colonies.

LEFT: *Spiranthes odorata*

The small, spirally arranged flowers of *Spiranthes* species may be seen in most parts of the world except Africa. In North America, most have white or cream flowers with the stems arising from a cluster of fleshy roots. *Spiranthes odorata* is very much of a plant of wet places especially in the coastal regions of the south eastern states, and flowering in the autumn and winter. It attracts bumblebees as pollinators and sometimes forms a dense colony of plants.

Bletia roezlii

Although a majority of tropical orchids grows as epiphytes, terrestrials are widespread and are found in many different habitats. While some plants show seasonal dormancy, in the manner of the European orchids, others are evergreen and depend on regular water supplies. Bletias have underground corms and are found from Florida to Argentina. This species occurs in Mexico, Guatemala and Honduras, growing in soil under scrubby vegetation or on rocks or in crevices in forests. The upright inflorescence produces a succession of flowers and the leaves are deciduous.

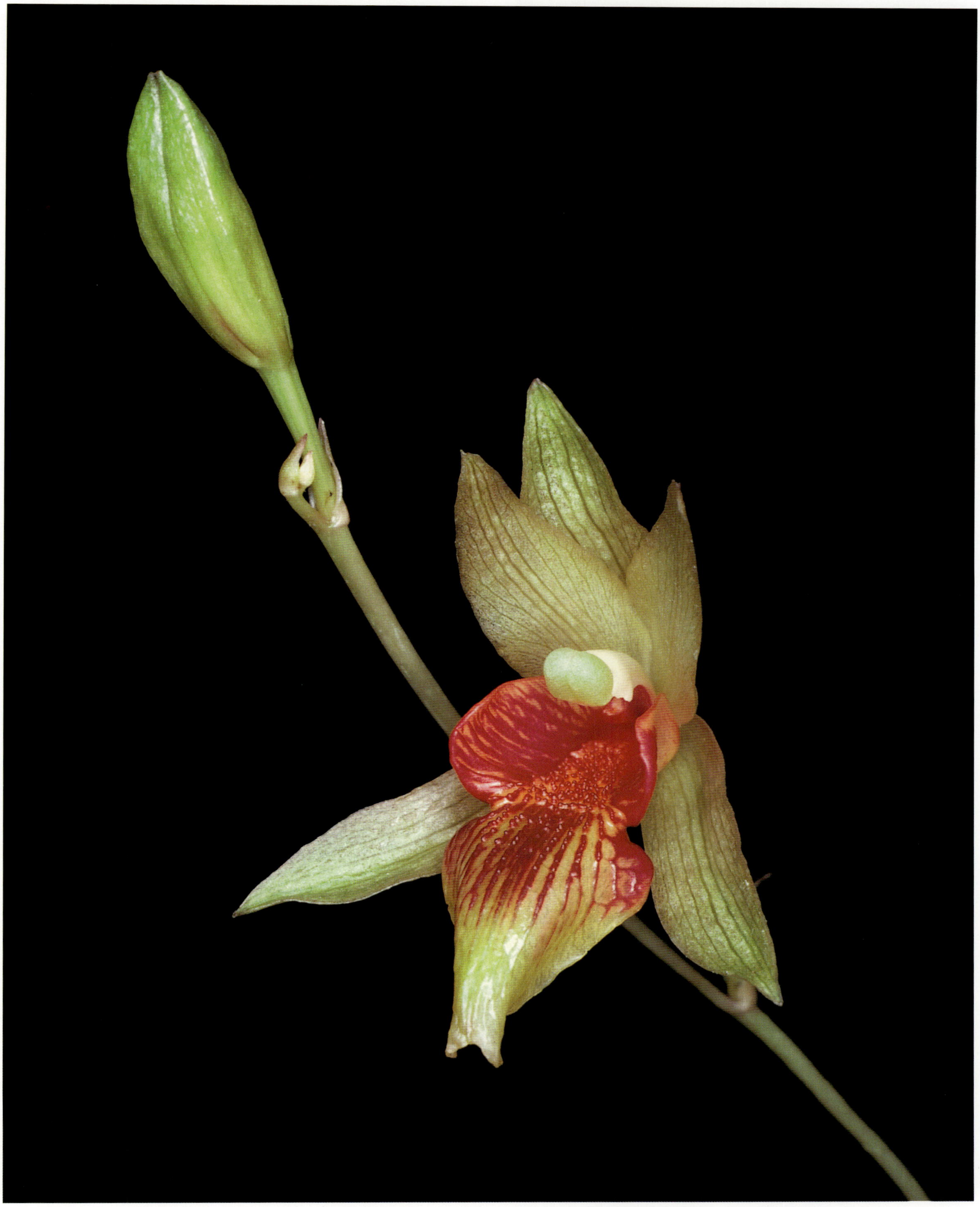

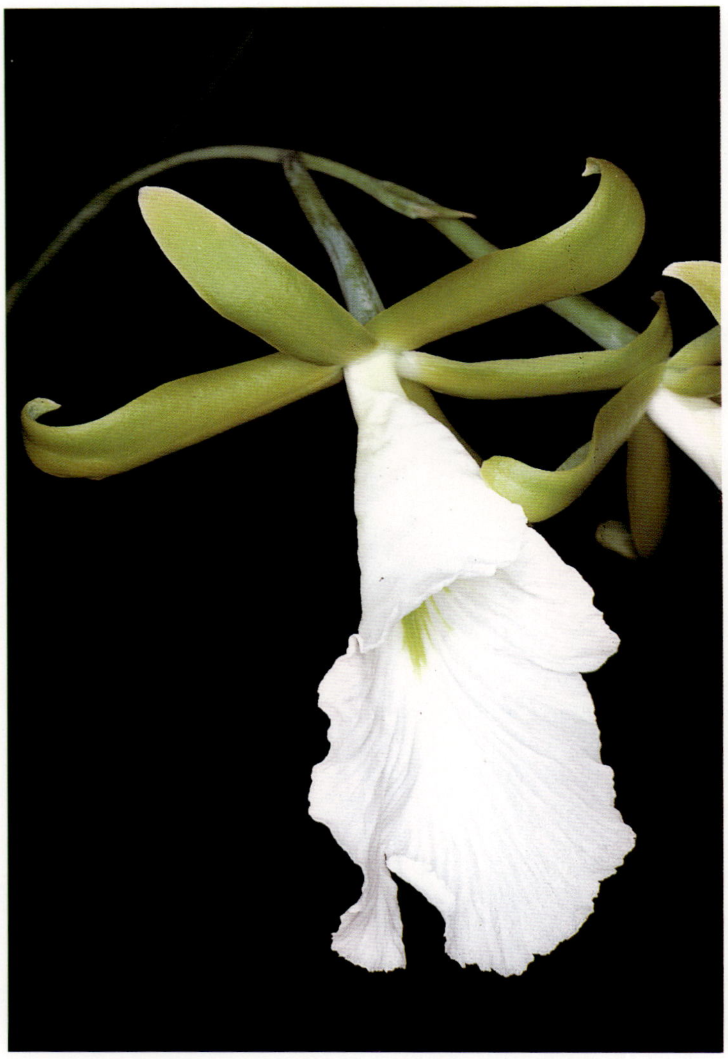

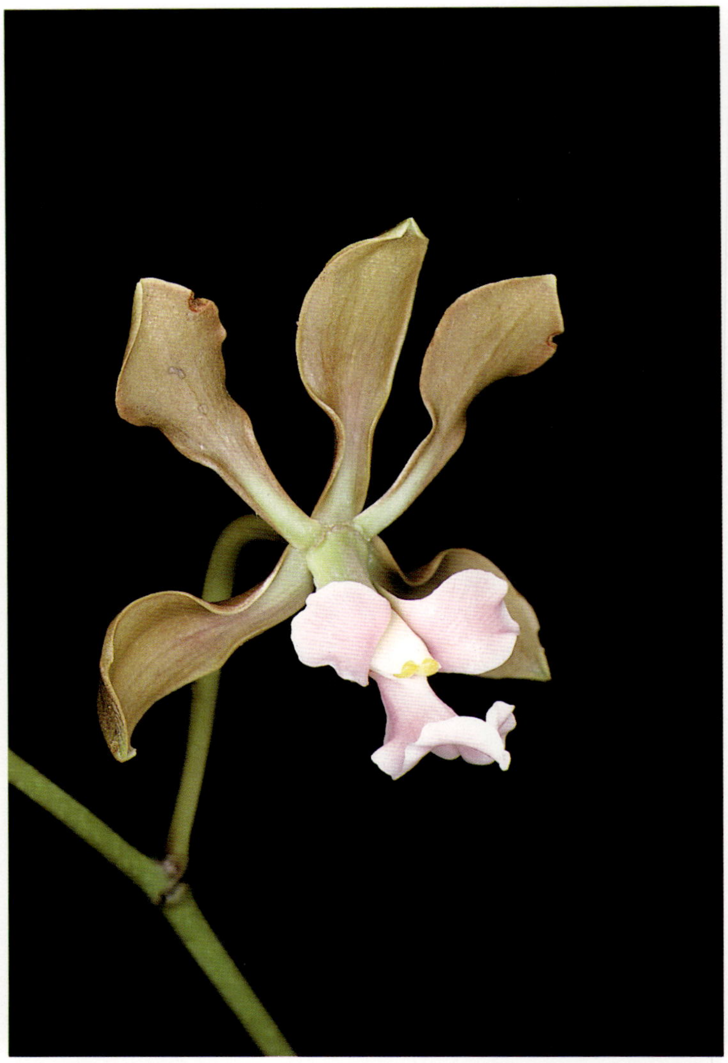

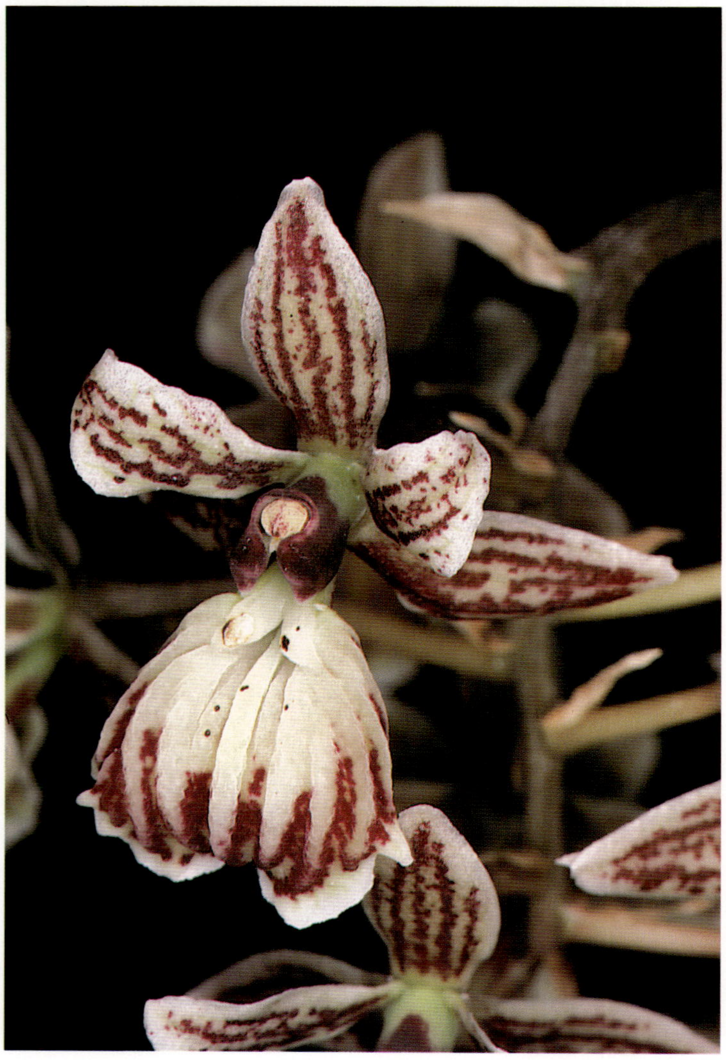

ABOVE LEFT: *Encyclia mariae*

The tropical American genus *Encyclia* is well represented in Mexico which has over 70 species. This beautiful one was described only in 1937, because it comes from an area in the north of the country where orchids were not expected to be found. Each inflorescence has up to four large flowers and the plants grow as epiphytes in dry oak forests at an altitude of around 1000m (3,300 feet).

ABOVE: *Encyclia selligera*

Many of the Central American encyclias are tough plants with hard pseudobulbs and leaves, and this obviously relates to their natural environment, which may be very dry at times. Although *Encyclia selligera* has smaller flowers than some, the inflorescence is tall and branching, so there are plenty of them and they are pleasantly scented. It is found in Mexico and Guatemala growing in dry forests at 1300-2200m (4265-7200 feet).

LEFT: *Epidendrum marmoratum*

The genus *Epidendrum* of sub-tropical and tropical America, rather parallels the genus *Dendrobium* of Asia and Australasia in its diversity of plant and flower forms, although considerably smaller with perhaps 400 species against 1400 for *Dendrobium*. *Epidendrum marmoratum* comes from Mexico, and is found growing on oak trees or rocks at quite high elevations, around 2000m (6500 feet), where conditions are cool and humid. The plant grows to about 30cm (12 inches) tall, and the flowers open in sequence over many weeks.

Epidendrum radicans

If some orchids could be described as roadside weeds, then this is one of them, being common on roadsides at higher altitudes in Mexico and Central America. The flowers, which have the lip lowermost, appear in succession at the top of a tall leafy stem, from which roots appear at each node. It is often confused in cultivation with *Epidendrum ibaguense* of Colombia and Venezuela, in which the flowers are similar although varied in color, and the plants form upright clumps rather than sprawling.

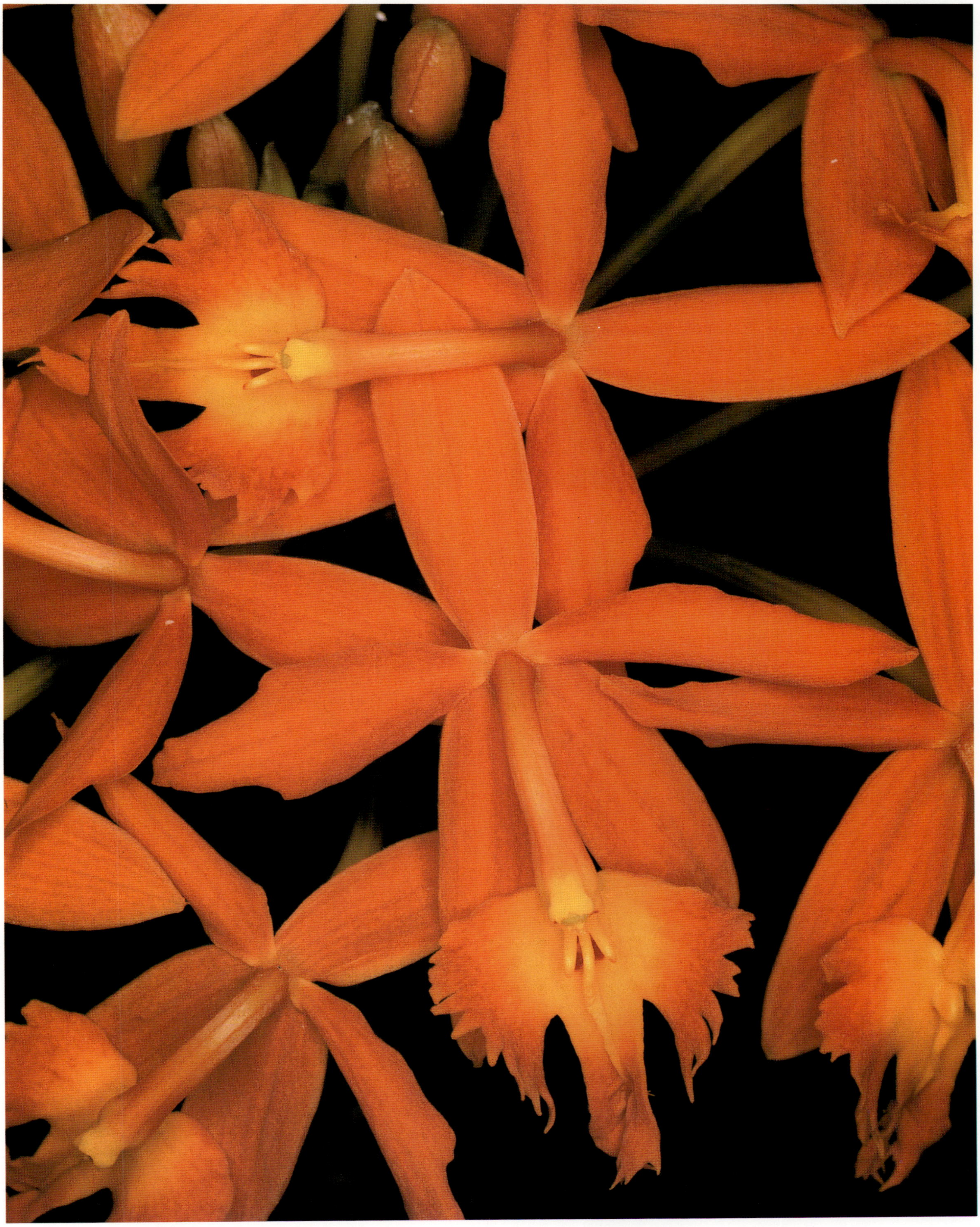

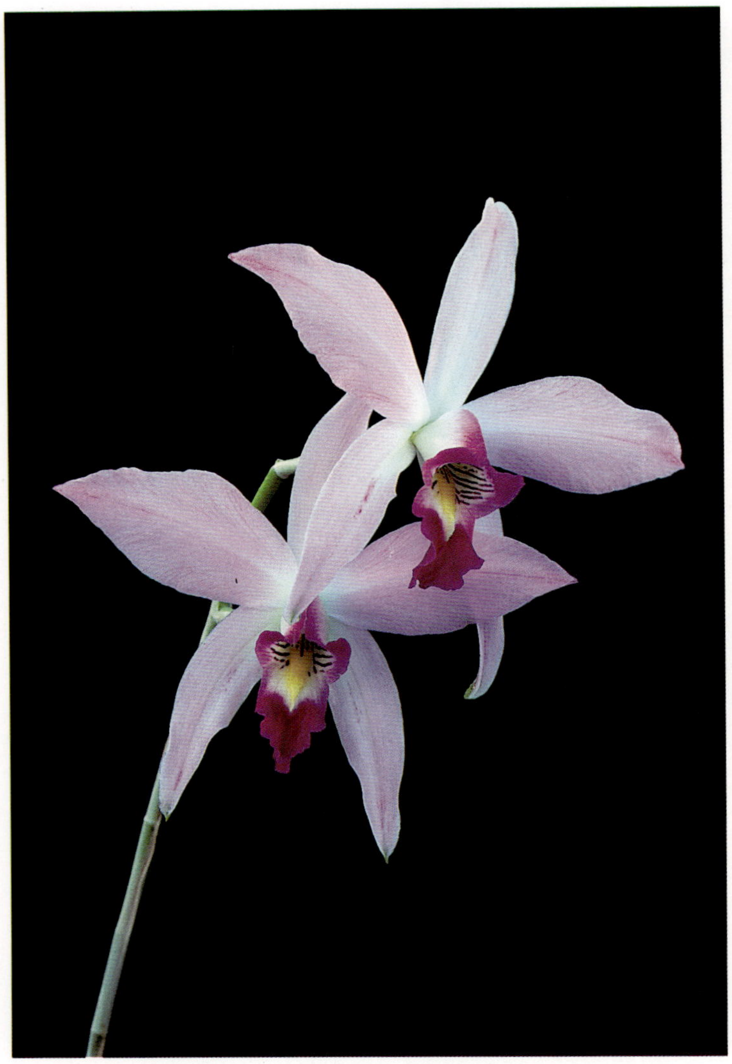

Laelia anceps

This beautiful winter-flowering species has been known in cultivation for more than 150 years. The 10cm (4 inches) flowers vary in the intensity of their colors and fine white forms exist. In its natural habitat in Mexico, it grows mostly as an epiphyte in situations where it receives a lot of light and strong contrasts, both in temperature and water supply.

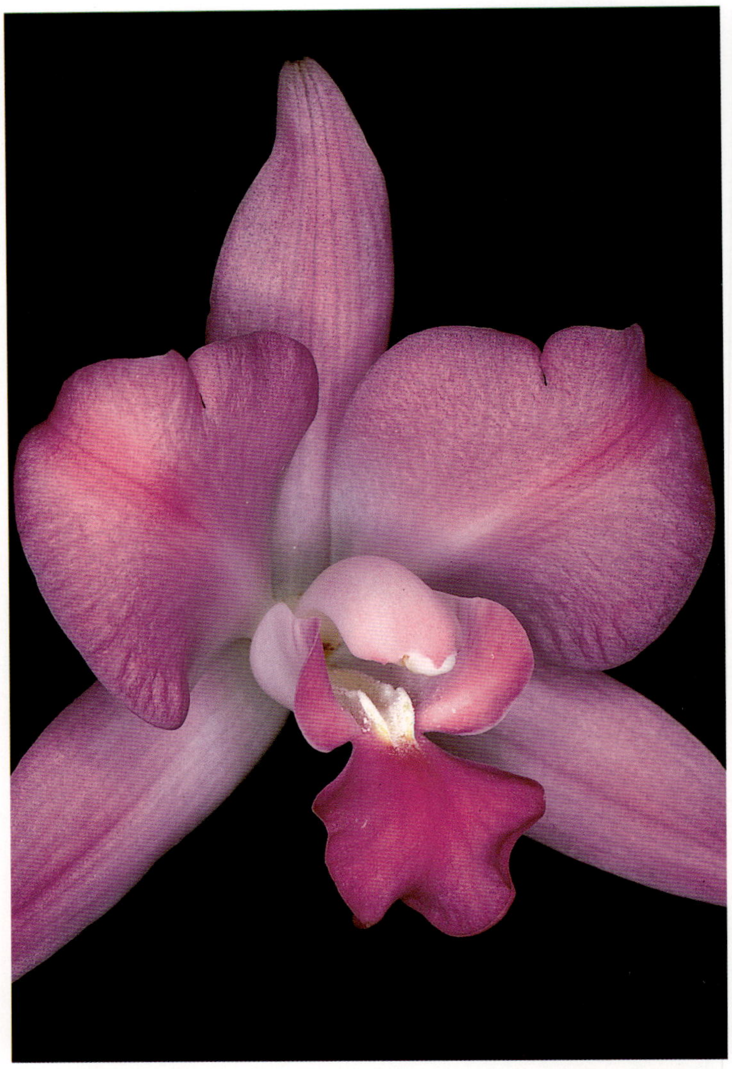

Laelia furfuracea

Another in the group of Mexican *Laelia* species which includes *Laelia anceps*, *Laelia autumnalis* and *Laelia gouldiana*. All of them grow as epiphytes or on rocks at altitudes between 2000 and 2500m (6560 – 7570 feet) where night temperatures may briefly fall below freezing and yet the days may be hot and sunny. Heavy rainfall is restricted to a five month period so that the climate overall is a dry one. The plants of *Laelia furfuracea* are more compact than those of *Laelia anceps*, but the flowers are of a similar size.

Lemboglossum bictoniense

Lemboglossum bictoniense from Mexico and Guatemala is one of a group of related species from this area which have prominent lips and are popular in cultivation. This is one of the larger species in terms of plant size, having a tall inflorescence opening in the late summer. It has been used very successfully as a parent in hybridizing in recent years.

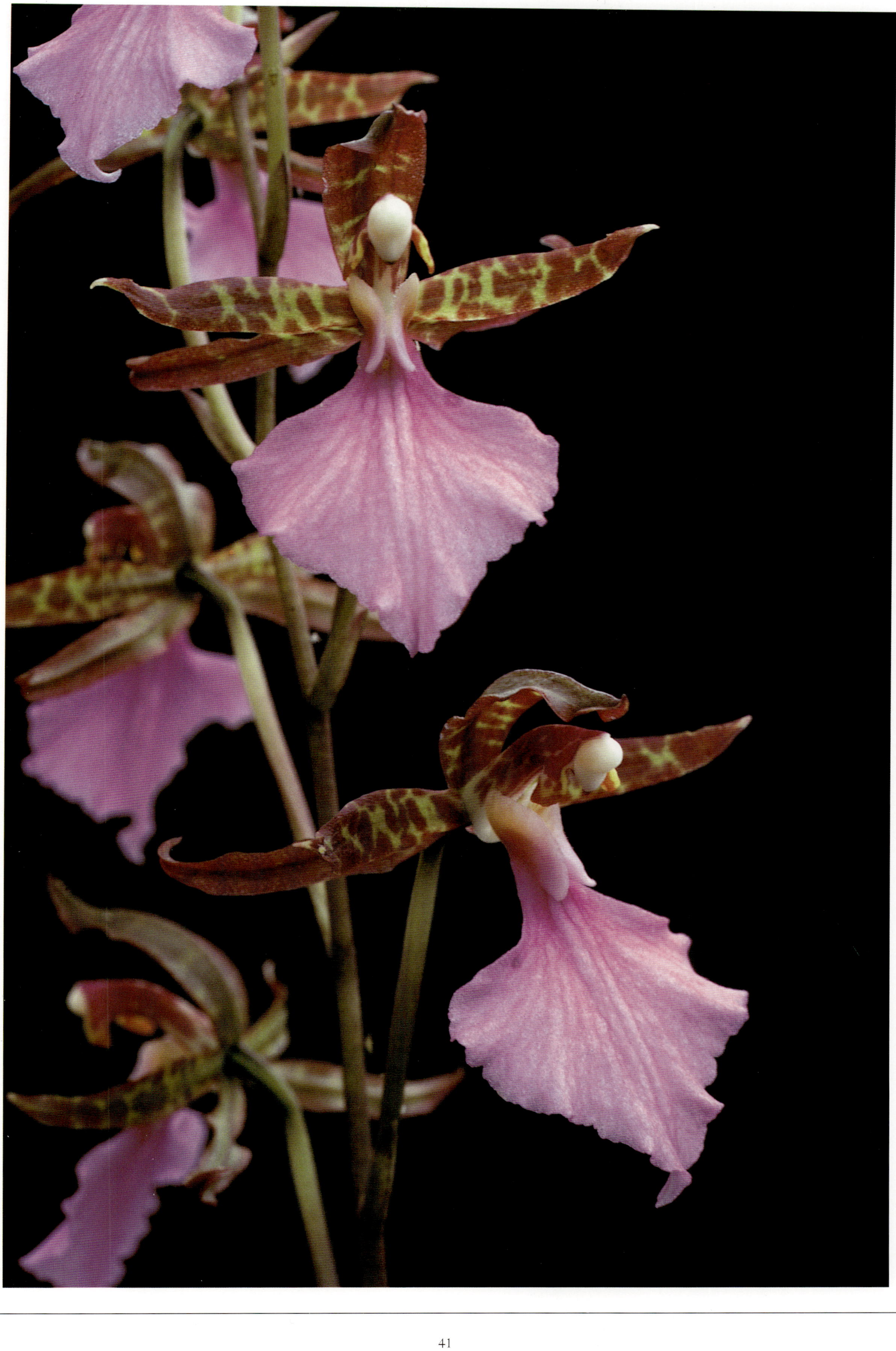

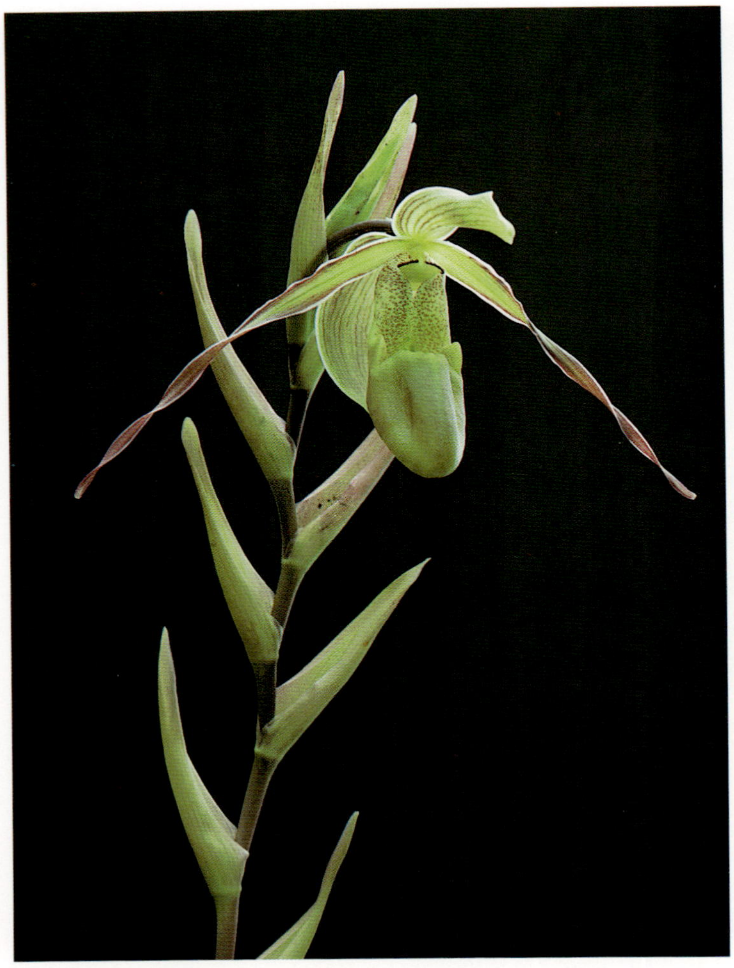

Phragmipedium longifolium

The slipper orchids of tropical America differ in a number of respects from their Asian cousins, but an obvious feature is the way in which the flowers open in succession up the stem. Occasionally, two will be present at the same time, but the older one will soon drop, always before withering. *Phragmipedium longifolium* is found in Costa Rica, Panama and Colombia, growing at medium altitudes as a semi-terrestrial in forest moss.

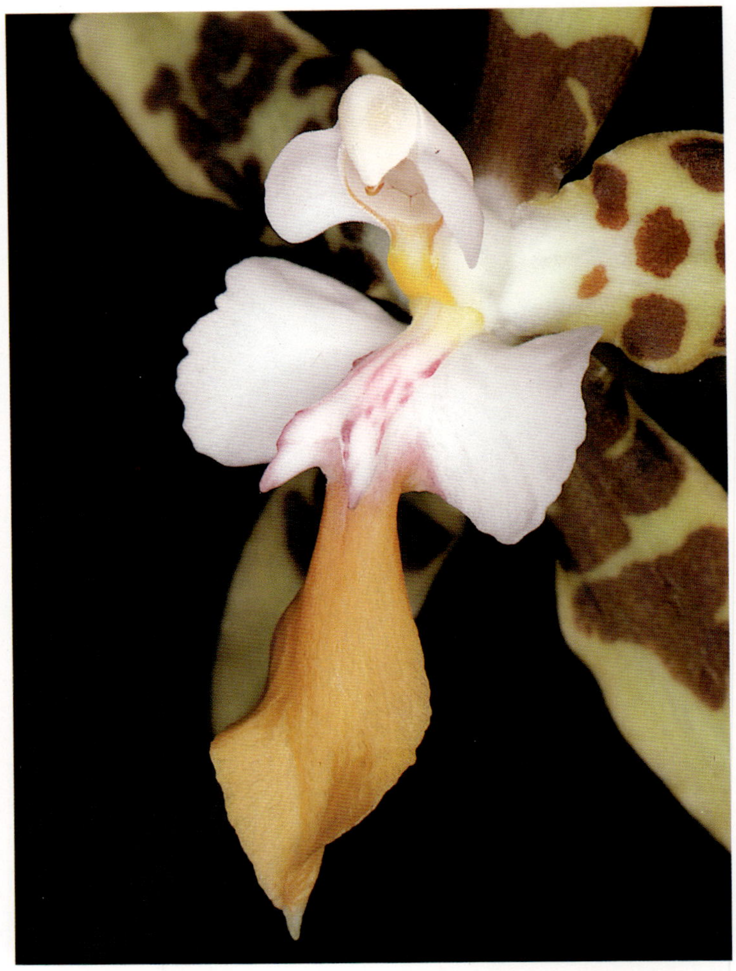

Oncidium hastatum

The genus *Oncidium* contains about 350 species, widely distributed in Central and South America. Most of them are of decorative value, with the predominant flower colors being yellow and brown. The Mexican species *Oncidium hastatum* is basically of these colors but, as can be seen here, the lip is white and orange. The numerous 4cm (2 inches) flowers are carried on a tall branching inflorescence.

Dresslerella pertusa

The genus *Dresslerella* is quite a new one, named in honor of the distinguished American tropical botanist, Dr. Robert Dressler. It is part of an alliance of which *Pleurothallis* is the largest genus, involving an enormous number of mostly small plants found throughout Central and South America. As seen here, the flowers are resting on the upper surface of a 7cm (3 inches) long leaf and is enclosed except for a small aperture. With its dull color and rough texture, it must still be attractive to a small insect somewhere in Panama.

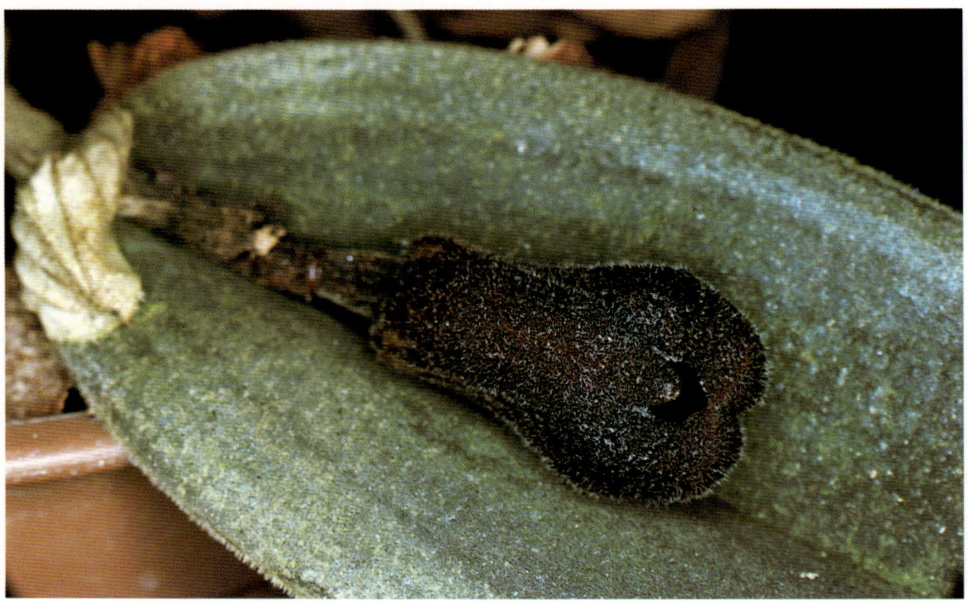

Arpophyllum giganteum

The thick leaves of *Arpophyllum giganteum* are up to half a meter (20 inches) long so that a mature plant is very large. For all its size, the flowers are tiny, but they form a solid column of color which is very attractive. The plants grow as forest epiphytes and are found over a wide area from Mexico to Costa Rica, Jamaica, Colombia and Venezuela.

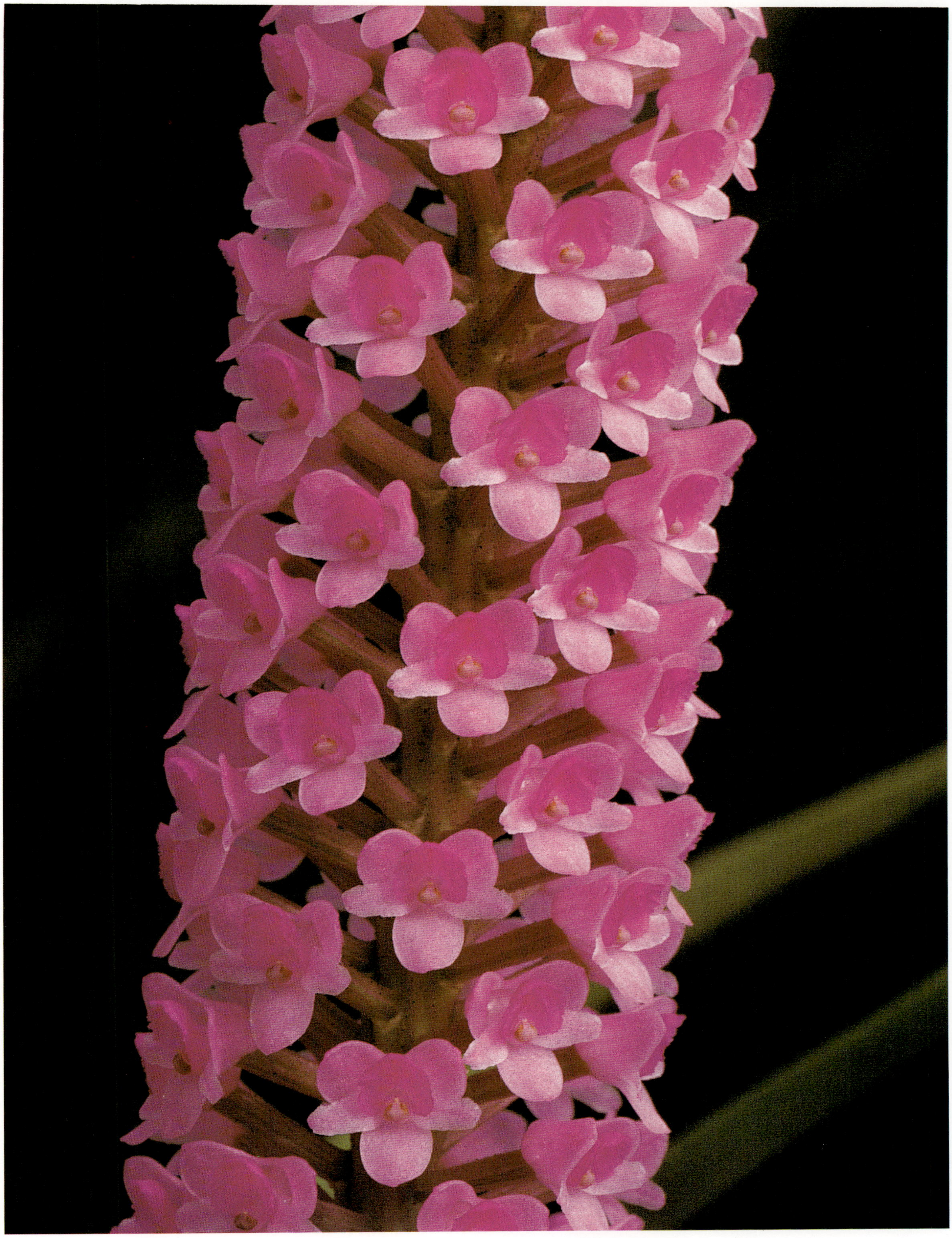

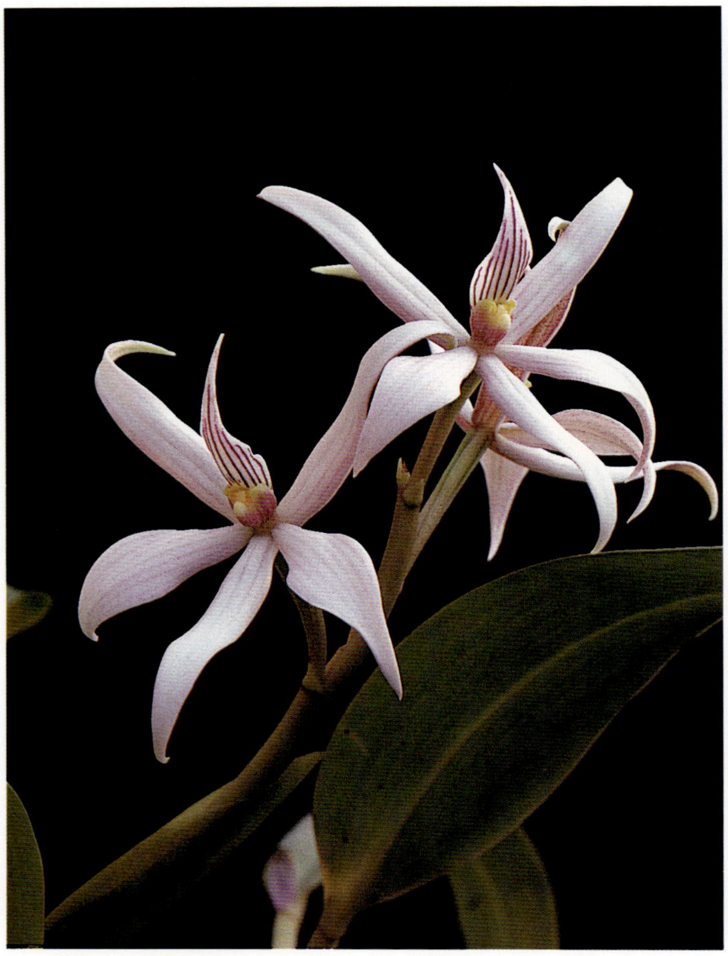

Encyclia sima

Apart from the tough Mexican encyclia species seen earlier, there is another group known sometimes as 'cockleshell orchids'. They are rather softer plants and the fragrant flowers have the lip uppermost. This species is found only in Panama, and was described in 1969 from plants collected in cloud forest near the summit of a mountain in Central Panama. The large flowers are produced in the spring and are long-lasting.

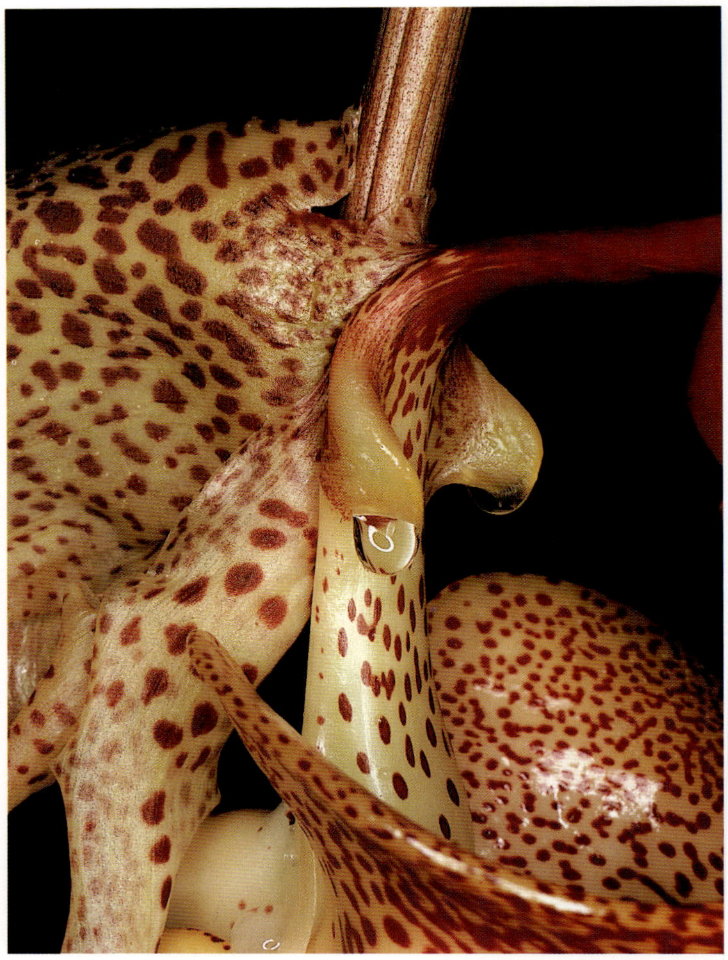

Coryanthes macrantha

The twenty or so species of *Coryanthes* are distributed from Guatemala to Brazil and they produce probably the most complex and specialized of all orchid flowers. The plants grow as forest epiphytes in association with other types of vegetation and nests of vicious ants. This makes them difficult to collect but they can be cultivated without the ants. Lasting only three or four days, the flowers are strongly scented and the sepals and petals soon fold back as they expand on opening.

Dimerandra emarginata

There are considered to be eight species of *Dimerandra* widely distributed in Central and South America. *Dimerandra emarginata* is found over much of that range, growing as a forest epiphyte at low to medium elevations. The plants grow to perhaps 40cm (16 inches) tall, but often less, and their slender stems bear several thin leaves. The attractive flat flowers are produced one or two at a time from the tops of the stems.

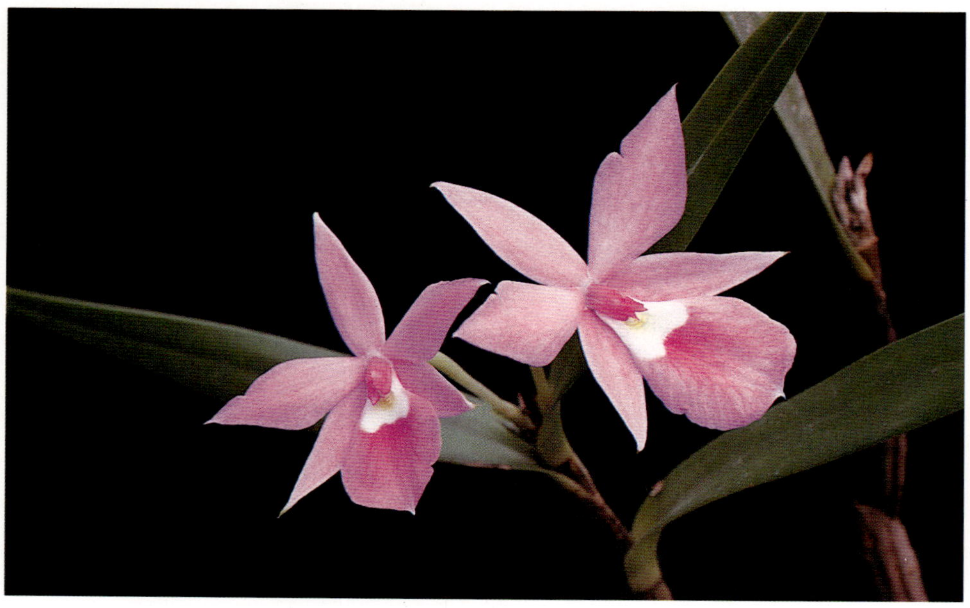

Coryanthes macrantha

Coryanthes macrantha is native to Trinidad, Venezuela and Guyana. The flower structure is dominated by the lip which is in the form of a bucket, suspended from the base of the column. Below this point, as seen here, are two horns which, when the flower is fully open, secrete a clear liquid so that the bucket fills to about a third where there is an aperture by the column tip. Bees attracted to the flower fall into the liquid and can escape only through the aperture, thus collecting the pollen.

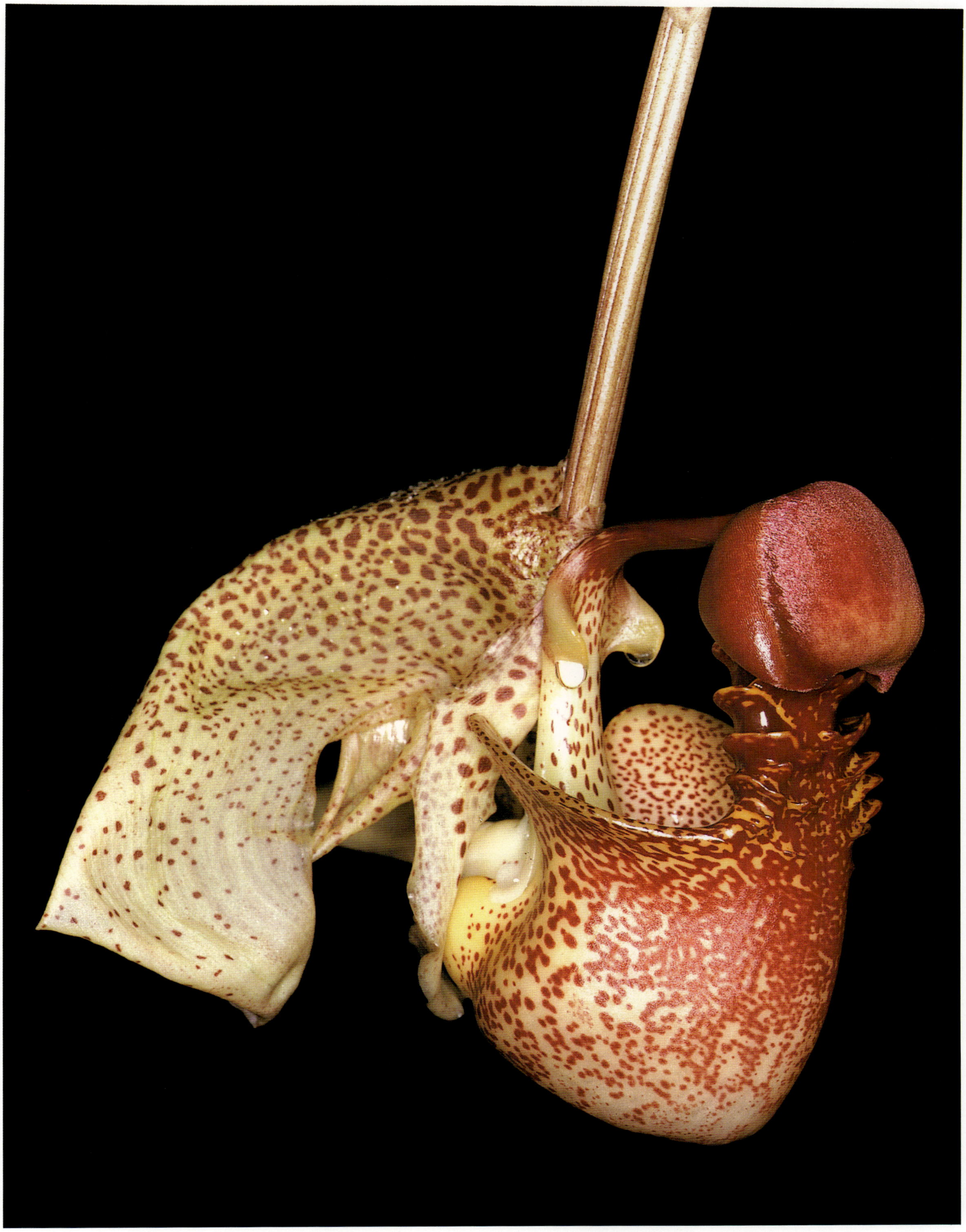

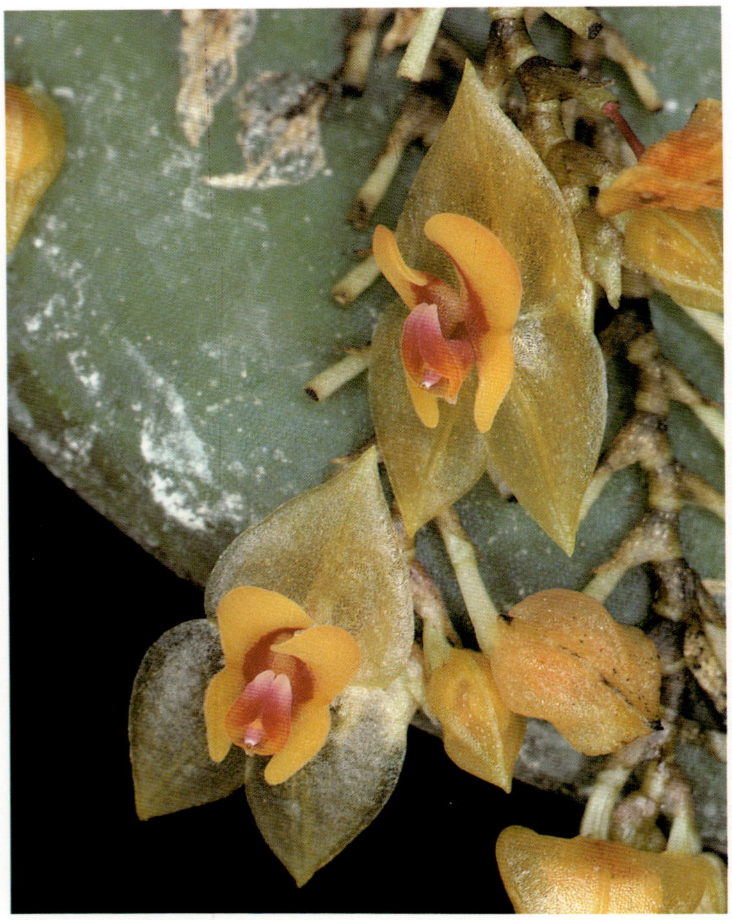

Lepanthes ovalis

Another of the small cloud forest genera of tropical America is *Lepanthes*, of which *Lepanthes ovalis* from Jamaica is a typical example. These are plants which grow amongst ferns and mosses on the branches and trunks of trees, under conditions where they never become dry. Although the flowers are tiny, they are brightly colored and exquisite in detail. In the case of this species, they open in succession on an inflorescence which lies against the leaf surface, but in other species they hang beneath the leaf.

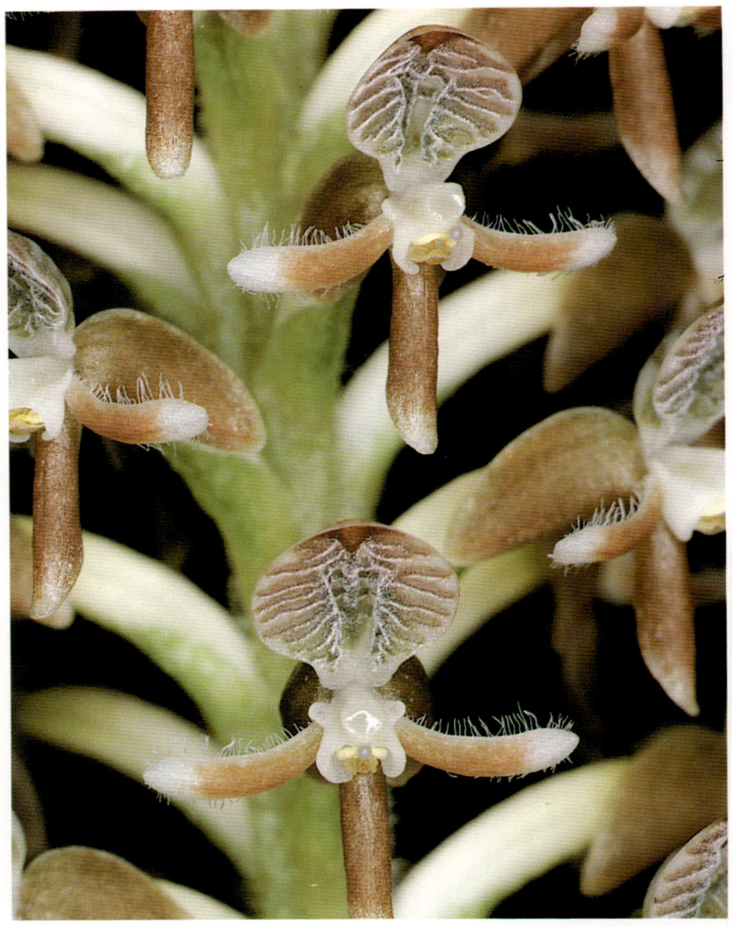

Cranichis ciliata

The genus *Cranichis* contains about 30 species of terrestrial orchids, distributed from Florida, south to Bolivia. *Cranichis ciliata* is typical of many tropical terrestrials in having fleshy roots to sustain it in dry periods. The erect inflorescence grows to 45cm (18 inches) tall, with the small flowers borne in a dense head on the upper part. They are simple in structure, although the concave lip is uppermost. It is found in rain forest at medium altitudes in Central America south from Guatemala, and in South America from Venezuela to Bolivia.

Sobralia lowii

The distinction between terrestrial and epiphytic orchids is not always clear in the tropics, as some plants can adapt to either growth habit. Sobralias are found throughout Central and South America, and in form the plants rather resemble clumps of bamboo. They grow on trees, in leaf litter or soil, and on rocks. Although the showy flowers last only a day or two, they appear in succession over a long period. *Sobralia lowii* comes from Colombia and is one of the smaller ones, with stems up to about 60cm (24 inches) tall.

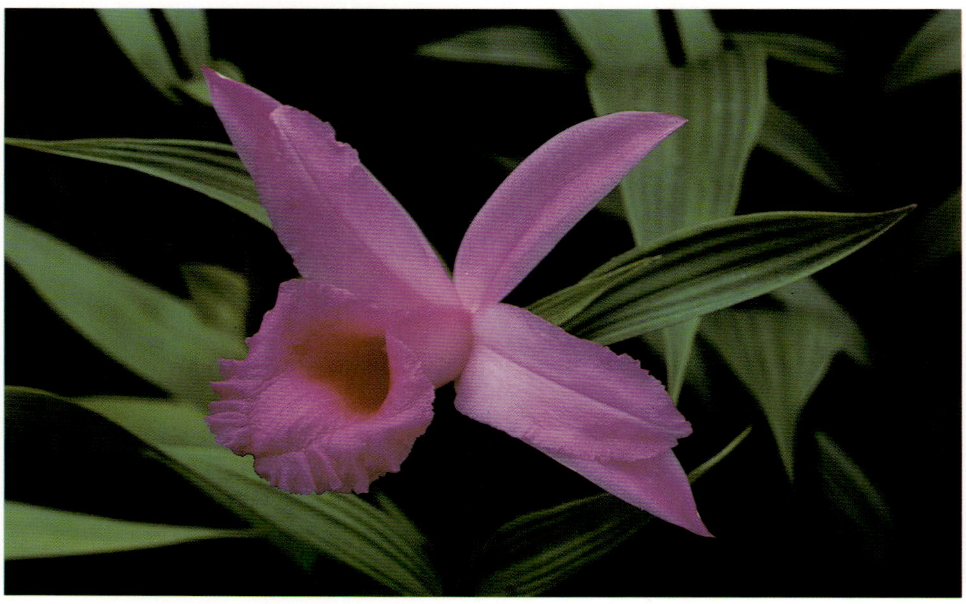

Epidendrum ferrugineum

While many *Epidendrum* species are rather large and even coarse, this one is almost dainty in appearance, standing less than 30cm (12 inches) tall and with a drooping inflorescence of small pretty flowers. These have extremely narrow petals, only a fraction of a millimeter wide. *Epidendrum ferrugineum* grows as a forest epiphyte in Trinidad, Venezuela, Colombia and Peru.

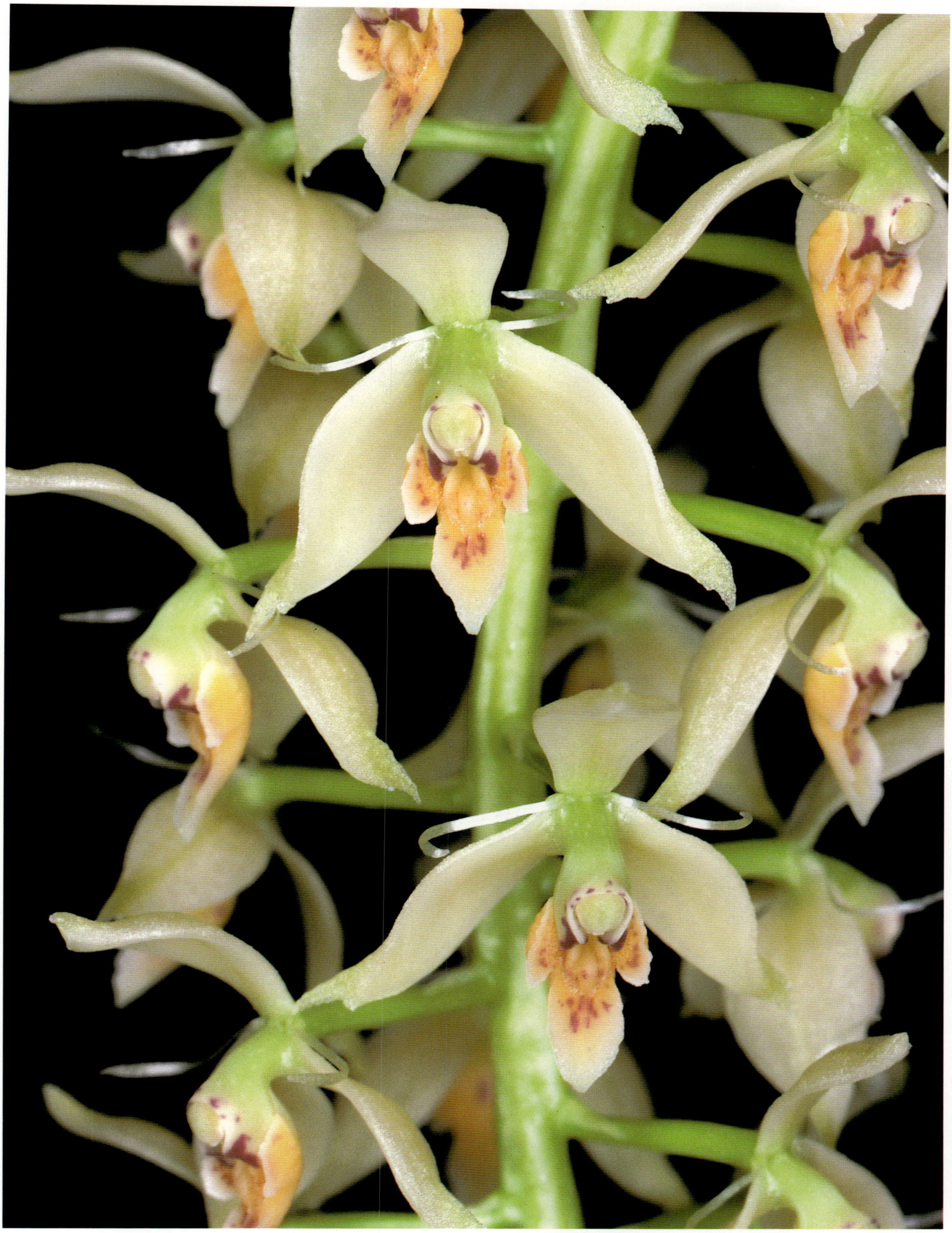

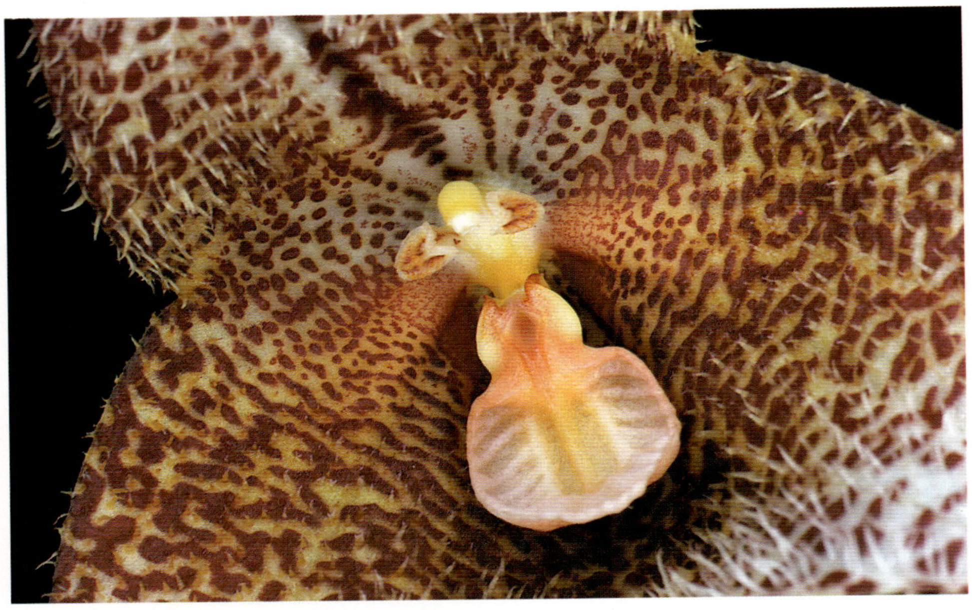

Dracula

With a name like dracula, meaning 'little dragon', a plant is bound to attract attention. There are about 90 species found mainly in northern South America, especially Colombia, and their favored habitat involves a lot of water, shade and high humidity. They grow as epiphytes on branches, and most cases, the inflorescences grow downwards so that the flowers hang free. This is a close view of the center of a dracula flower showing the shell-like lip, and the two tiny petals, one on either side of the column. The whole flower is about 10cm (4 inches) across, and the dominant sepals extend into tapered tails.

Masdevallia coccinea

Pleurothallis, *Dracula* and *Masdevallia* are closely related tropical American genera, but it is the species of *Masdevallia* which are the most popular in cultivation. This is due to their generally compact growth habit, and the range of color and form of their flowers. *M. coccinea*, which grows at around 3000m (9840 feet) in Colombia, is one of the best known species. The flowers are large, and vary in color from magenta and crimson, to yellow and white. The sepals form the visible parts as the petals and lip are tiny.

Pleurothallis talpinaria

Pleurothallis talpinaria, from Venezuela, Colombia, Ecuador and Peru, produces its striking flowers in succession, from the junction between the plant's leaf and stem. As in a majority of pleurothallis flowers, the two lateral sepals are fused together, but the petals are more prominent than many. However it is the elaborately sculptured lip which catches the eye of the observer.

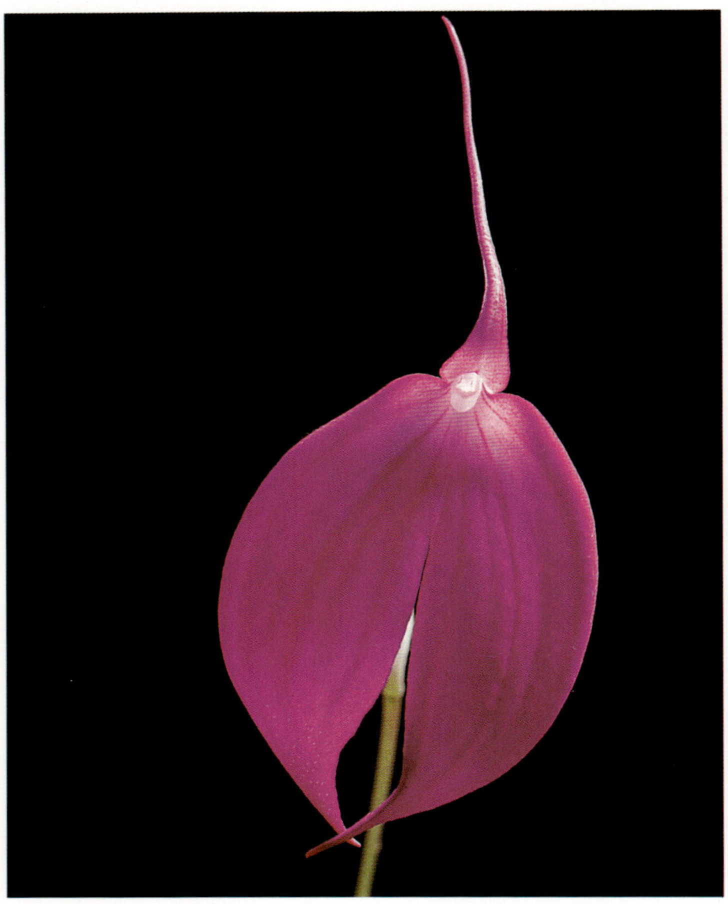

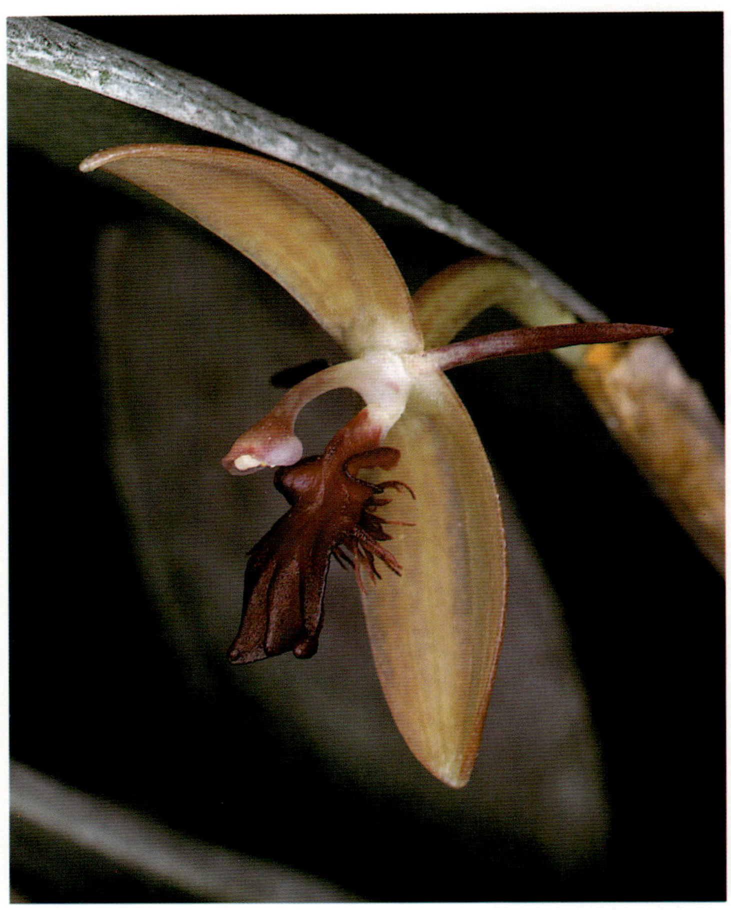

Maxillaria fulgens

The large genus *Maxillaria* is another of those which is widespread in Central and South America. The species usually grow as forest epiphytes and most of them have pseudobulbs and tough leathery leaves. Each infloresence produces a single flower, but as in the case of *Maxillaria fulgens* from Costa Rica, Panama, Venezuela and Colombia, a great many flowers may appear from each growth. This species is unusual in having a cluster of pseudobulbs, from which extending leafy stems grow upwards, and it is from between these leaves that the flowers are produced.

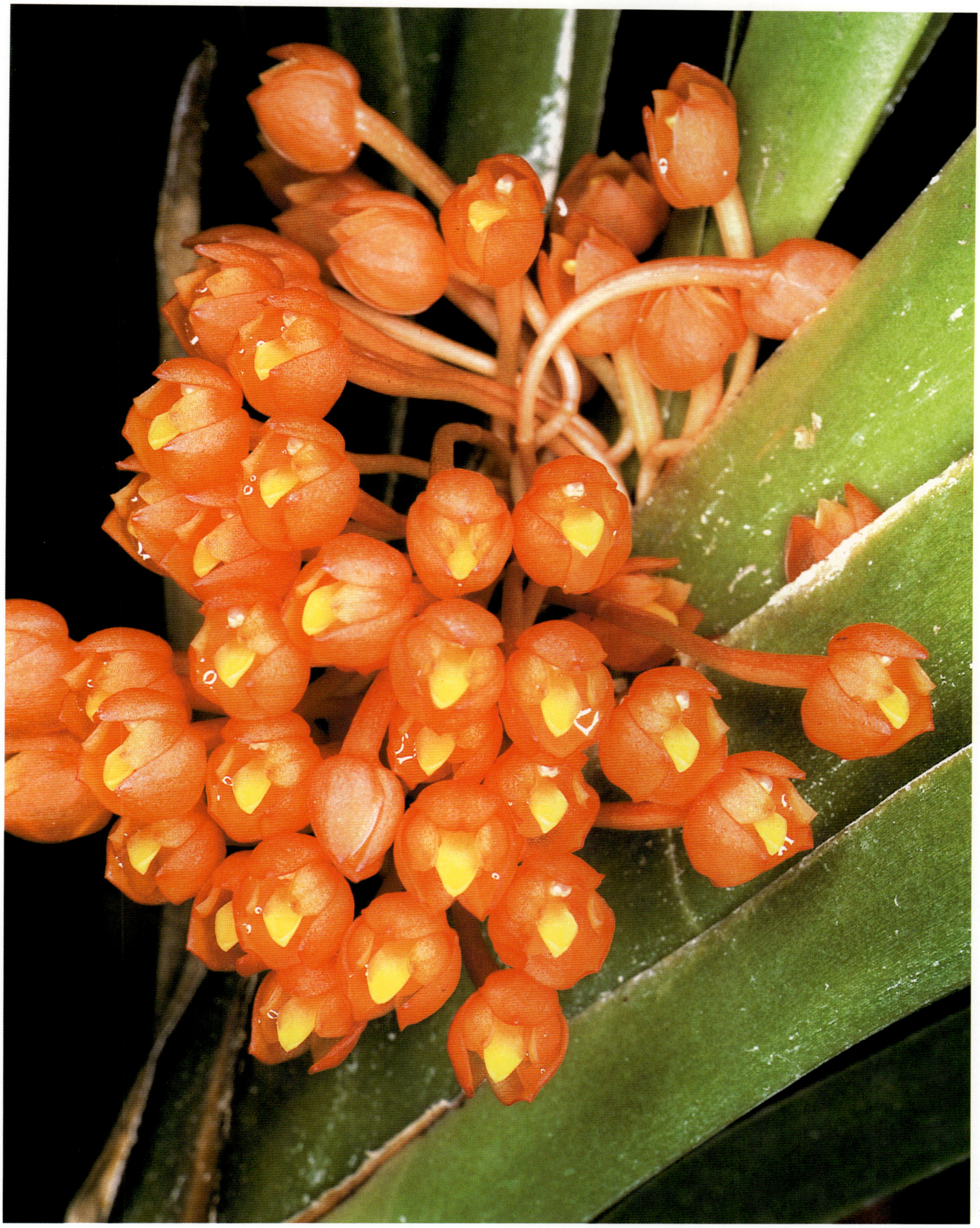

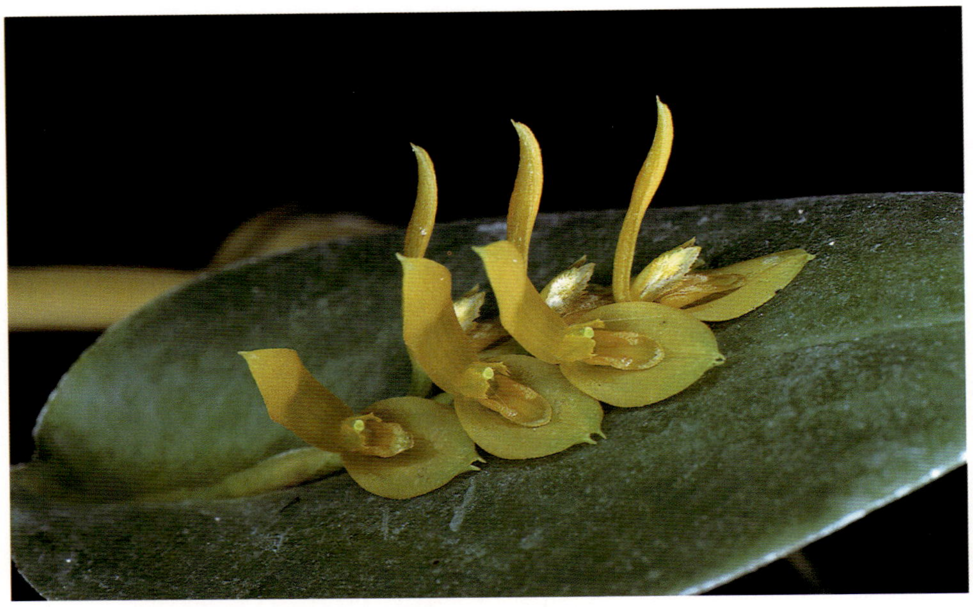

Pleurothallis chamensis

At least a thousand *Pleurothallis* species have been described from Central and South America. They are mostly small plants growing mainly as epiphytes in montane forest where they are never subjected to drought. Although showing great diversity in both plant habit, and in flower shapes and colors, there are certain features common to most species. *Pleurothallis chamensis* occurs in South America, from Venezuela to Bolivia, and the 8mm long flowers only appear to grow from the leaf surface.

Neomoorea wallisii

This rare species from Colombia and Panama has about the largest leaves of any orchid, each one being up to a meter (40 inches) long and 18cm (7 inches) wide. The size of the plant rules it out for most amateur growers, but when the inflorescences appear at the side of the new growth in the spring, the inconvenience is forgotten. *Neomoorea* grows as a forest epiphyte at moderate elevations, and mature plants tend to grow vertical roots which act as traps for dead leaves and other sources of nutrient.

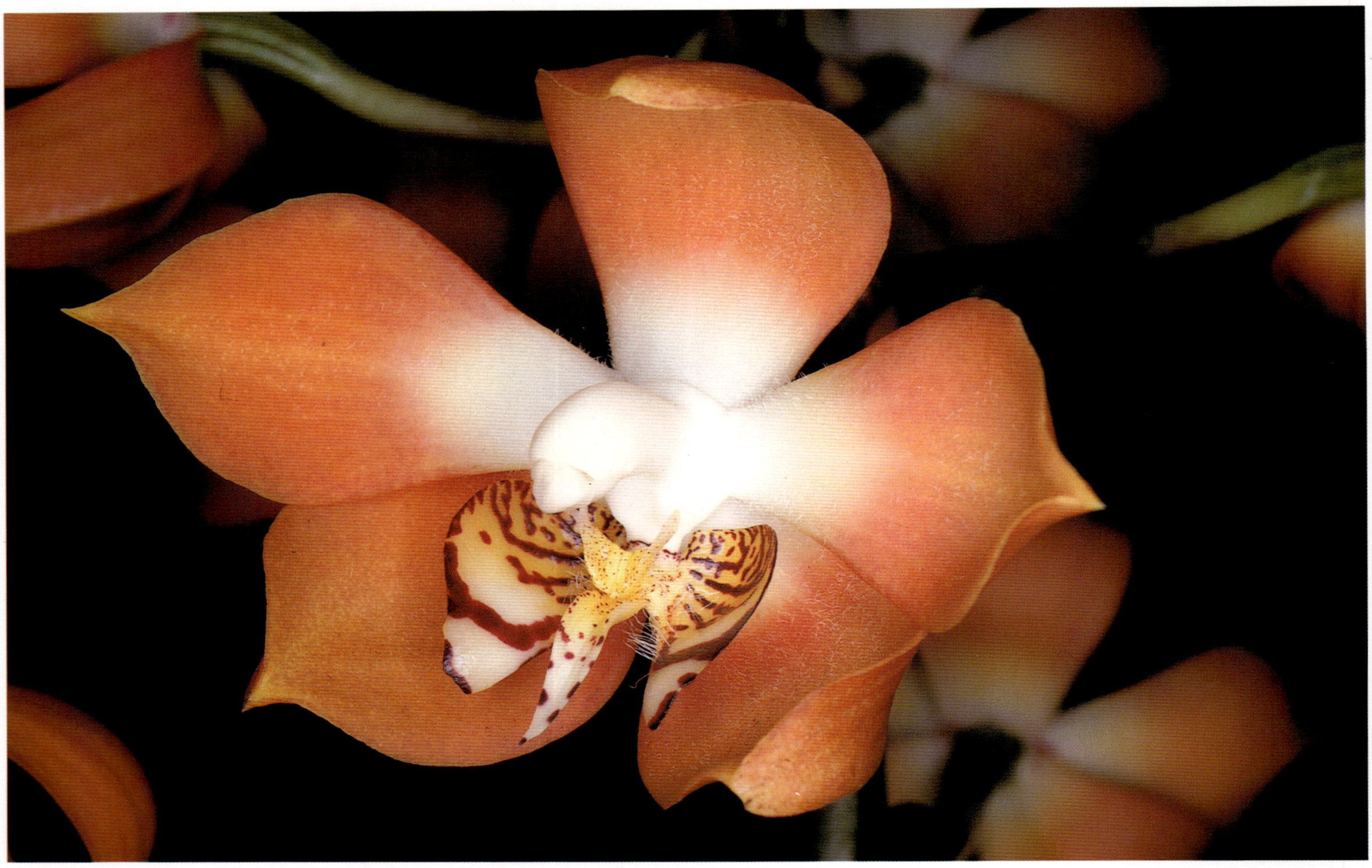

Polycycnis ornata

Some orchid flowers were never meant to be decorative, but still have a certain fascination. *Polycycnis ornata*, which grows as an epiphyte in Venezuela, Colombia and Ecuador, produces a long pendent inflorescence, bearing about a dozen flowers. These have an interesting structure which is clearly seen here. The three spotted brown sepals hang down, while the green column arches gracefully above. Between them are the two ribbon-like petals and the narrow, rather spiny lip.

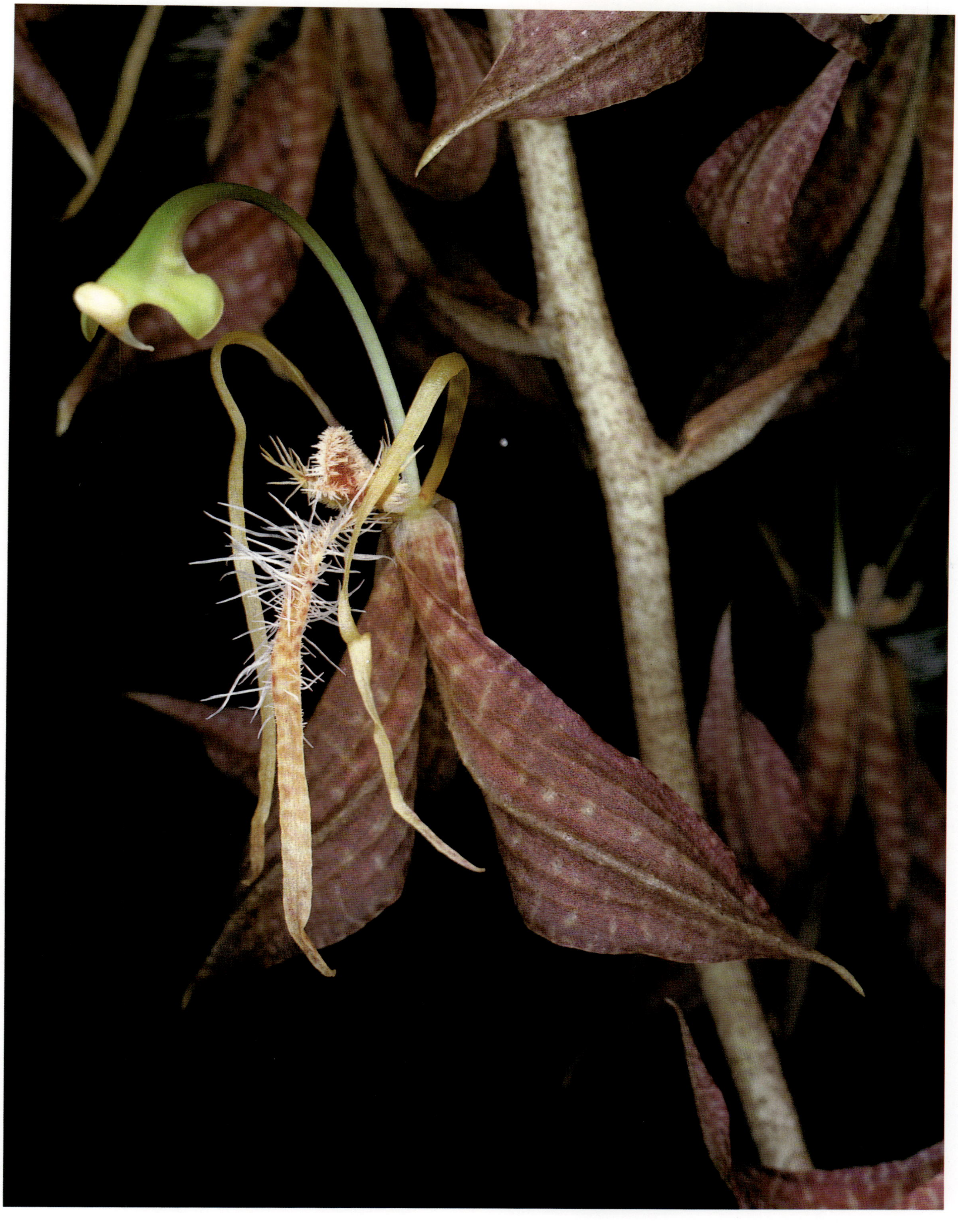

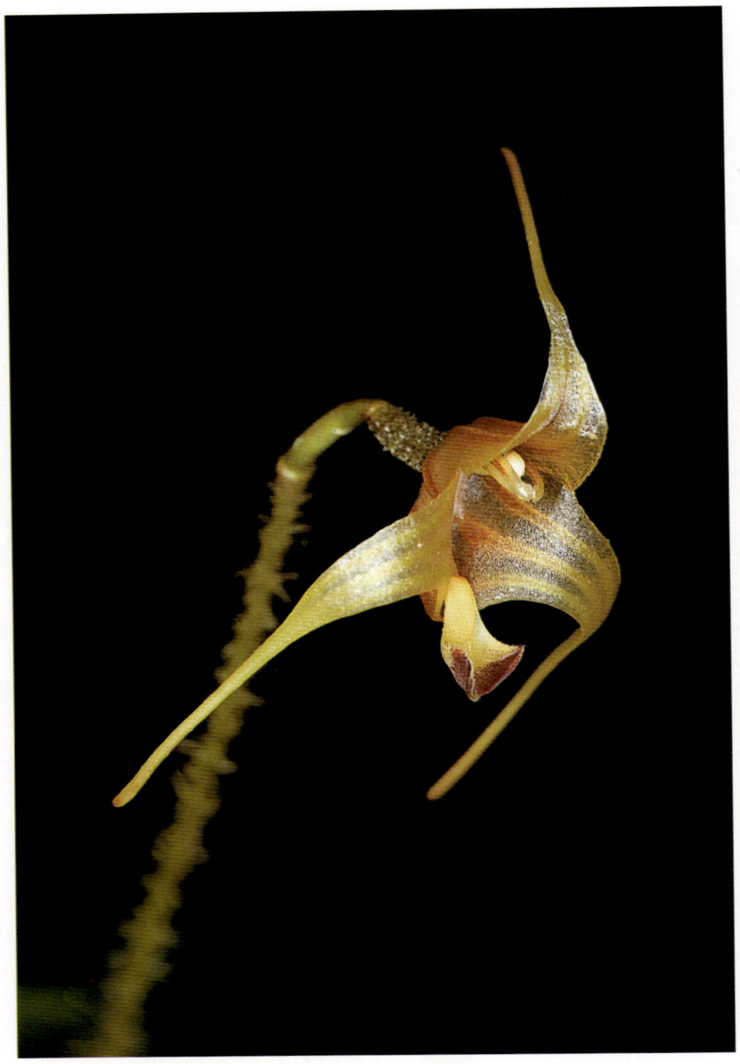

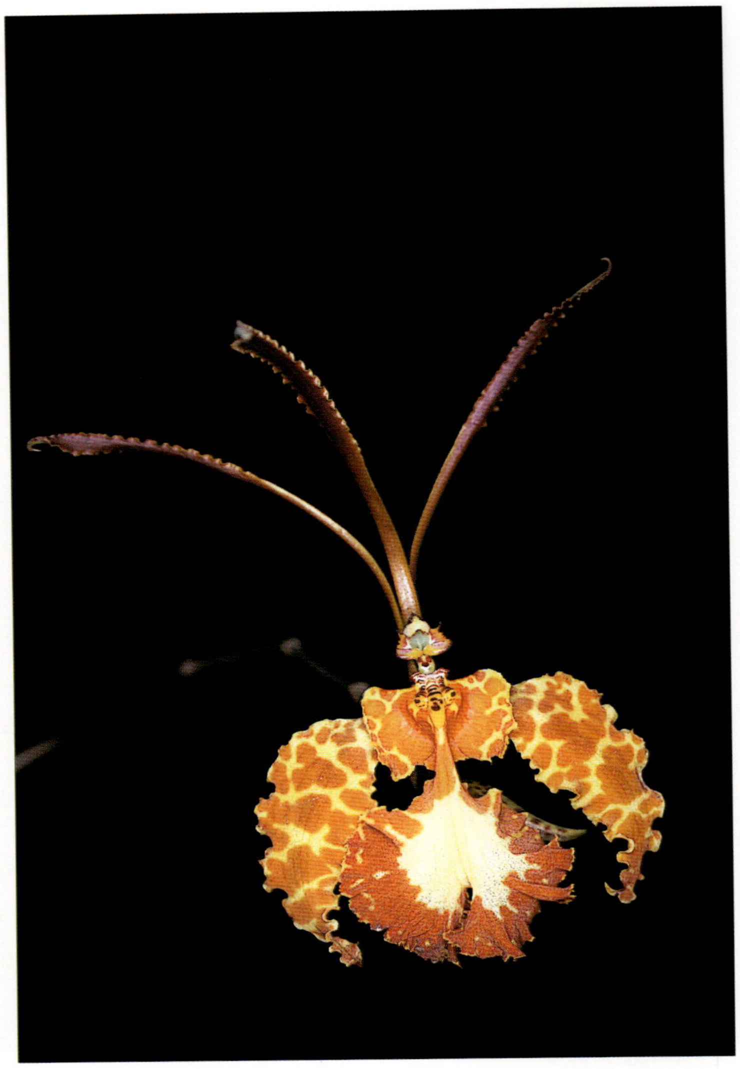

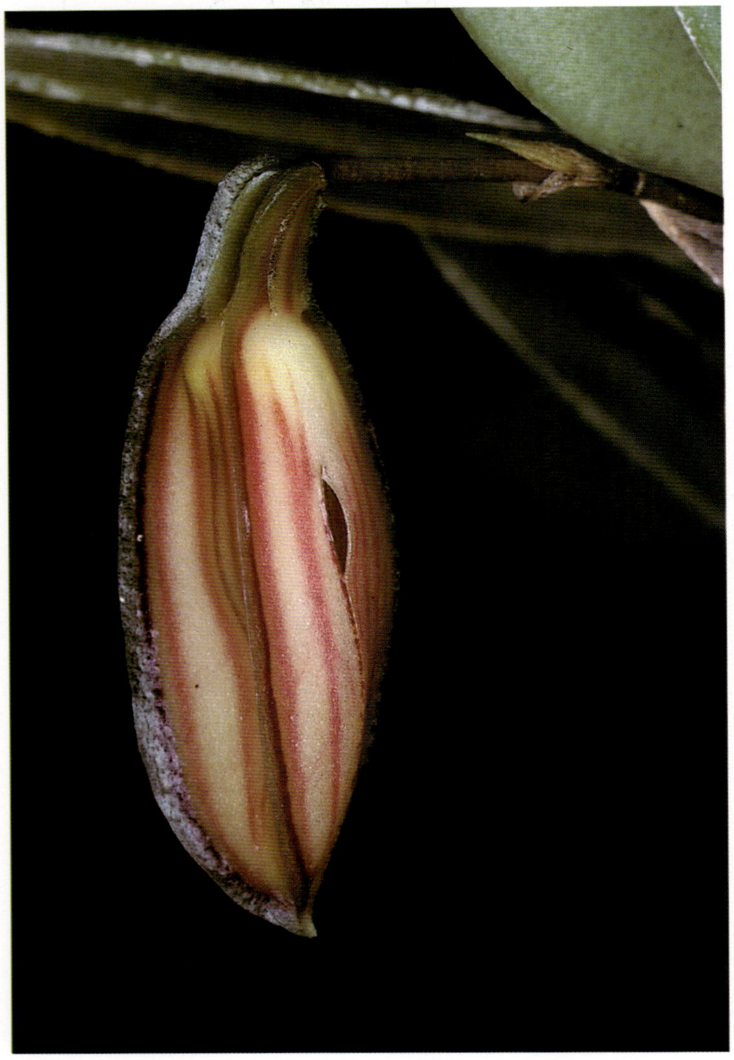

ABOVE LEFT: *Porroglossum echidnum*

The forests of the South American Andes are home to thousands of small but often intriguing and attractive orchid species. This one comes from Venezuela, Colombia and Ecuador, growing mostly as a cloud forest epiphyte but occasionally on stream boulders, at altitudes around 2500m (7570 feet). The plant consists of a cluster of 10cm (4 inches) tall leaves, from the base of which arises the 15cm (6 inches) inflorescence. The three sepals form the main part of the flower, but the hanging lip moves rapidly upwards on contact, to briefly trap pollinating insects.

ABOVE: *Psychopsis krameriana*

The tropical American genus *Psychopsis* contains several spectacular species, sometimes known as butterfly orchids. The large flowers are borne, usually singly, at the end of a long rigid stem so that they appear to hang in the air. *Psychopsis krameriana* is found in Costa Rica, Panama, Ecuador and Peru, and grows as a forest epiphyte at altitudes of up to 1000m (3300 feet). It was a similar species, *Psychopsis papilio*, which, it is said, inspired the Sixth Duke of Devonshire to establish a famous orchid collection at Chatsworth Park.

LEFT: *Zootrophion oblongifolium*

Zootrophion species are distinguished by the fact that their flowers are almost entirely closed, leaving only a small slit or aperture on either side. The flowers of *Zootrophion oblongifolium* from Ecuador, hang downwards, and are about 2.5cm (1 inch) long. Apart from revealing one of the apertures, the illustration shows the ribbed ovary at the top of the flower. These plants are yet other examples of cloud forest epiphytes.

Prescottia plantaginifolia

Not all terrestrial orchids are small slender plants, although the larger ones cannot rival the bigger epiphytes in size. *Prescottia* is a small genus distributed from Florida to Brazil, and the Brazilian species *Prescottia plantaginifolia* is probably the largest of them. The numerous soft leaves form a fleshy rosette from which the 60cm (24 inches) inflorescence arises, and this is densely covered with tiny green flowers. These look strange because the globular lip is the most prominent feature, while the sepals are crumpled underneath.

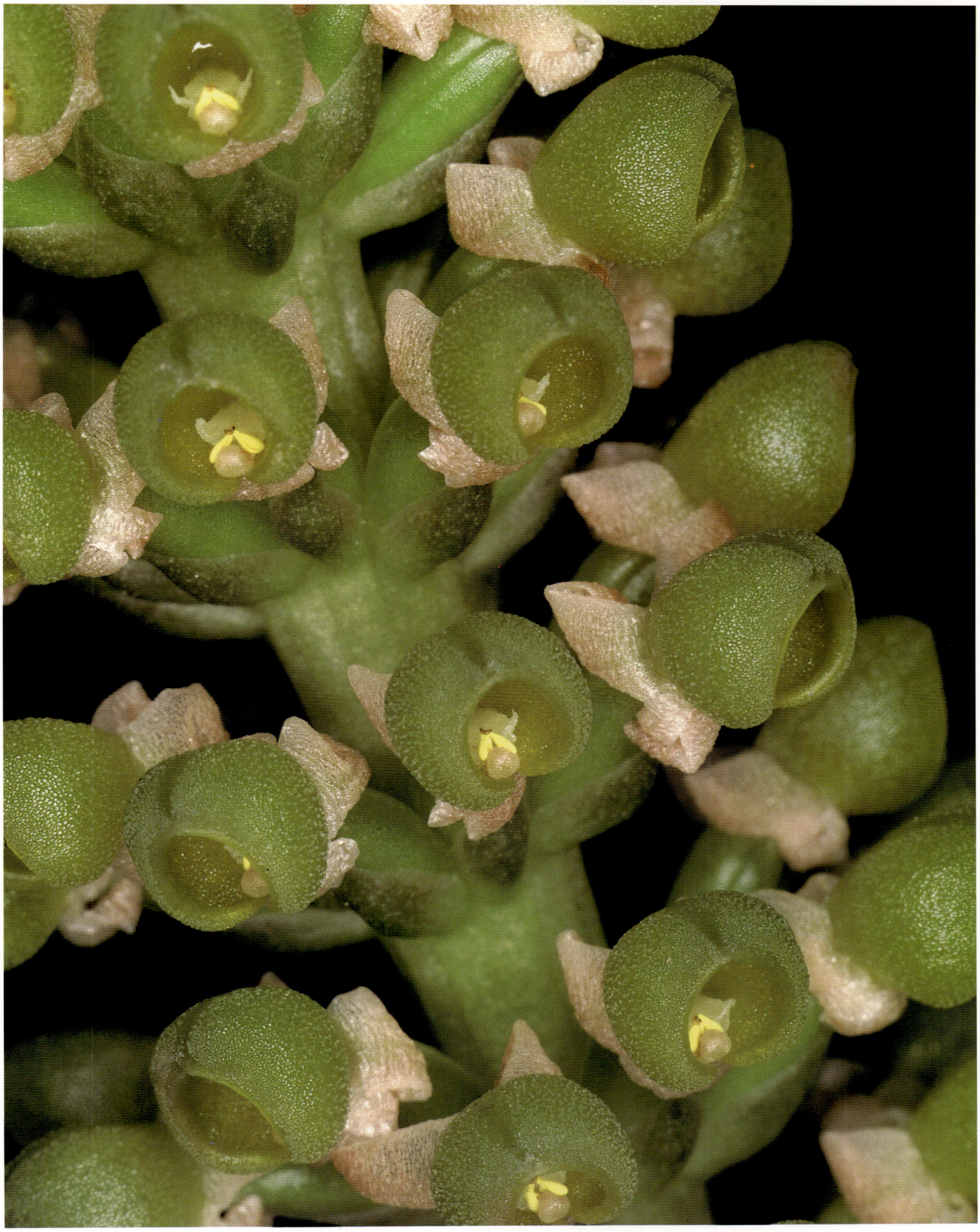

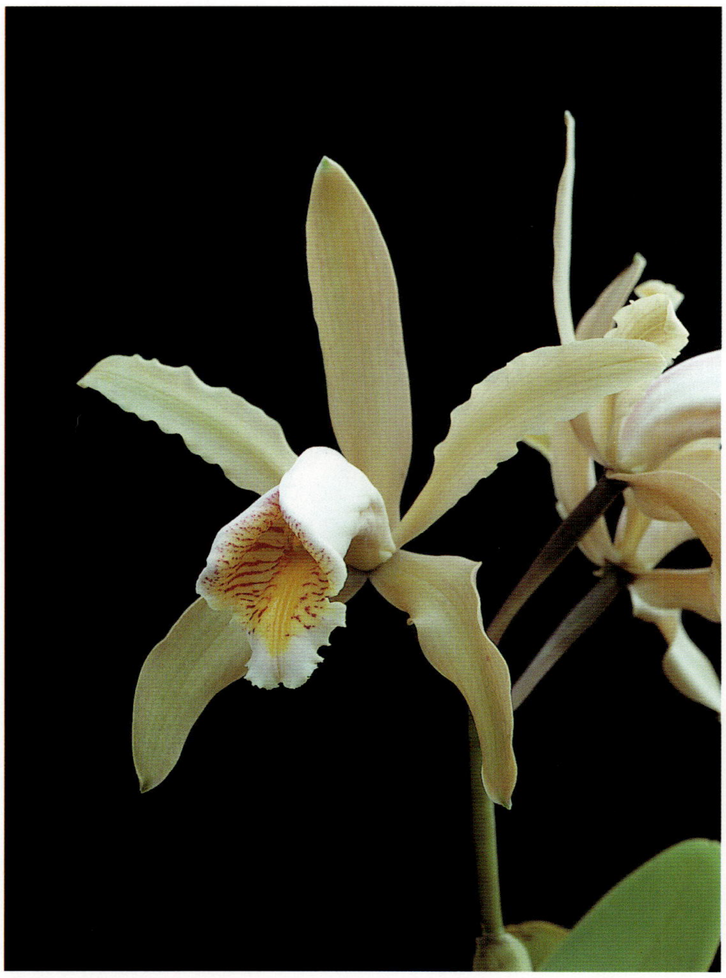

Cattleya forbesii

If there were to be one group of plants identified in the public mind with the word orchid, it would have to be the cattleyas of Central and South America. There are about 30 *Cattleya* species, dividing naturally into two groups; those with a single leaf and those with two or three on each stem. *Cattleya forbesii* from coastal Brazil is a tough epiphyte with two leaves on each pseudobulb. The 9cm (3.5 inches) flowers last for two or three weeks and usually appear in the summer months.

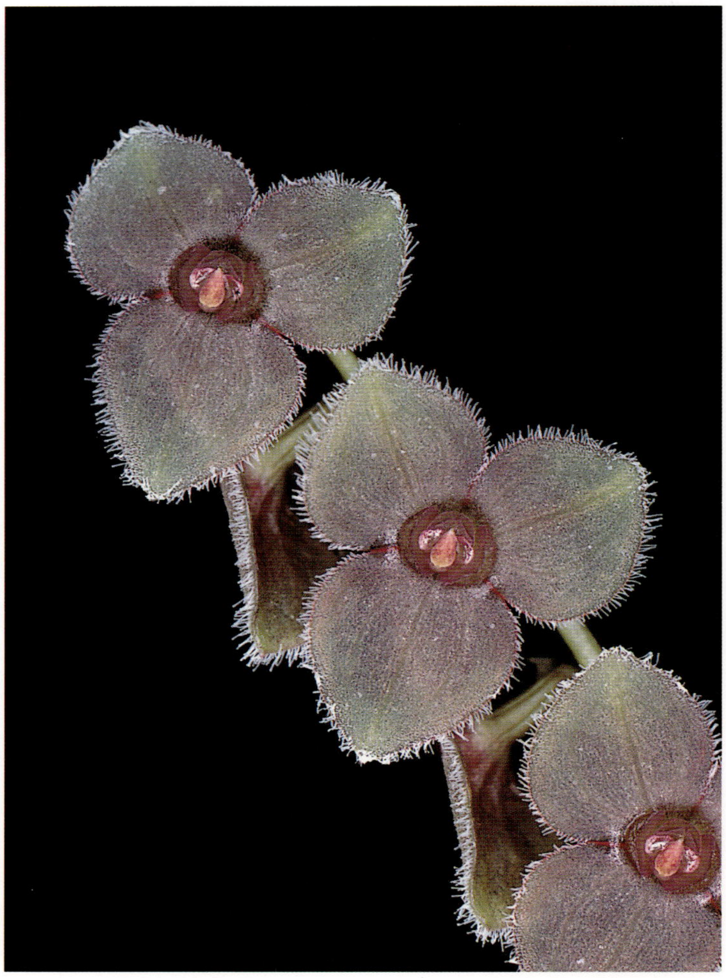

Stelis fragrans

Another of those small-flowered tropical American genera, related to *Pleurothallis*, which is found growing epiphytically in cloud forest from Mexico to Brazil and Peru. The flowers are distinguished by their flat spreading sepals, while the minute petals and lip are mostly lost in the center. *Stelis fragrans* comes from Brazil and the 8mm flowers are delicately attractive when enlarged.

Cattleya labiata

The single leaved cattleyas, of which this is the typical example, have larger flowers which are pleasantly scented. *Cattleya labiata* grows as an epiphyte, often high up in trees in the eastern states of Brazil. It was the first such species to be introduced to cultivation in Europe, and is a parent of numerous hybrids. Up to five 15cm (6 inches) flowers are carried on each inflorescence, and they are to be seen in the fall and winter.

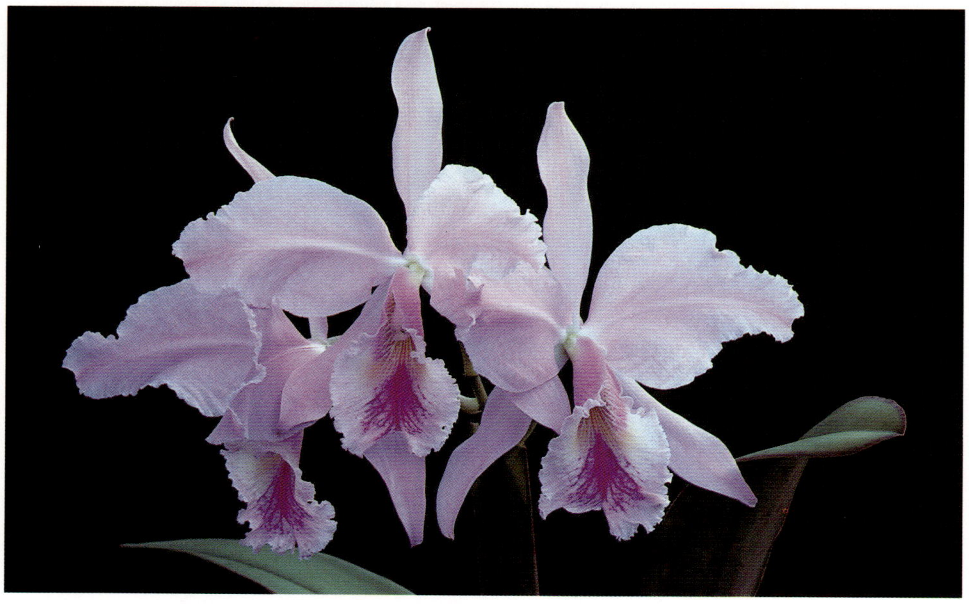

Sophronitis coccinea

The dwarf Brazilian species *Sophronitis coccinea* enjoys a reputation far greater than its size would suggest. Its fiery color soon attracted hybridists anxious to create large red cattleyas, and in this they have succeeded. However, size is not everything, and many other hybrids have emphasized its compact nature to good effect. The species itself grows as an epiphyte in mossy forest on coastal ranges in Brazil. Here there is always plenty of moisture and temperatures are never extreme.

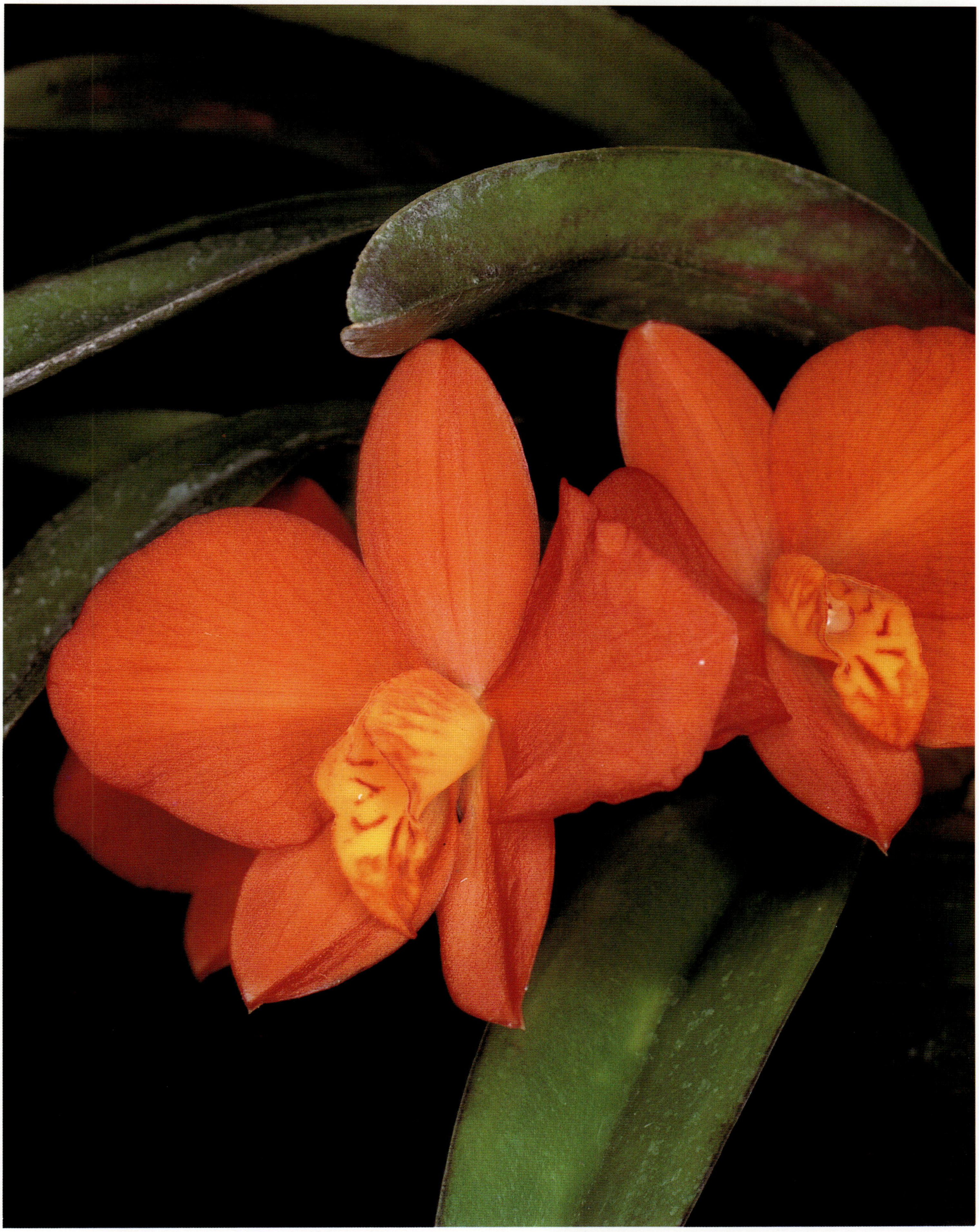

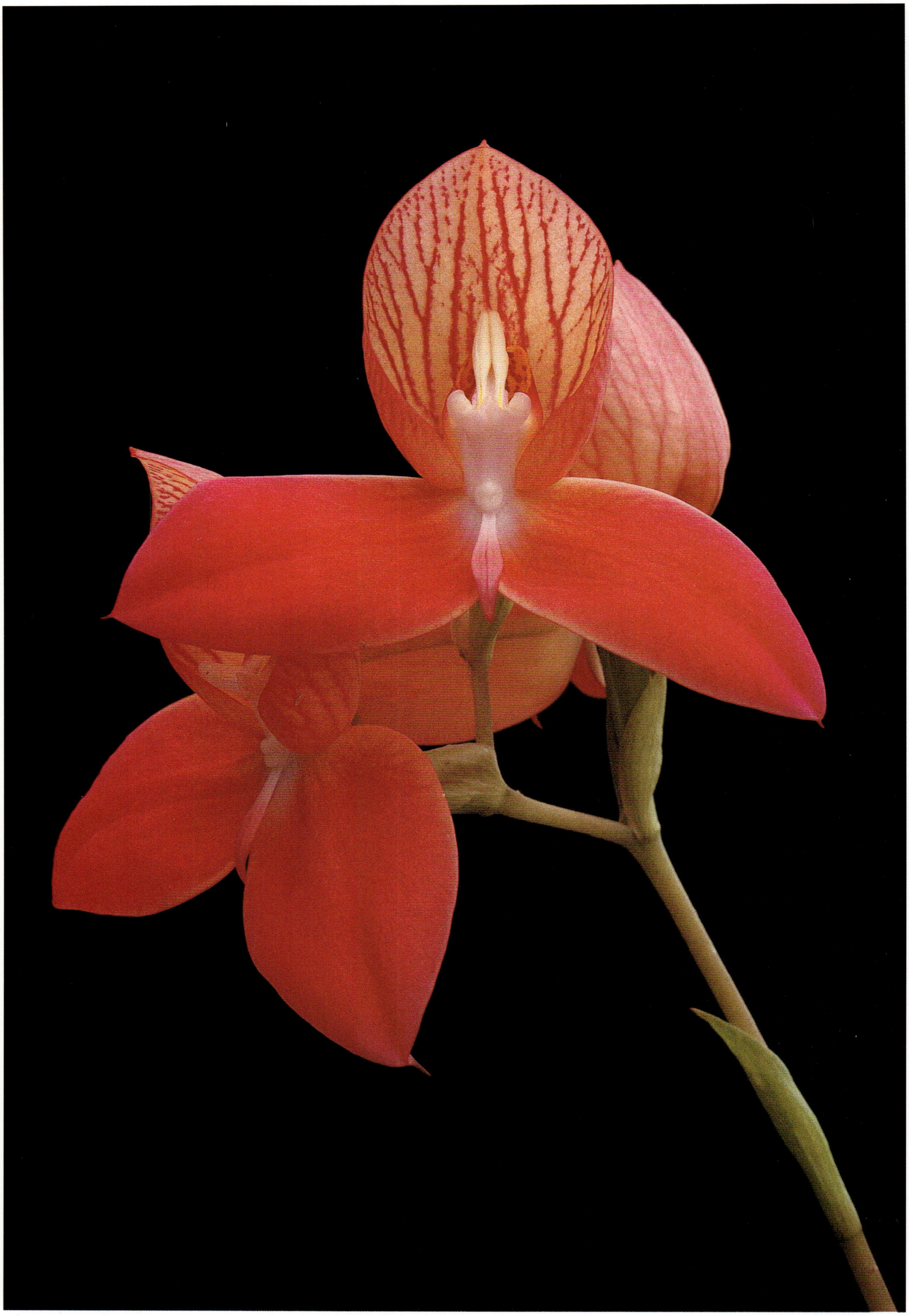

— 3 —
Climates and Habitats of Africa

Disa uniflora

Disa uniflora enjoys a special place among terrestrial orchids, both for its large colorful flowers and for its long and not always successful history in cultivation. Its natural home is in South Africa, beside the mountain streams and waterfalls of the South Western Cape. Here, the roots are always cool and moist, even in the summer heat, and the air is fresh; difficult conditions to maintain in a glasshouse. The flower structure is dominated by the three sepals, the petals and lip being small and insignificant.

In terms of climate, the simple feeling about the great continent of Africa is that it is a hot place. While this is a fair generalization, there are other factors, such as rainfall and altitude, that need to be considered when looking at plant life. The equator passes through the center of the continent, with symmetrical tropical and then temperate zones to the north and south. Equatorial day temperatures are uniformly high through the year, although lower at night, and rain falls during every month with corresponding high humidity. Such a climate encourages the growth of tropical rain forest with its great diversity of plants. These forests are also found along the eastern side, from Mozambique to Natal in South Africa where there is also a greater seasonal difference in temperature. To the west of this area, and to the north of the equatorial zone, lie enormous regions where rainfall is confined to one period only, and the remainder of the year, which may last up to eight months, suffers total drought. Also during this time, the clear skies allow night temperatures to drop sharply. The vegetation here is open woodland and grassland, where during the rains, growth takes place rapidly in preparation for the coming drought.

The majority of epiphytic orchids grow in forests where rainfall is reliable, but because of the dense canopy, they are found high in the trees or lower down in clearings such as along streams in order to get enough light. In the woodlands, the trees are deciduous in the dry season, so that only a few epiphytes, such as *Ansellia africana*, are tough enough to withstand the high light intensity and drought. Montane forests in East Africa are often relatively dry, but temperatures are moderated and the trees shorter and more uniform. Many orchids are found here, and are adapted to alternating periods of rain and drought. With their underground tubers and other storage organs, terrestrial orchids are better adapted to dry conditions, so are found in large numbers in the open woodland and grassy areas. A few can cope with the heavy shade in forests, while many others are found either in swamps or seasonally waterlogged grasslands.

The large tropical and mountainous island of Madagascar lies to the east of Mozambique and shows great variation of rainfall and consequently of vegetation, in habitats ranging from rain forest to semi-desert. It is the eastern side which receives the most consistent rainfall and this both decreases and becomes more seasonal further west. Only remnants of forest remain here, but they contain many epiphytic and some terrestrial plants. High in the mountains, the trees are dwarfed and a more limited range of orchids grows among shrubs and rocks.

The orchids of temperate North Africa are closely related to those of the Mediterranean region in general, while South Africa has a rich and unique orchid flora of which nine tenths are terrestrial. These plants are found in a wide variety of habitats from swamps and sandy scrub, to grassland, rocky outcrops and various forests. Most are adapted to a period of drought, either in summer or in winter.

Disperis fanniniae

It would not be difficult to think of a fanciful name for these curious flowers with their hooded appearance due to the dorsal sepal and petals coming together over the other parts. Found in the eastern regions of Southern Africa, the plants grow on the forest floor or in pine plantations at altitudes of up to 2000m (6560 feet). The slender stems carry up to eight flowers during the summer months.

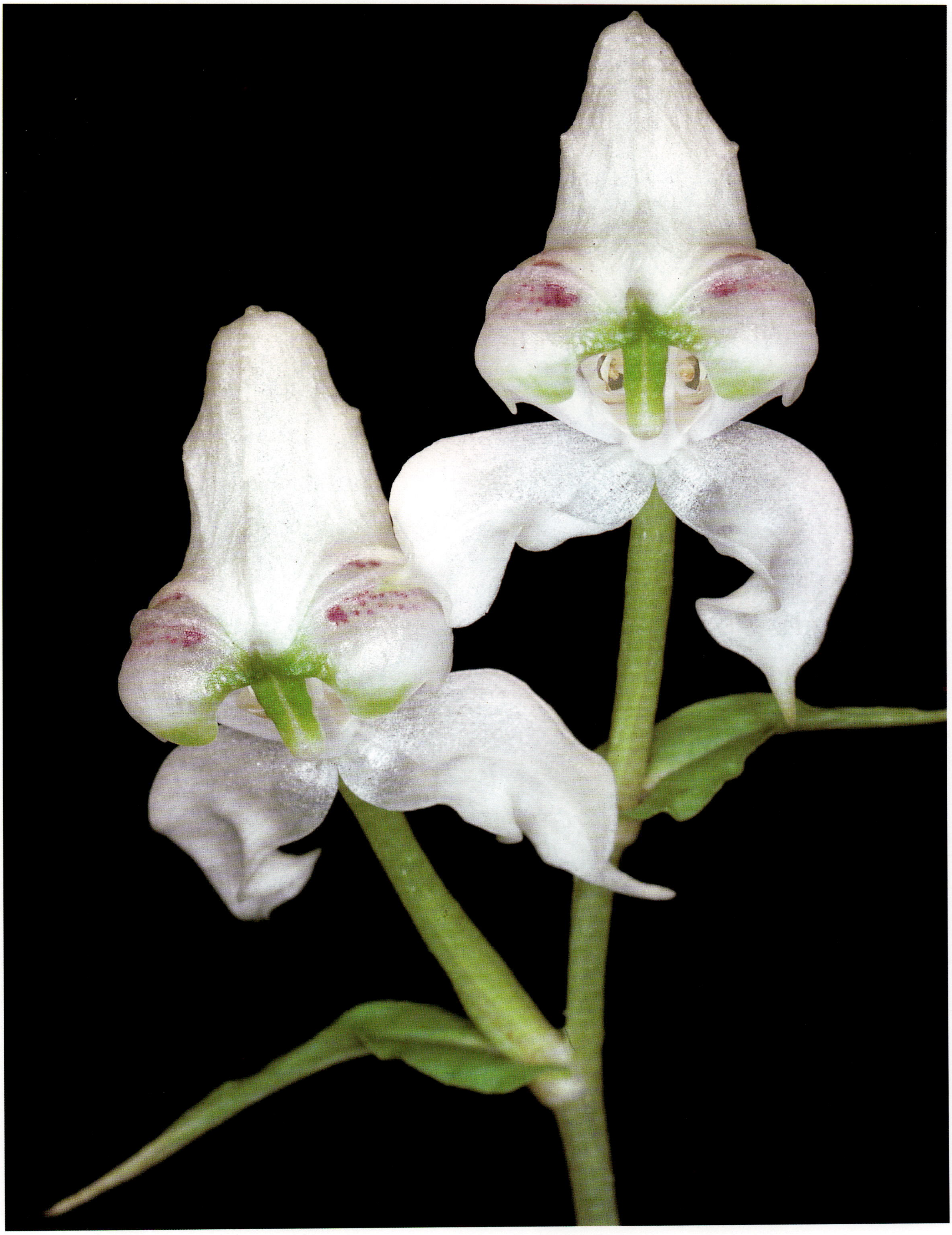

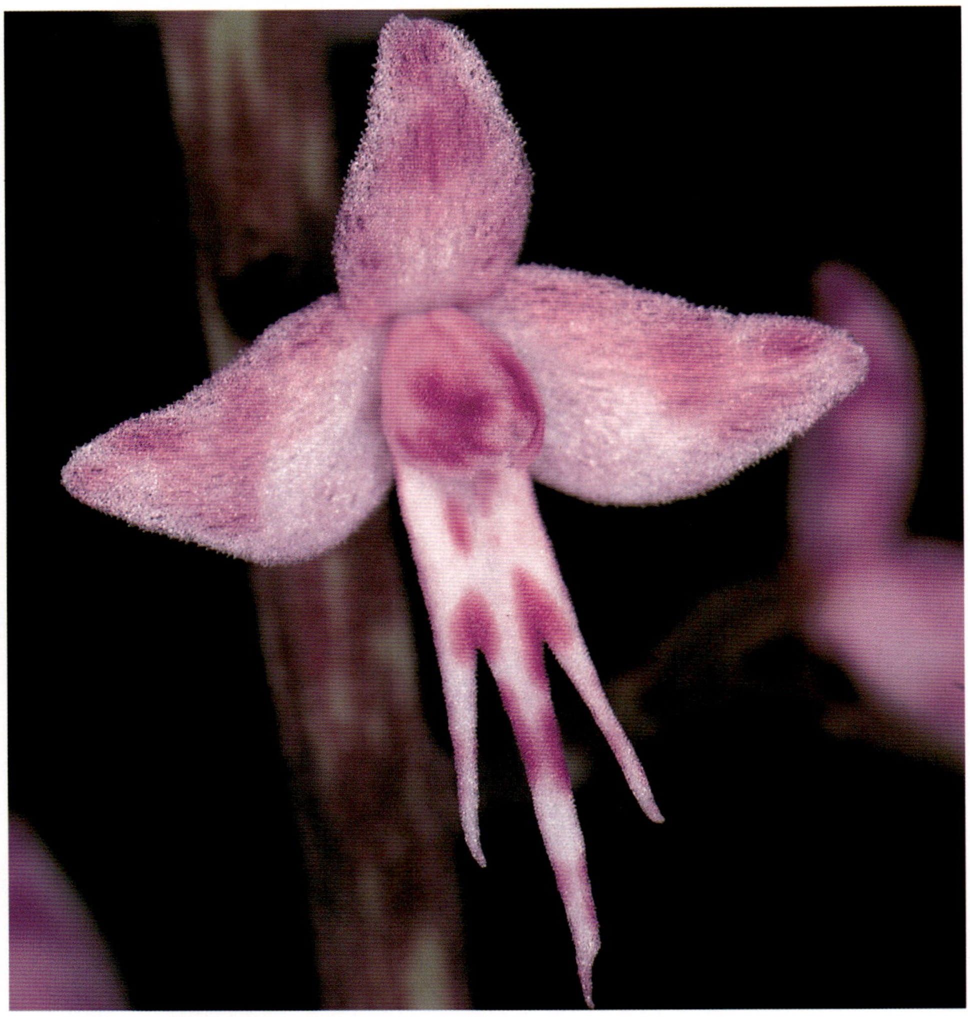

Stenoglottis fimbriata

From looking at plants of this species, native to Transkei, South Africa and Swaziland, it should be terrestrial in habit as it has rosettes of soft spotted leaves and fleshy roots. In fact it prefers to grow on the surface of forest rocks, or lower down on tree trunks. The erect flower stems may be up to 40cm (16 inches) tall with up to 30 or more flowers opening in succession. As with so many African plants, *Stenoglottis* species have adapted to a dry season when the leaves wither and the plants are sustained by their roots.

Polystachya ottoniana

In comparison with most orchid flowers, those of the mainly African genus *Polystachya* stand out because they appear upside down with the lip uppermost. Among the 200 or so species are many attractive ones, and although the flowers are mostly small, they are often pleasantly scented and may be produced in great numbers. *Polystachya ottoniana* comes from the eastern part of Southern Africa where it commonly grows in forested areas on rocks and trees.

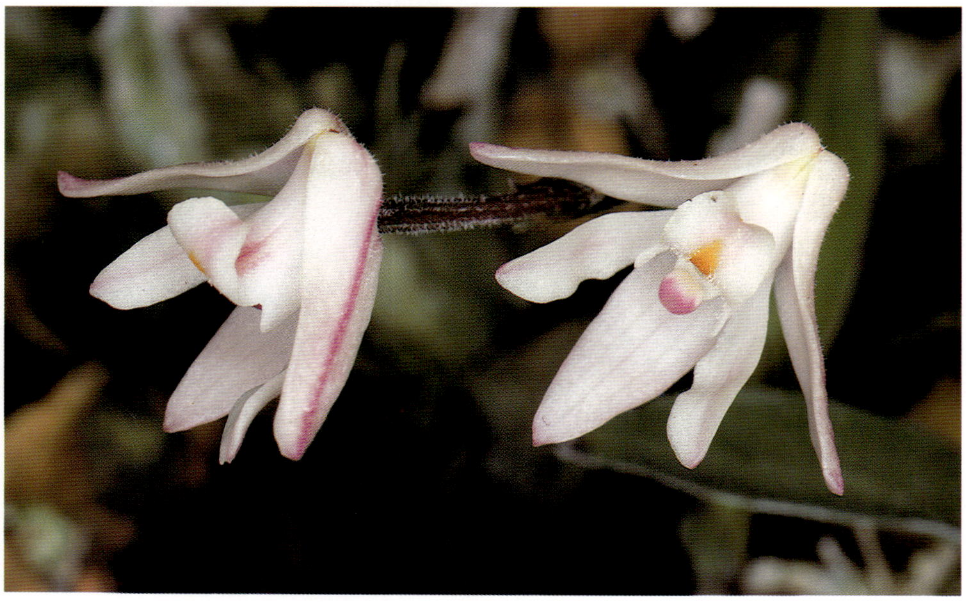

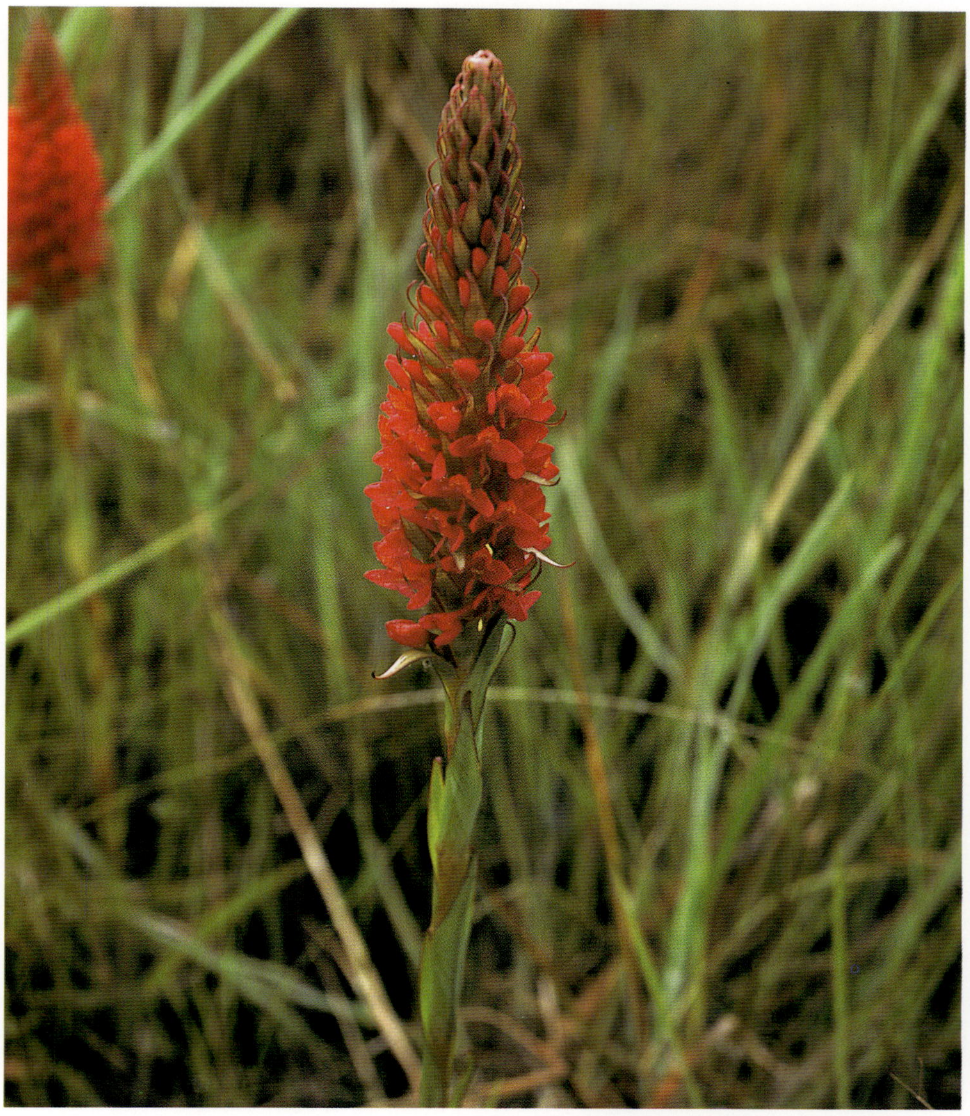

Disa welwitschii

Although of a similar color to the South African *Disa uniflora*, this species is very different in appearance, having numerous small flowers on a tall stem. It favors open grassland which is seasonally wet and the edges of boggy areas. The plant shown here was growing in such a habitat in Malawi but is also occurs in Zambia and Angola.

Aerangis kirkii

A fine plant of Aerangis kirkii growing in its natural home on the shady branch of a forest tree in Tanzania. The white flowers, with their long nectar-filled spurs and night perfume, are obviously moth pollinated. Unusually, the flower furthest from the plant is the first to open, and is larger than the others. *Aerangis* species are mostly very short stemmed so that the leathery leaves are close together.

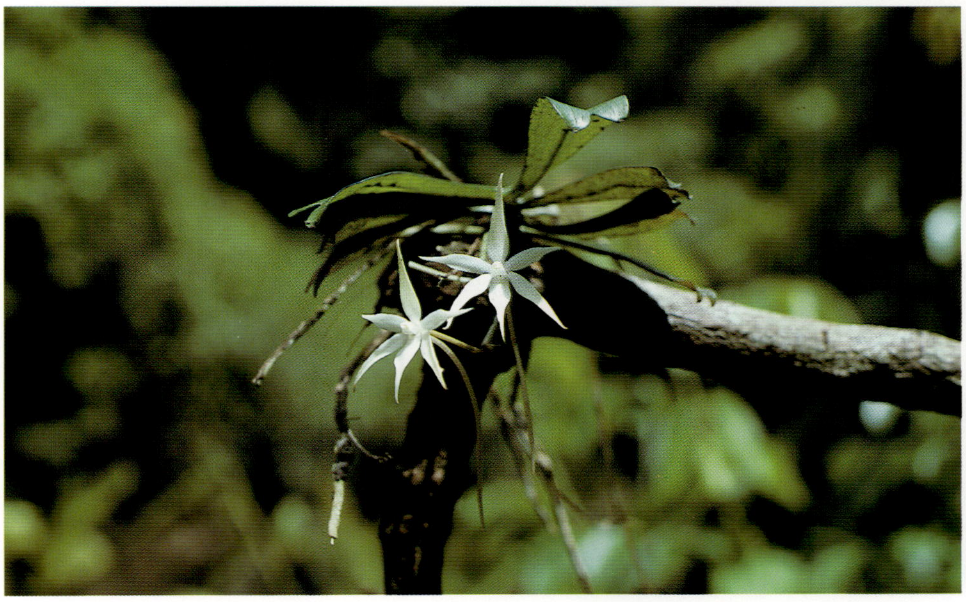

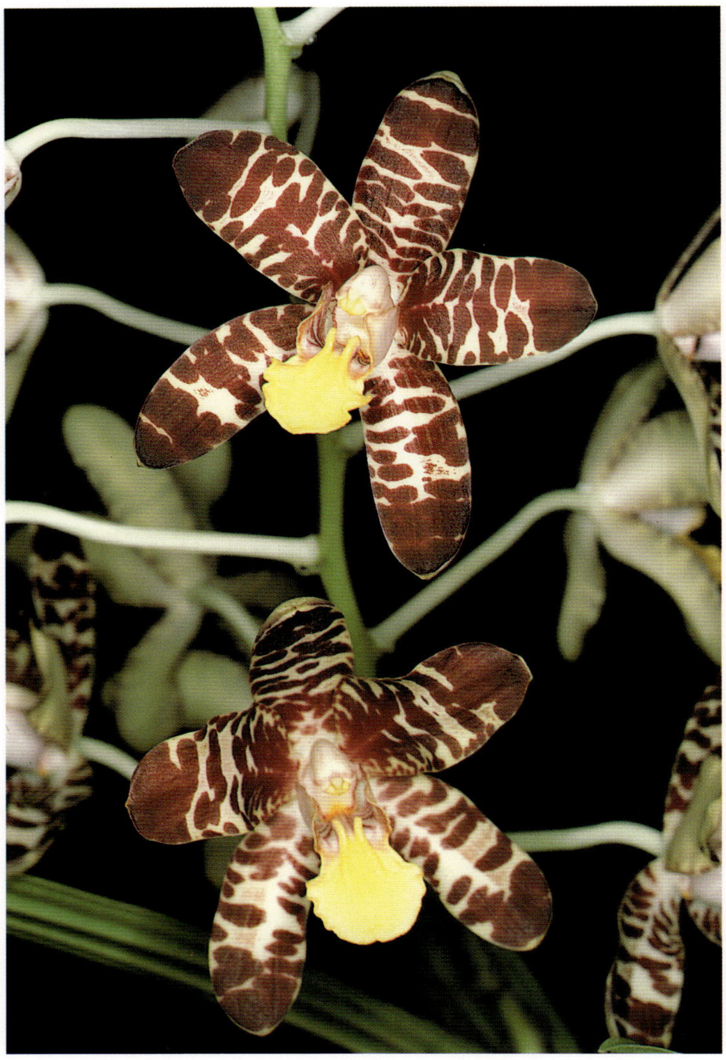

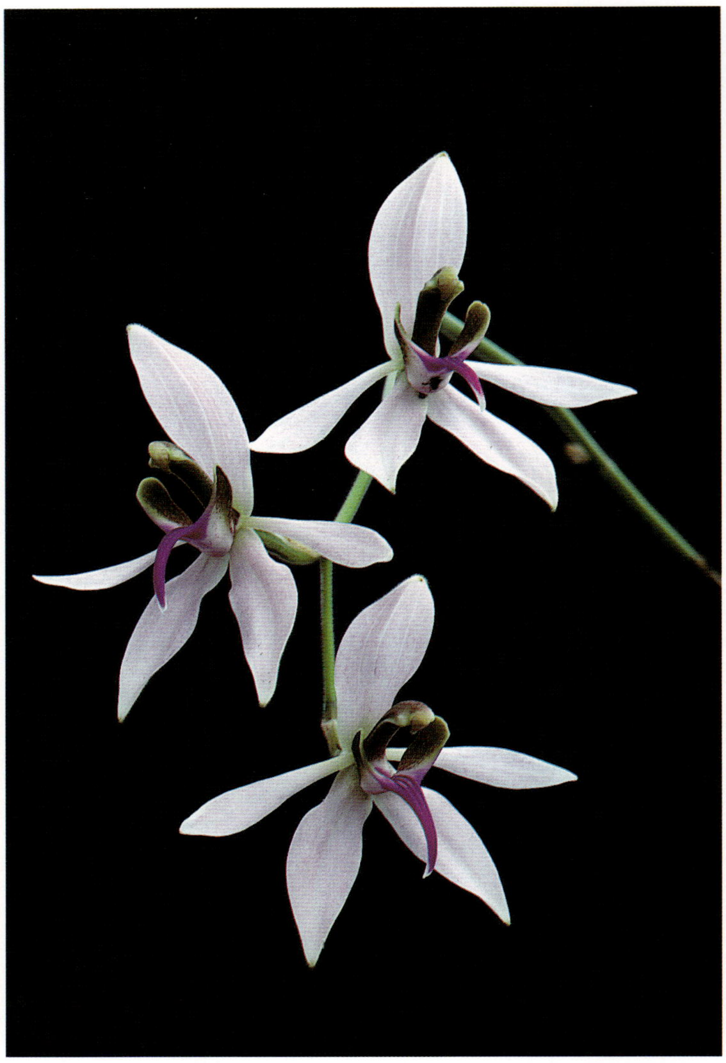

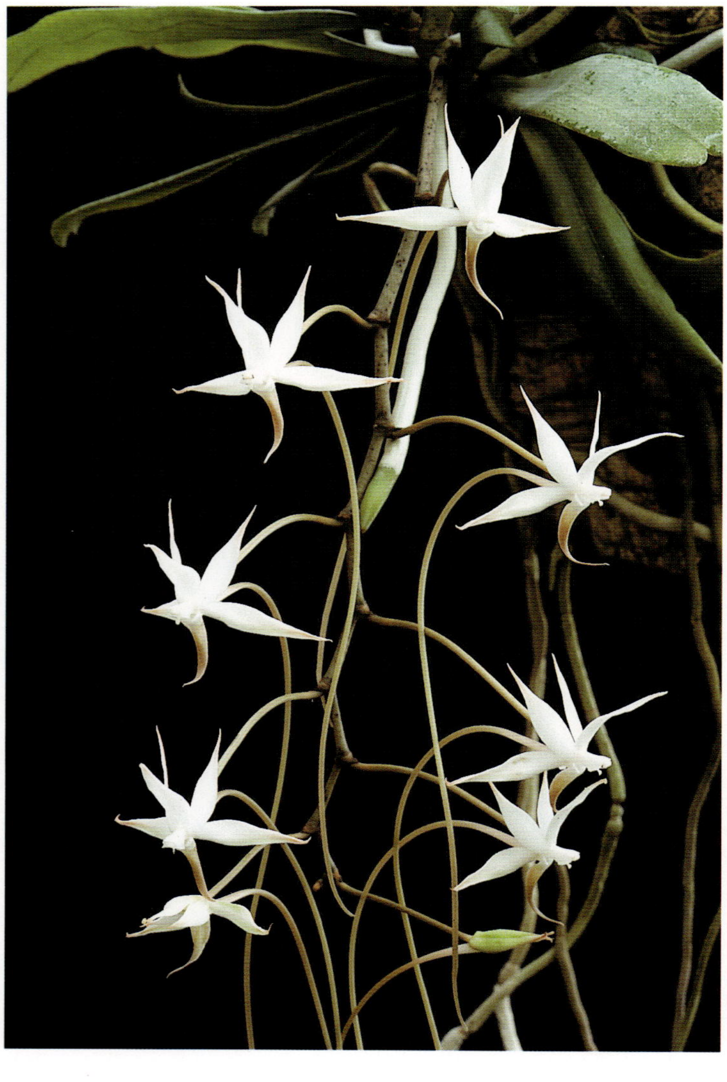

ABOVE LEFT: *Ansellia africana*

From some of the small African orchids to one of the largest, at least in terms of plant size. There is some debate amongst botanists as to whether they are looking at one variable species or several, because ansellias are found throughout Tropical Africa and in parts of Southern Africa. The plants grow epiphytically in mainly semi-arid conditions forming large clumps. The pseudobulbs may grow up to a meter (3 feet) tall but usually less, and the numerous flowers vary in color from pure yellow through various degrees of spotting to almost black.

ABOVE: *Ancistrochilus rothschildianus*

Very much an exception among African orchids, this beautiful species was named in honor of the Hon. Walter Rothschild in whose collection at Tring Park it flowered in the early years of the century. The flowers which are up to 8cm (3 inches) across, arise from the base of conical pseudobulbs which grow close together. In the wild, the plants are difficult to find, as they are covered by mosses and ferns on the trunks and lower branches of forest trees. While mainly distributed in West Africa, it has also been collected in Uganda.

LEFT: *Aerangis brachycarpa*

An altogether larger plant than *Aerangis kirkii* this one is also more widespread in its distribution, being found in East Africa from Ethiopia to Tanzania and across to Angola in the west. The spurs are up to 20cm (8 inches) long making a very graceful impression when all of the flowers are open. It prefers to grow low down on tree trunks or branches in dense shade, and nearer the equator, may occur in forests up to 2300m (7550 feet).

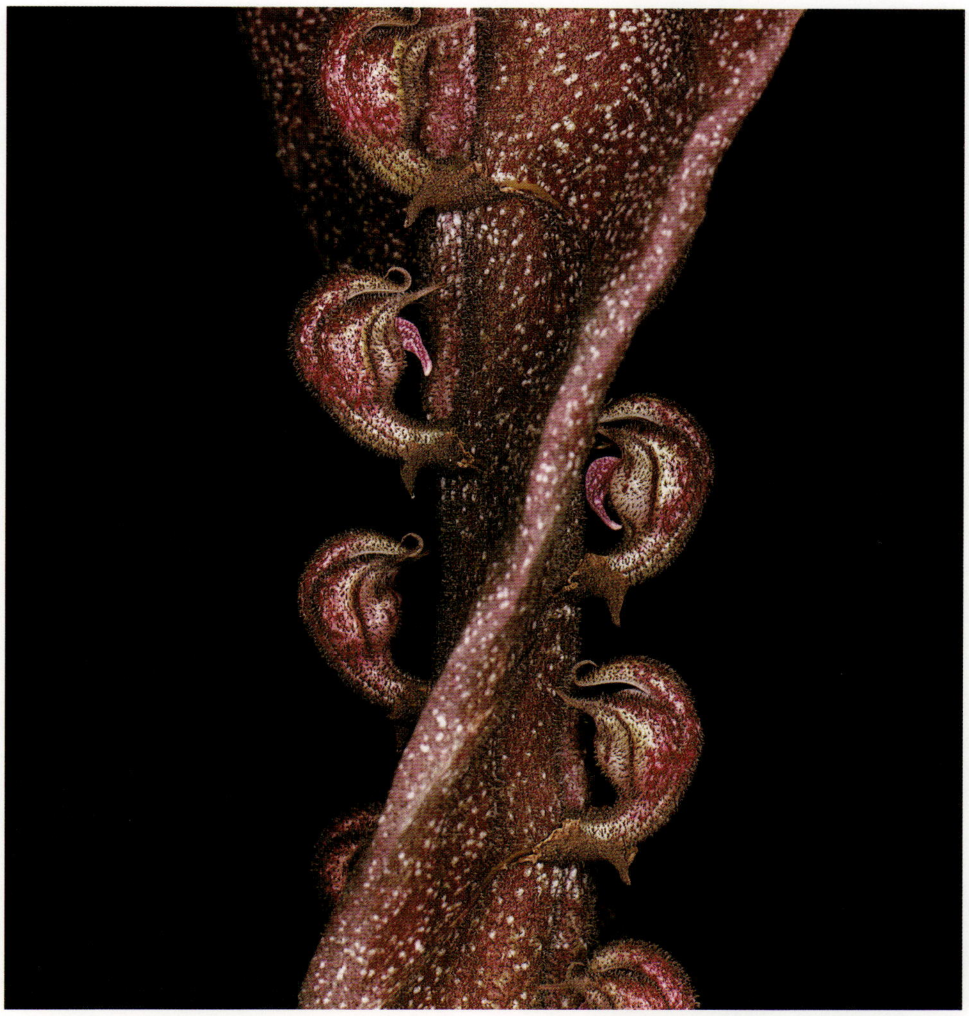

Bulbophyllum purpureorhachis

The genus *Bulbophyllum* is one of the largest in the orchid family, containing at least 1000 species. Although Africa has only about 70 of them, they are very distinct from those found in Asia. This particular plant has been growing at Kew Gardens for at least fifty years, and while the small flowers do not attract the eye, they are strikingly presented on either side of a twisted blade, up to 60cm (24 inches) tall. This species grows as an epiphyte in West African lowland forest.

Angraecum distichum

The predominantly African and Madagascan genus *Angraecum* includes about 200 species, varying in size from dwarf miniatures to substantial specimens a meter (3 feet) high or more. *Angraecum distichum* is very much in the former category and although the slender stems may be up to 25cm (10 inches) long, the single flowers are only 8mm across. It is found growing as an epiphyte in upland rainforest at altitudes of around 1500m (4900 feet) in Uganda and in West Africa, from Sierra Leone to Zaire.

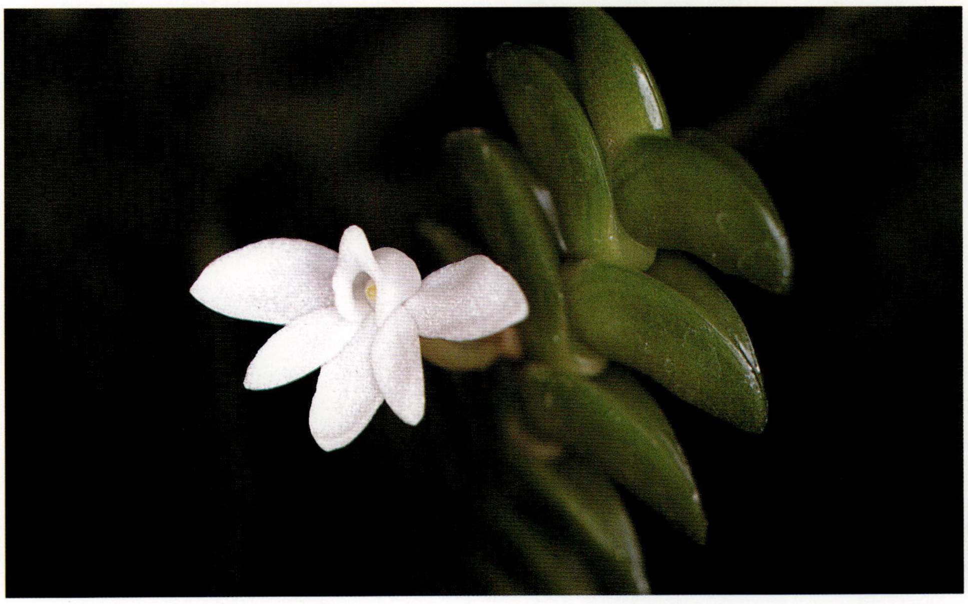

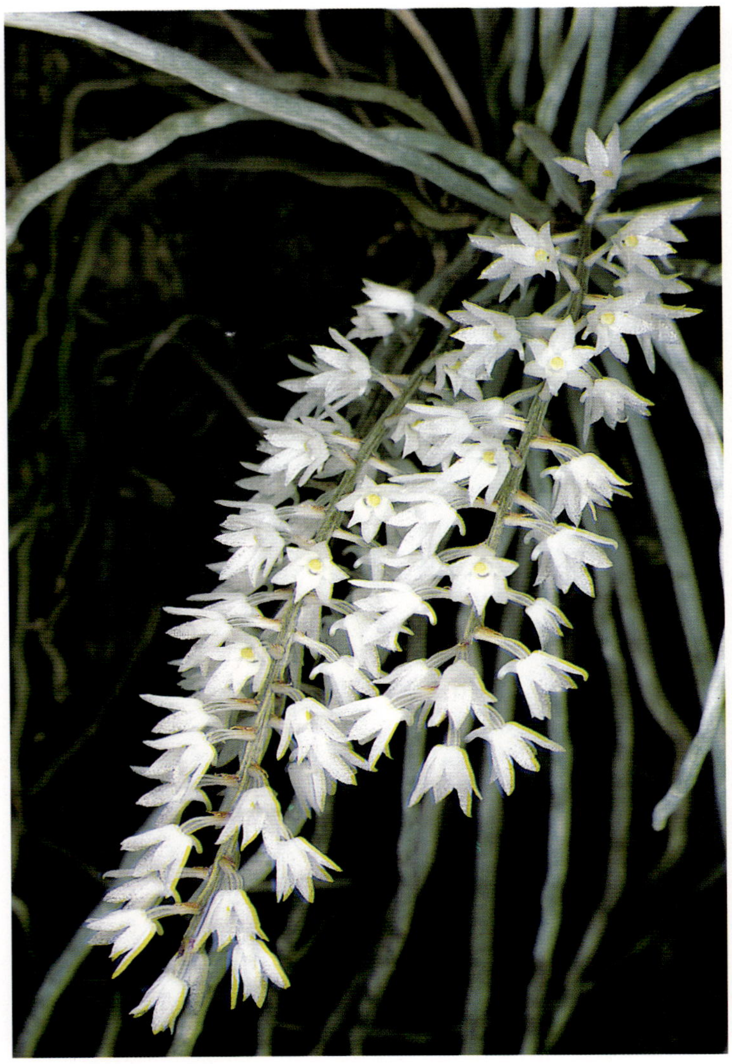

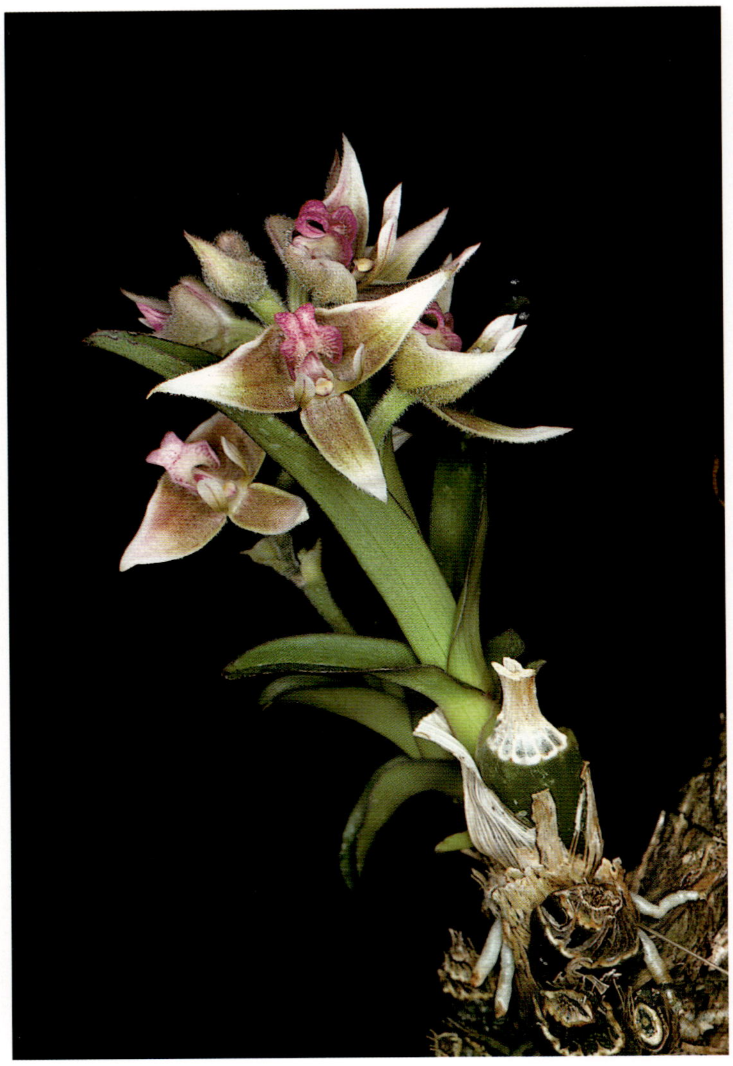

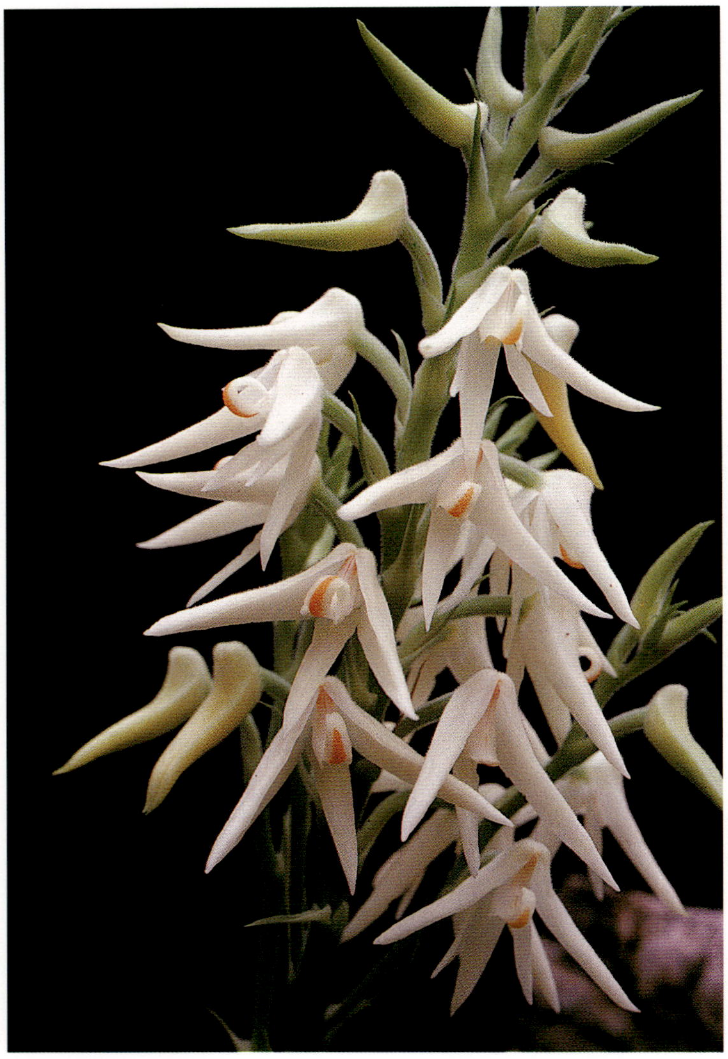

ABOVE LEFT: *Microcoelia stolzii*

Epiphytic leafless orchids, consisting of only a stem and roots, are found throughout the tropics of the world, although microcoelias are confined to Africa and Madagascar. The silver-gray roots function as leaves, in that they contain chlorophyll to convert light energy into food for the plant. *Microcoelia stolzii* occurs throughout East Tropical Africa as an epiphyte on the smaller branches and trunks of bushes and trees in medium altitude forest. The flowers are very small but numerous enough to make a good show.

ABOVE: *Polystachya johnstonii*

This beautiful little plant is found only in Malawi, where it grows exclusively as an epiphyte on the fibrous stems of *Xerophyta* species. The roots are able to penetrate the fiber to give good anchorage and protection in exposed situations. The plant itself is very neat, with its centimeter round pseudobulbs and the inflorescence arising from the center of the new shoot.

LEFT: *Polystachya laurentii*

Polystachya laurentii is much larger in all respects than the preceding species, growing to about 28cm (11 inches) tall. The flattened pseudobulbs grow close together on an ascending rhizome which may become pendulous as the plant gets taller. The usually branching inflorescence carries many elegant white flowers which are pleasantly scented. This species grows as an epiphyte in rainforest in Zaire and Uganda.

Bulbophyllum cochleatum var. gravidum

Coming from Malawi, this is a much smaller plant and the whole inflorescence is only about 8cm (3 inches) long. As with many African bulbophyllums, the lip is finely hairy and delicately hinged so that it moves in the slightest breeze. The natural habitat is either growing among lichens on rocks, or as an epiphyte on tree trunks and lower branches in open woodland.

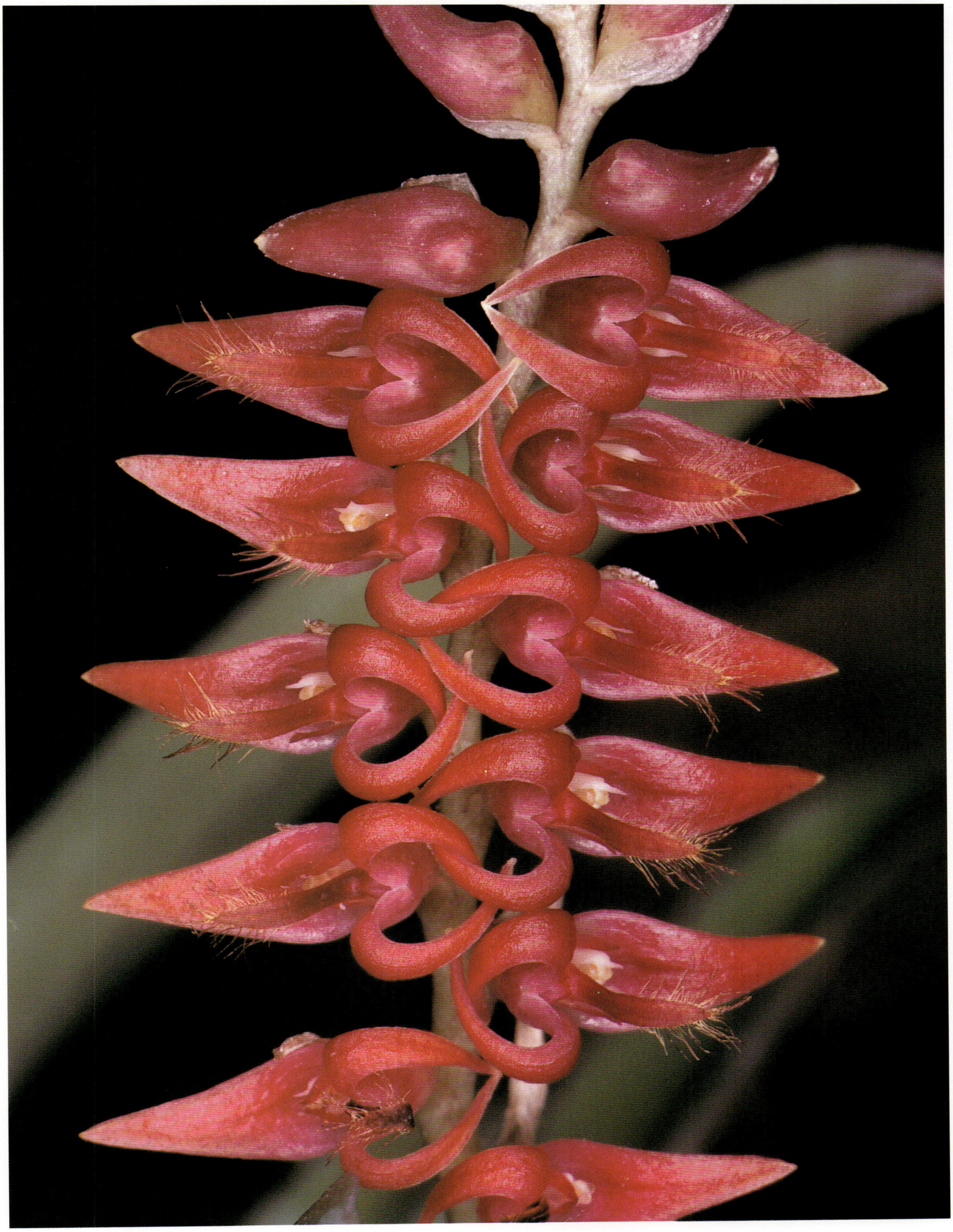

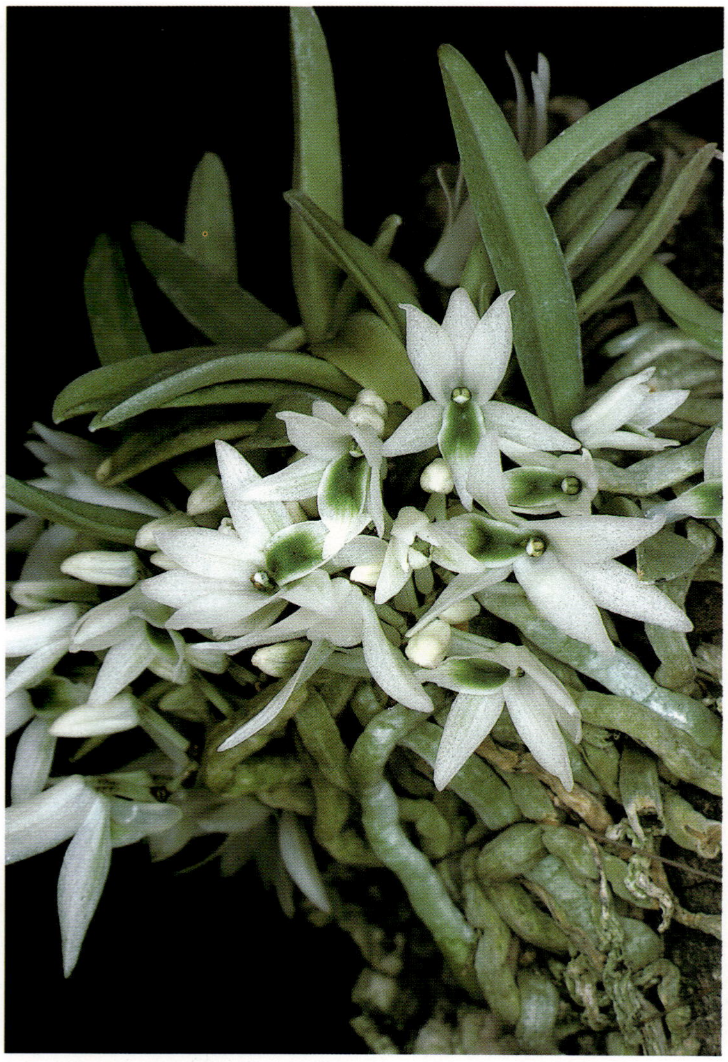

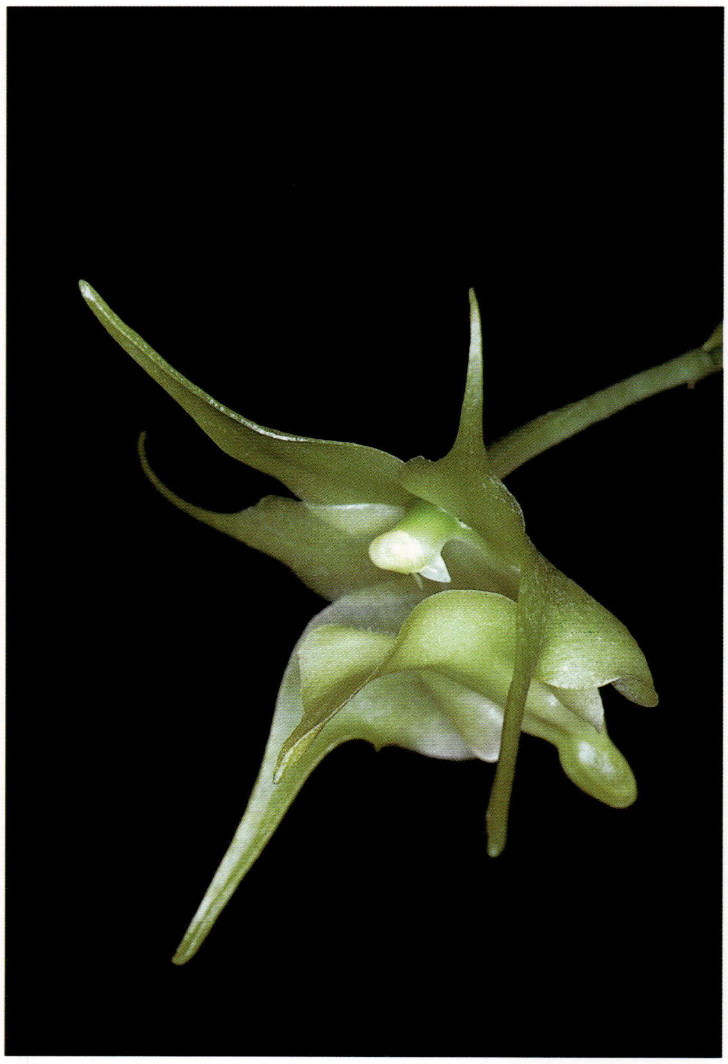

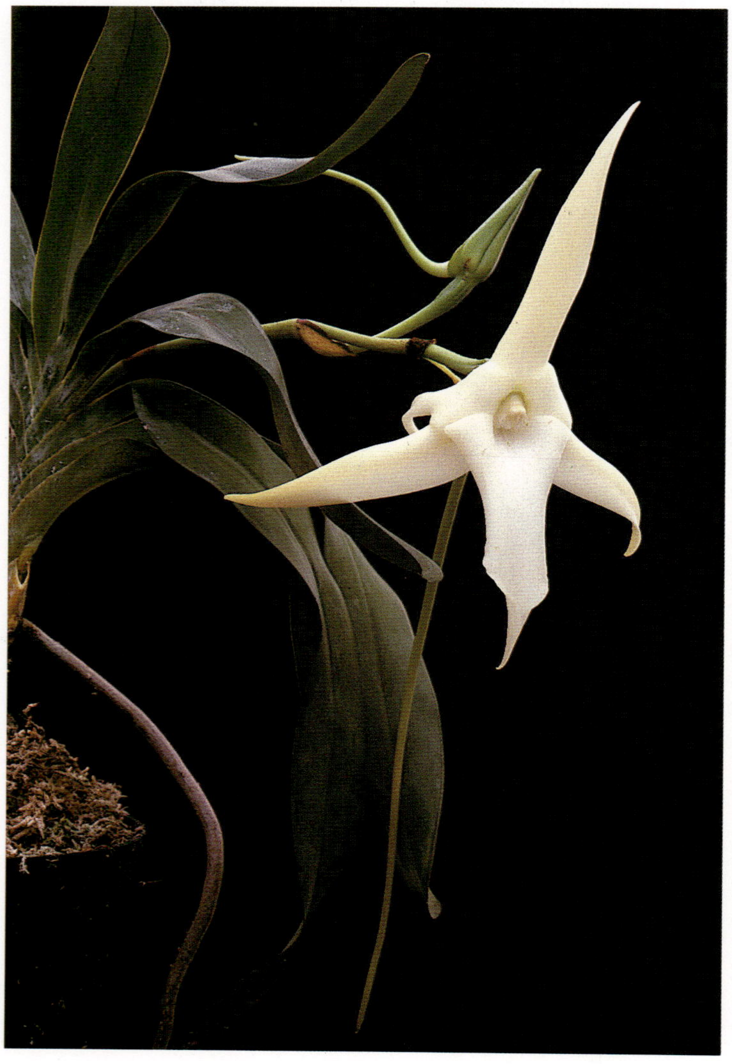

ABOVE LEFT: *Sphyrarhynchus schliebenii*

A true miniature species, found only in Tanzania, the whole plant shown here is only about 8cm (3 inches) across, and roots leaves and flowers are equally prominent. As with many African epiphytic orchids, the flowers are mainly white, and have a nectar-filled spur at the base of the lip to attract pollinating moths. Its natural habitat is in evergreen montane forest at altitudes of up to 1600m (5250 feet).

ABOVE: *Aeranthes arachnites*

At first sight, *Aeranthes arachnites* presents a fantastic appearance, with its neat fan of leaves and the long wiry dangling flower stems, bearing spidery green flowers. Although most *Aeranthes* species come from Madagascar, this one is found only on Réunion Island, to the east of the country. It grows as an epiphyte under rather shady conditions in lowland forest.

LEFT: *Angraecum sesquipedale*

The Madagascan species, *Angraecum sesquipedale*, is graced by one of the longest orchid flowers, typically being up to 22cm (9 inches) wide, and 45cm (18 inches) top to spur tip. Each inflorescence may carry up to six such beauties but often less, especially on young plants. The long spur contains nectar for the pollinating moth which is initially attracted by a strong nocturnal perfume. A full grown plant is around a meter tall, and may grow in dense clumps on tree trunks in the wet lowland forst on the eastern side of the island.

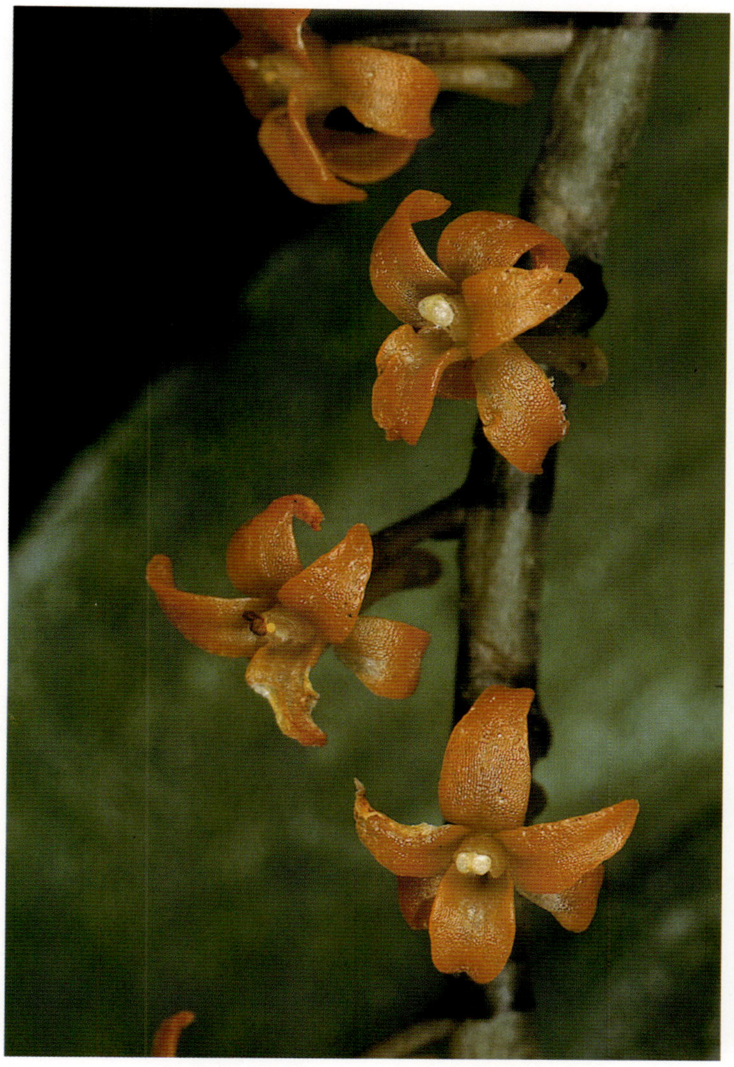

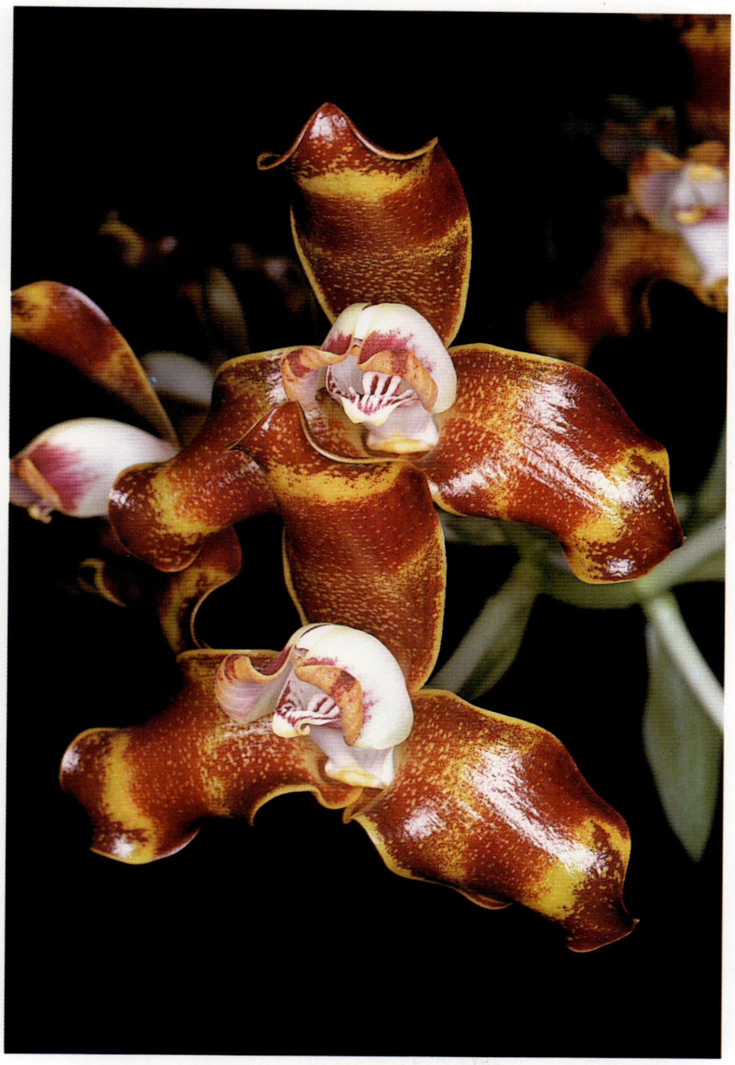

ABOVE: *Chamaeangis hildebrandtii*

Chamaeangis hildebrandtii comes from the Comoro Islands, to the north west of Madagascar. It grows epiphytically as a fan of fleshy leaves, below which hang the small slender inflorescences. The flowers are only a few millimeters across, but show all the characteristics of their larger cousins, including fat spurs for nectar. There are about 15 *Chamaeangis* species spread through Africa and adjacent islands, and they all have similar coloring, varying between green orange and yellow.

ABOVE RIGHT: *Grammangis ellisii*

The island of Madagascar is home to many spectacular orchids and this is surely one of them. It grows as an epiphyte on trees in very humid forest on the eastern side of the island where it is never dry for very long. The flowers are long lasting, and with their prominent glossy sepals, provide a good show for the grower. Many such plants are disappearing in the wild as forests are cut down, so it is important for seedlings to be raised and distributed around the world.

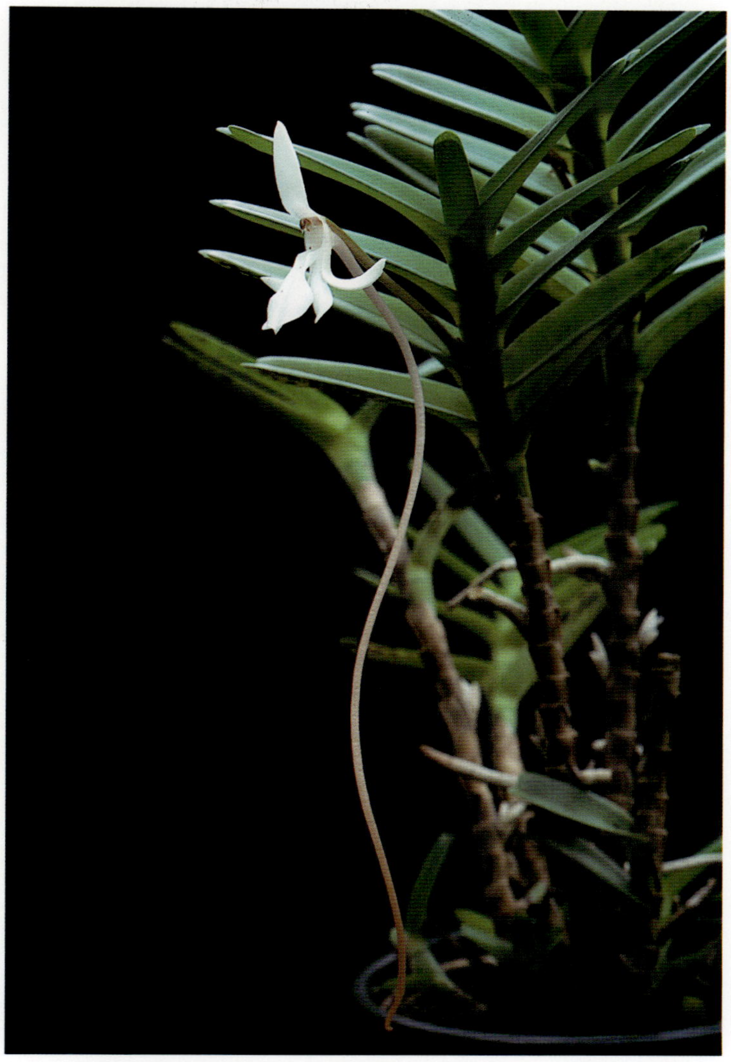

RIGHT: *Jumellea henryi*

Apart from two species in East Africa, the delightful genus *Jumellea* is represented in Madagascar and neigboring islands. The Madagascan *Jumellea henryi* shows the characterstics well, with its pure white flower, borne singly on the inflorescence, the upturned dorsal sepal, and the long spur hanging down. It grows in Central Madagascar as an epiphyte on bushes, at medium altitudes up to 1500m (4920 feet).

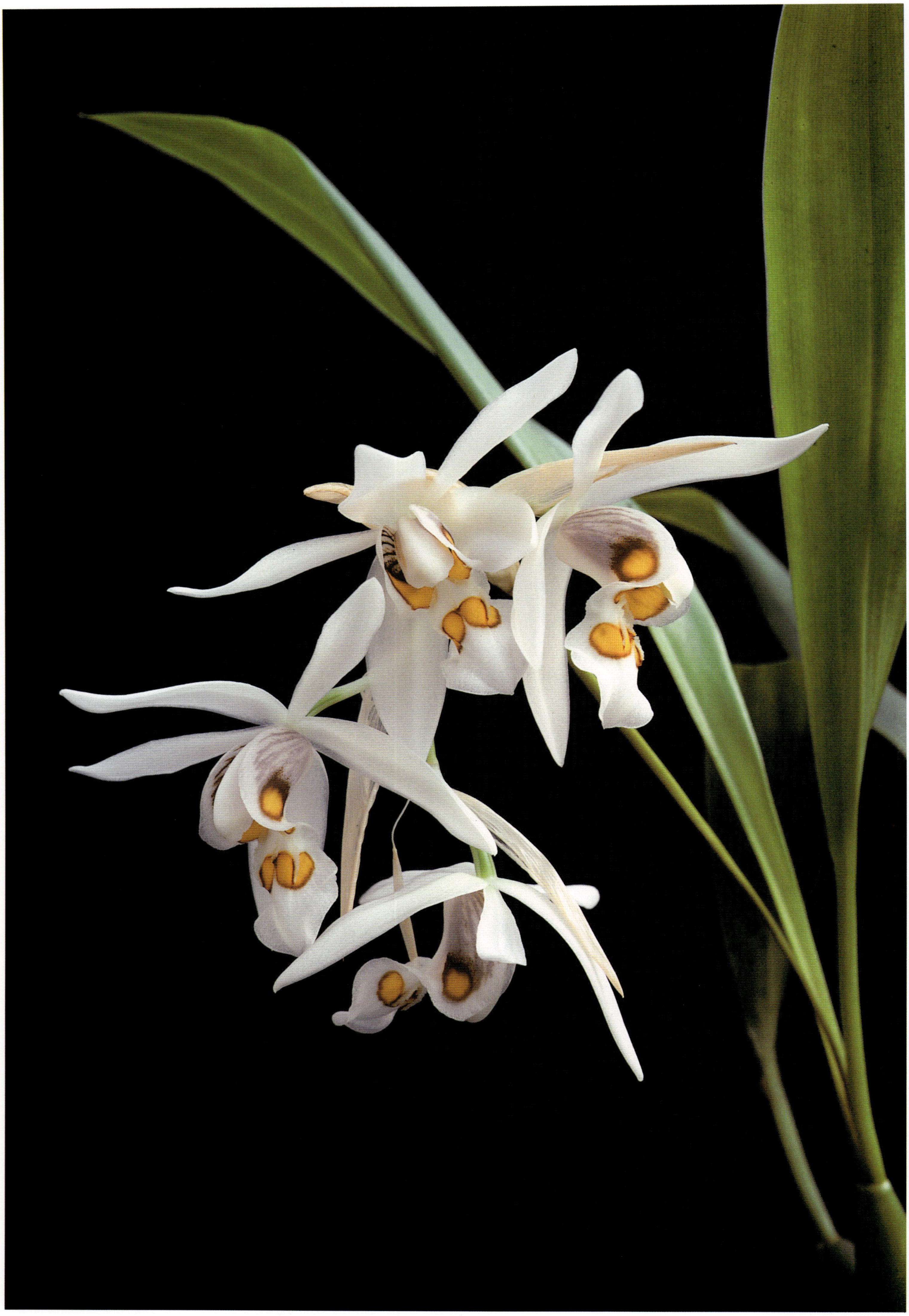

— 4 —
Climates and Habitats of Tropical Asia and Australasia

Coelogyne punctulata

The genus *Coelogyne* is wide spread in Asia and the islands of the Pacific with a number of species popular in cultivation. Although the flowers last only two or three weeks, they are attractive and often pleasantly scented. *Coelogyne punctulata* from Northern India, blooms in winter from the top of mature pseudobulbs. It resembles *Coelogyne nitida* from the same area and from Thailand, but that species is spring-flowering and the flower stems arise in the center of the new shoots.

Major orchid habitats of Asia begin in the forested foothills of the mighty Himalayas, including Nepal, Sikkim and Bhutan, as well as the ranges in the north east of India, including Assam. Here the rainfall tends to be high for much of the year, but with a marked dry period of cooler conditions when plant growth ceases. Further south, in the mountains and uplands of Burma and Thailand, these monsoon conditions are more pronounced, with a warm wet season being followed by a long dry one. However, in the mountains, there is a sharp drop in temperature at night, so that even epiphytes in the forest receive moisture from condensation. Towards the equator, in the Malay Peninsula, Singapore, Indonesia and the Philippines, the climate is much more equable, with high temperatures and well distributed rainfall throughout the year. This is obviously modified at higher elevations, when night temperatures are lower. Forests in this region support a very varied and interesting orchid flora. To the north, in South China, Taiwan and southern Japan, subtropical forests are home to many epiphytes, but northern Japan and much of China have cold winters which confine orchids to terrestrial species.

The tropical island of New Guinea, which is divided between the Indonesian territory of Irian Jaya and the independent state of Papua New Guinea, has a particularly rich orchid flora, especially in the wet forests of the high mountains which are a significant feature of the landscape. While there are both epiphytic and terrestrial orchids to be found in the hot lowlands, it is the cloud and moss forests up to 3000m (9840 feet), which provide the most extensive range of species. Here, day temperatures may be quite high, but it is always much cooler at night, and mists and showers are frequent.

Acampe papillosa

Species of *Acampe* are found in Africa, Madagascar and South East Asia, and the plants have a similar appearance, with thick rigid leaves on woody stems. The waxy flowers are usually on short inflorescences and are strongly scented. *Acampe papillosa* grows as a forest epiphyte over a wide range in Asia from Nepal and Bhutan, through Burma and Thailand to Indochina.

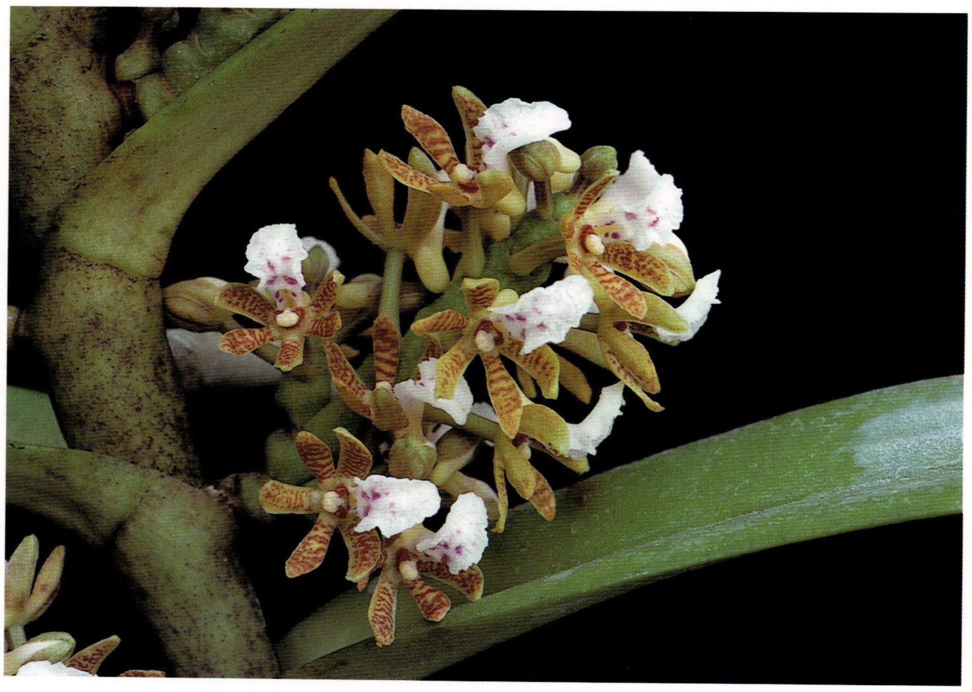

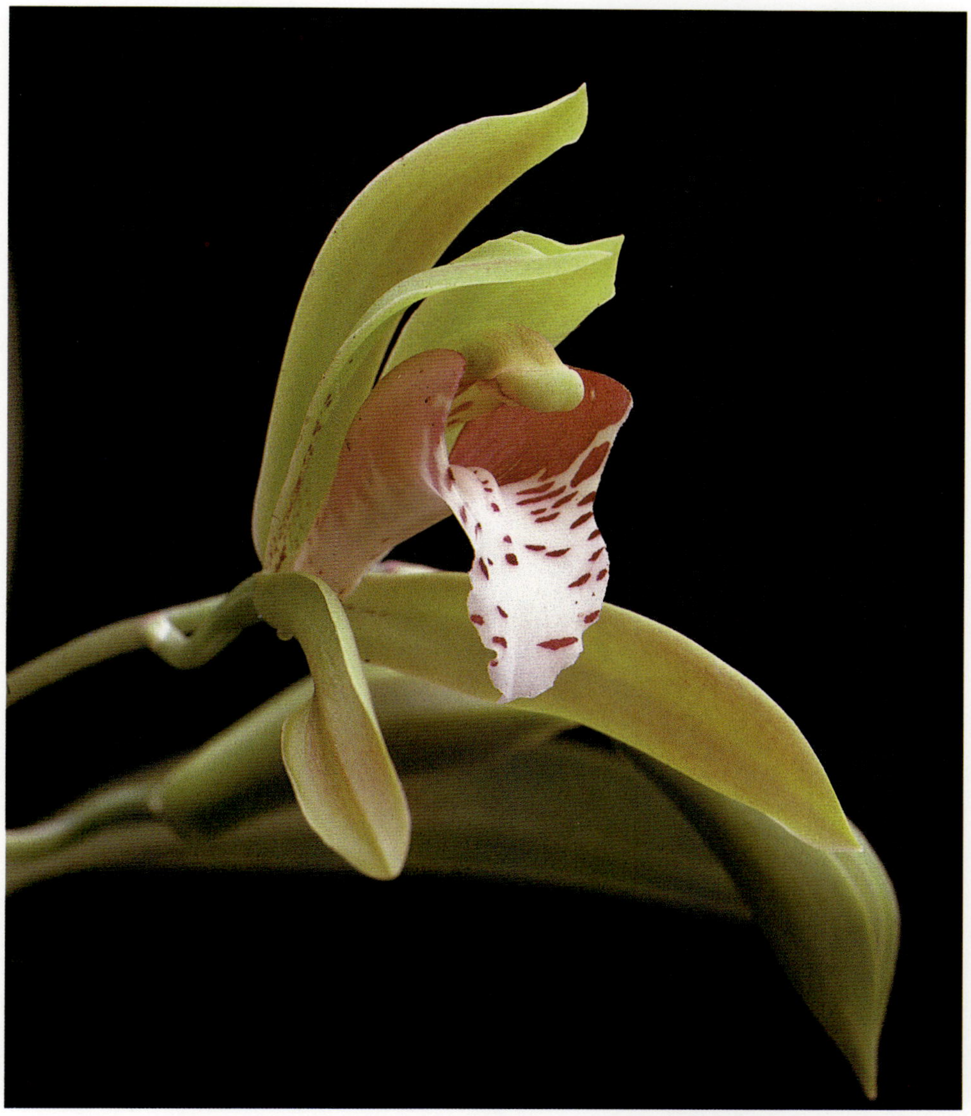

Cymbidium tigrinum

A dwarf growing plant with relatively large flowers, *Cymbidium tigrinum* comes from North-east India and Burma, where it grows on bare rocks and in rock crevices at altitudes of up to 2700m (8860 feet). It has never been common in cultivation, but in more recent years, has been used in hybridizing to produce smaller plants with flowers having interesting shapes and colors.

The Republic of Vanuatu consists of numerous islands lying to the east of Papua New Guinea, and varying from tropical in the north to subtropical in the south. Mainly volcanic in origin, the largest islands are mountainous and naturally forested, with composition varying according to altitude. Rainfall is higher in the northern islands, while in the south, it is lower and temperatures show more seasonal range. Epiphytic orchids are found at all altitudes from sea level to the mountain tops, and a wide range of terrestrials occupy various habitats throughout the forests.

As a continent, Australia has vast areas in the interior which are entirely without orchids. In fact suitable habitats are never far from the coast, and while terrestrial species are found in Western and South Australia, epiphytes are confined to the north and east, as far south as Tasmania. In tropical Queensland, there are still areas of rainforest, both on tablelands up to 1000m (3300 feet) and in the lowlands, where rainfall occurs through the year. Other forests are more open and seasonal, with a marked dry period. Both epiphytes and terrestrials are found in these habitats. More restricted habitats are provided by the

Dendrobium longicornu

Dendrobium longicornu belongs to a group of ornamental dendrobium species notable for the short black hairs on their stems and young leaves. It comes from Nepal and grows naturally as an epiphyte in open forest at moderate elevations. The slender stems grow up to 30cm (12 inches) tall and the long lasting flowers appear from the upper parts before or after the thin leaves have fallen.

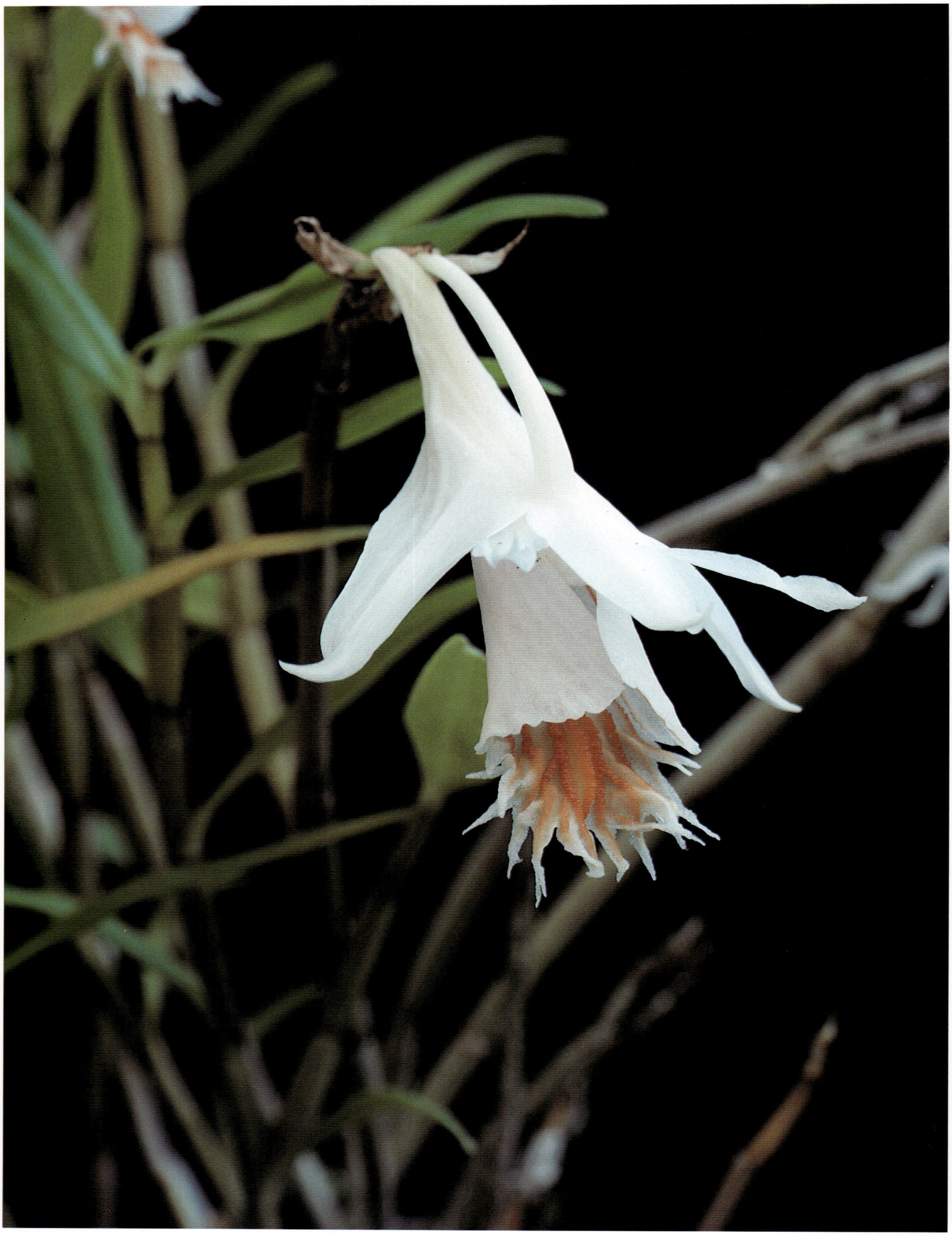

coastal mangroves, and the monsoon forests which extend across the north. Here, the dry season is very long and harsh, and only a few orchid species are adapted to it, although they may occur in large numbers. Coastal New South Wales and Tasmania have a seasonal temperate climate, and in protected forest areas on trees and rocks, many orchids are to be found. Terrestrial species are more widespread in a variety of habitats, from open woodland or scrub, to grassland and sandy coastal areas. With their underground tubers, they are able to survive dry summers and even fire on occasion.

No part of New Zealand is far from the sea, and this results in a temperate climate; subtropical in the north and cooler in the south. The prevailing westerly winds bring rain to that side, so that the east is drier, but not enough to discourage plant growth. The natural vegetation over much of the country was dense mixed forest, and that which remains is still home to epiphytic orchids, although introduced trees have also been acceptable. However, the majority of orchid species here are terrestrial in habit, and may be found particularly in open scrubland on poor soils, along paths and under trees in open forest, in rough pasture, and unexpectedly, in very large numbers in man-made conifer plantations. A few species must have water, and so are confined to wetlands or in some cases, to mossy river boulders which are flooded at times.

Pleione praecox

The large and beautiful flowers of *Pleione praecox* always create a good impression, appearing as they do from small bare pseudobulbs in the fall. This is in contrast to the majority of pleiones, which flower in the late winter or spring. This species grows at medium to high altitudes in North India, Bhutan, Burma, Nepal, Thailand and China. In drier areas it prefers rocks and cliffs, but in West Bengal, it grows as an epiphyte on tree trunks and branches.

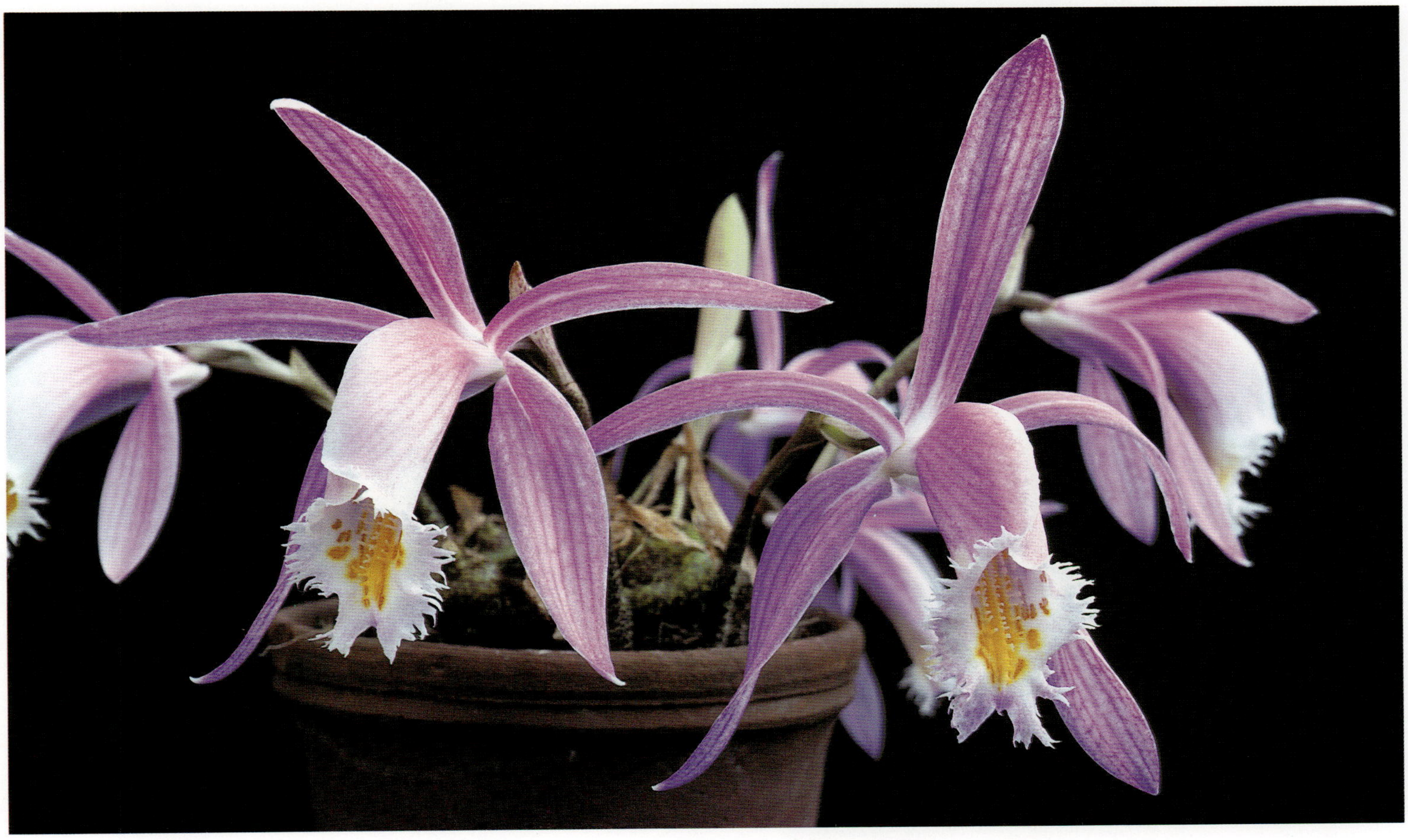

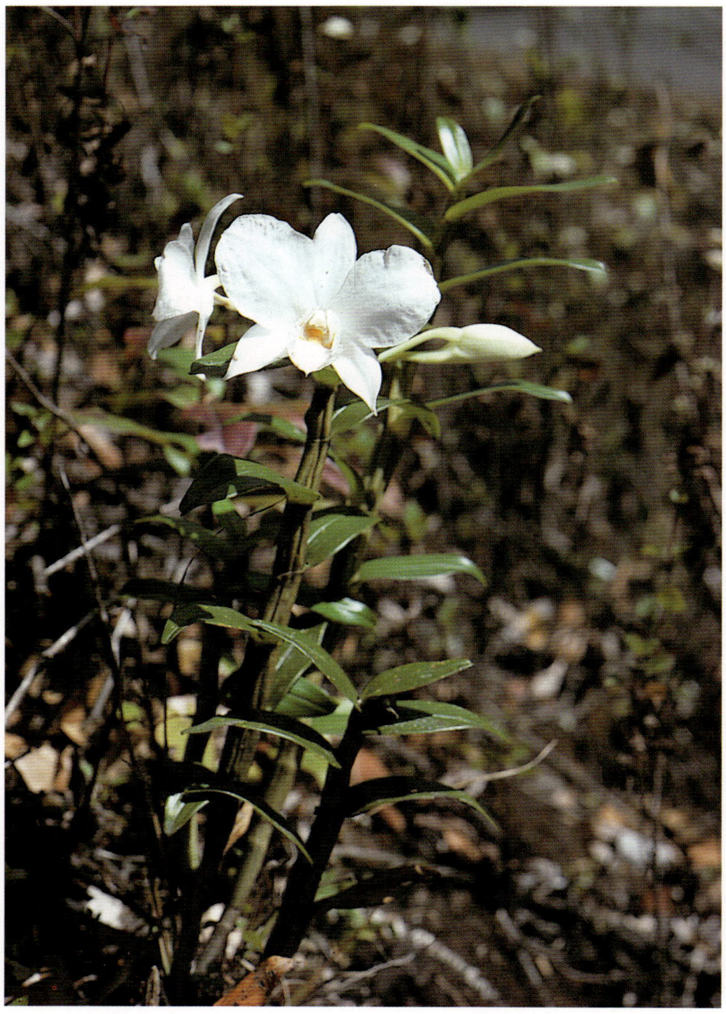

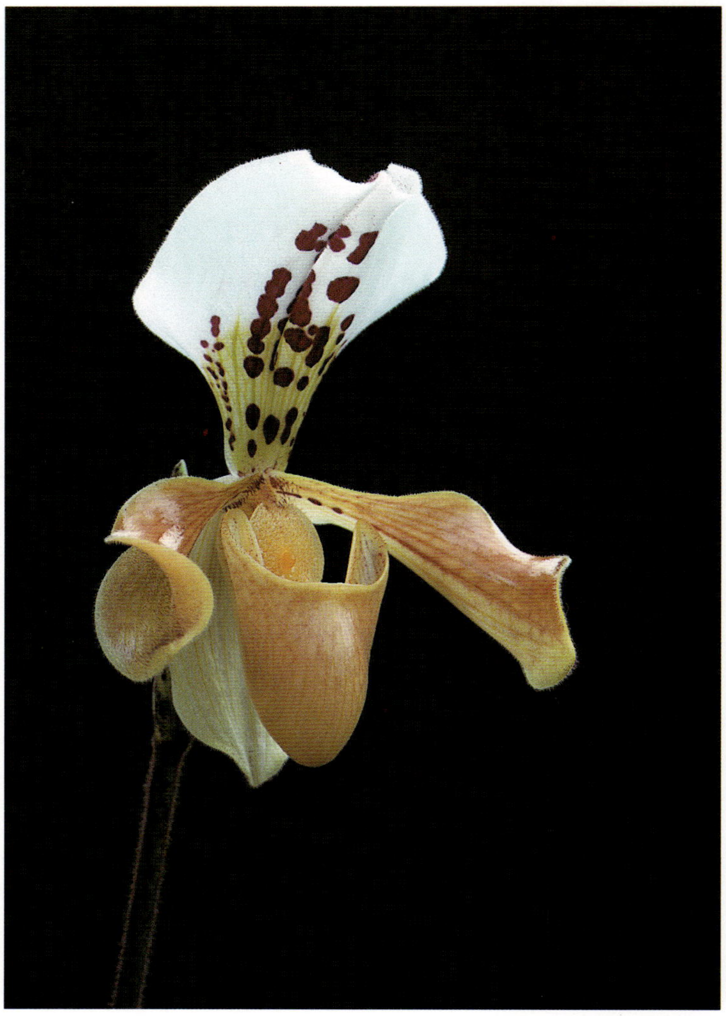

Dendrobium infundibulum

Here is a good example of a species which is normally epiphytic, growing on a road cutting in North Thailand at an altitude of over 2000m (6560 feet). *Dendrobium infundibulum* is closely related to *Denrobium longicornu*, but the stems are often stouter and the flowers larger. Although thin in texture, they are very long lasting and appear in clusters of two or three from upper nodes on the stems in the summer.

Paphiopedilum gratrixianum

Many of the Asian slipper orchid species are well-known in cultivation but this one is not. *Paphiopedilum gratrixianum* comes from Laos, where it grows as a terrestrial, and was first described in 1905. It is distinguished by its narrow green leaves, purple spotted on the underside towards the base, and the relatively small flower, carried on a tall hairy stem. Such plants grow in clumps which may be divided in time, although seedlings are becoming more available.

Paphiopedilum sukhakulii

This beautiful slipper orchid was first described in 1965 and named after Prasong Sukhakul, the Bangkok nurseryman who first introduced it into cultivation. Its natural habitat is restricted to a mountain area in North-east Thailand where it grows terrestrially in sandy loam, often beside shady forest streams. Although greatly depleted in the wild, it is widely grown by orchid lovers around the world.

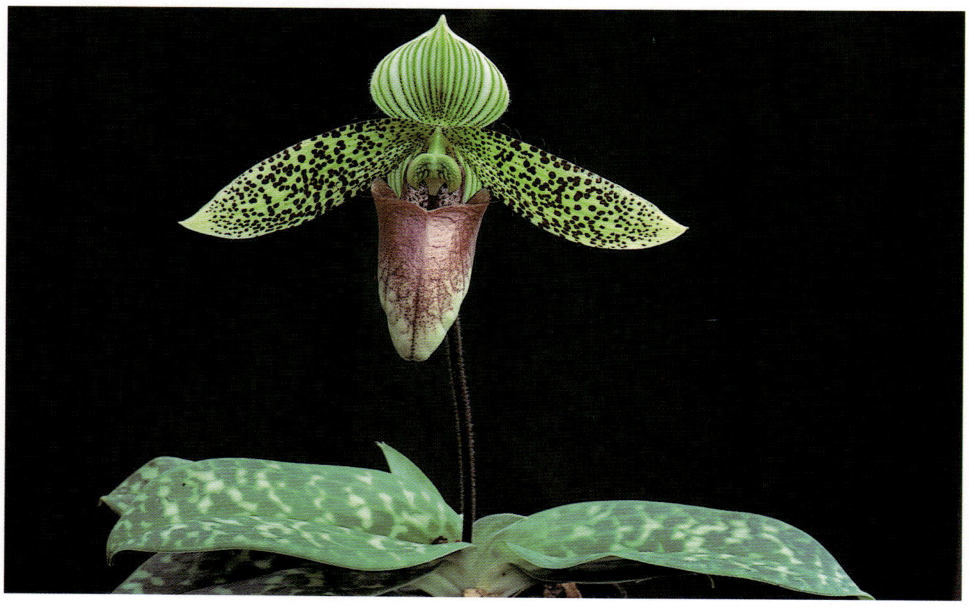

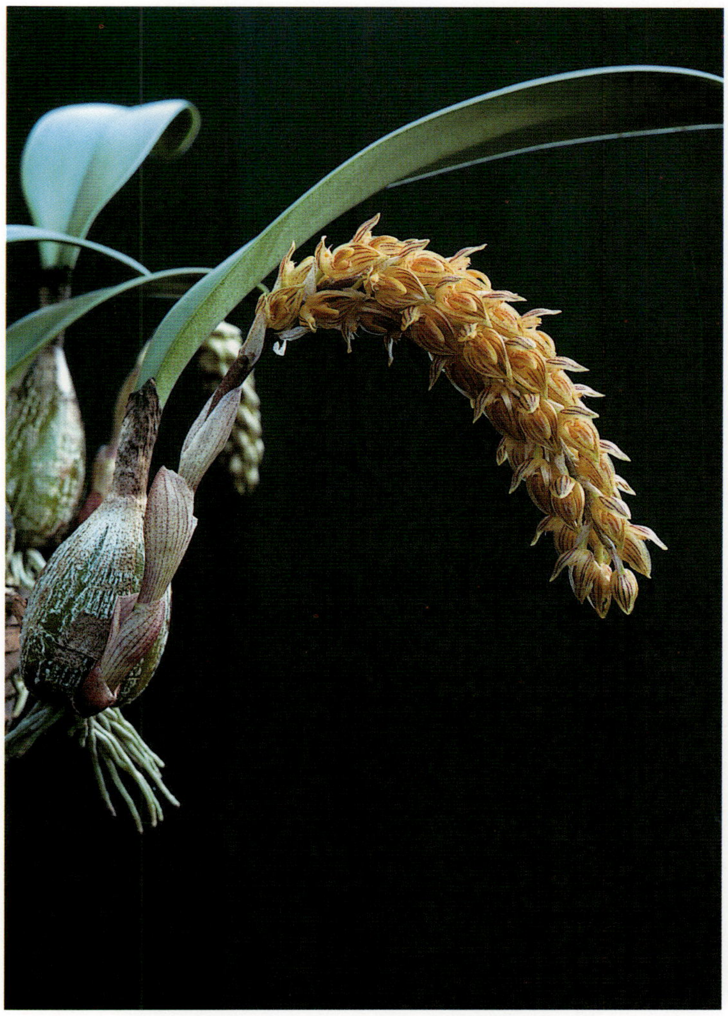

Bulbophyllum careyanum

In Thailand alone, there are at least 130 *Bulbophyllum* species. A majority of these has small flowers, although through adaptation to fly pollination, their shapes and smells are interesting, if not repugnant. *B. careyanum* is known from Nepal to Assam, and in Burma. It grows as a creeping epiphyte on tree branches, and has a single tough leaf on each pseudobulb. The unpleasant smelling flowers are presented on an inflorescence arising from the base of mature growths.

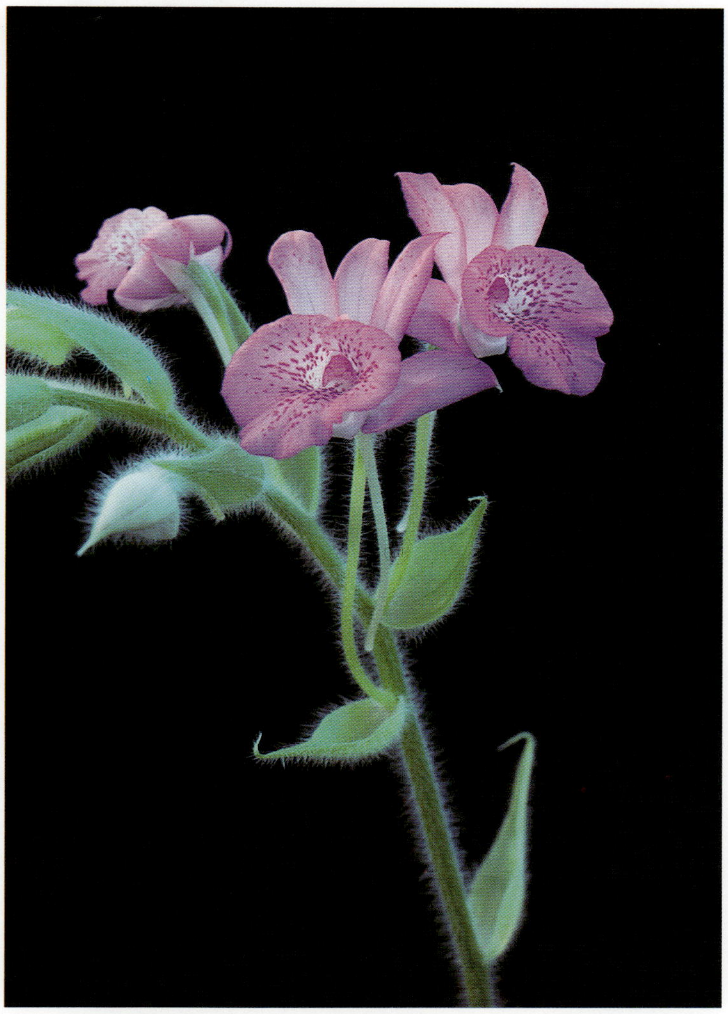

Calanthe hirsuta

Calanthe hirsuta, found only in Thailand, belongs to a group of plants which is strongly adapted to alternate dry and wet seasons, and widely cultivated in Victorian times. When in bloom, this species is leafless, consisting only of a clump of large silver-gray pseudobulbs, each with a distinct neck in its upper part. During this time it is completely dry, but during the spring and summer, new pseudobulbs are formed beneath large soft leaves.

Bulbophyllum dayanum

These flowers, native to Burma, Thailand and Cambodia, have been likened to a nest full of fledgling birds with open mouths. They appear on a short stem, near the round purple pseudobulbs, and apart from a fishy smell, their fringed sepals and petals make them attractive. Bulbophyllums are often grown in botanic gardens because of their ease of cultivation and their diversity of form.

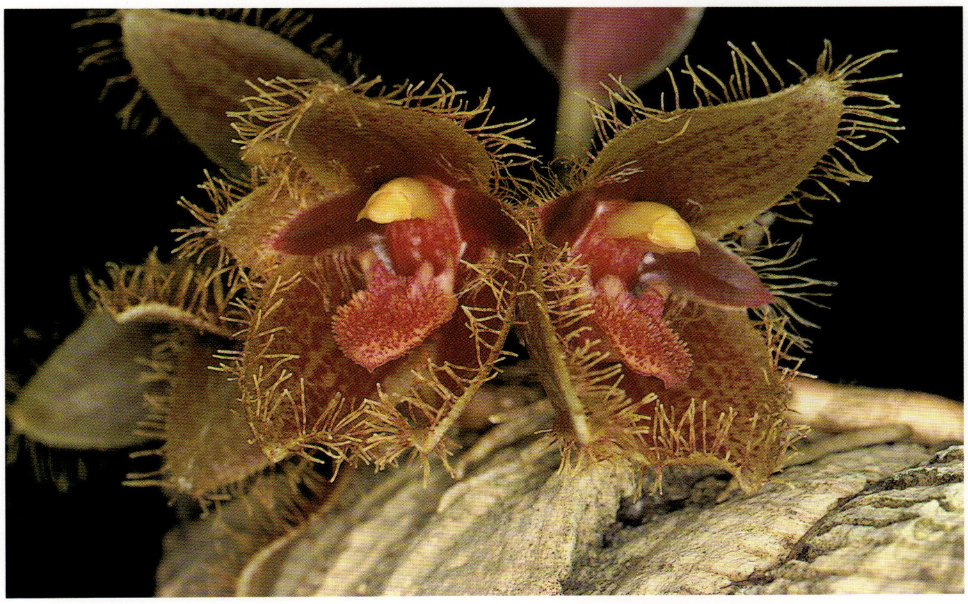

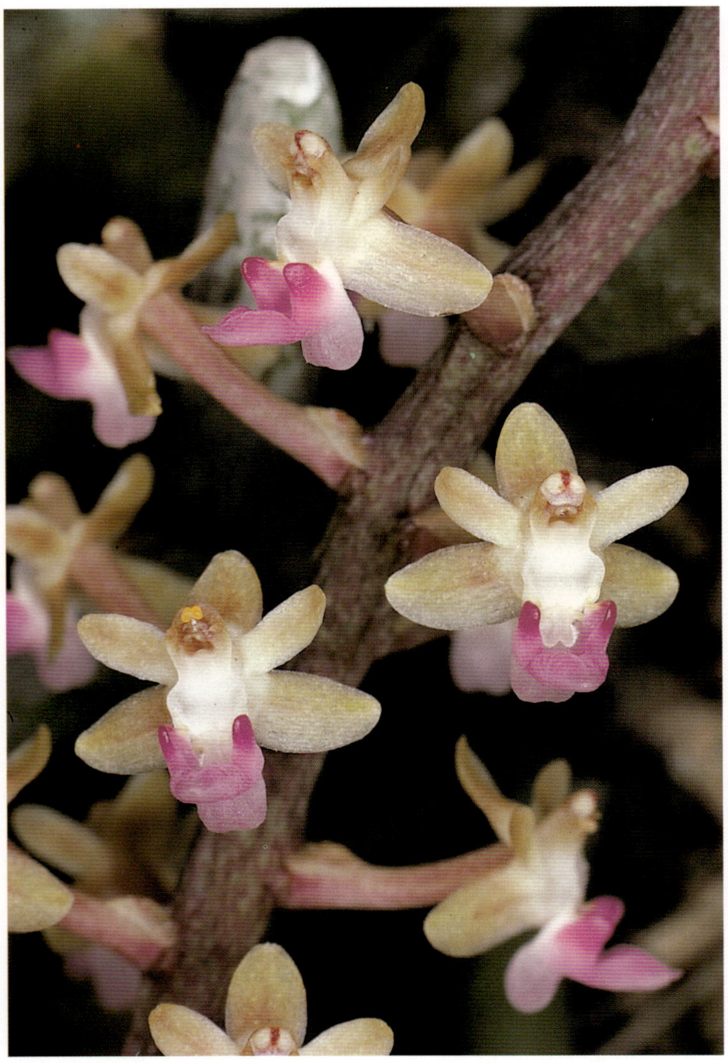

Cleisostoma arietinum

Included in the orchid flora of Thailand are many species of small plants bearing tiny colorful flowers, and *Cleisostoma arietinum* is one of them. The plants look tough with their thick curved leaves arising either side of a short stem. In the wild, they often grow hanging downwards beneath branches of trees in dry forest.

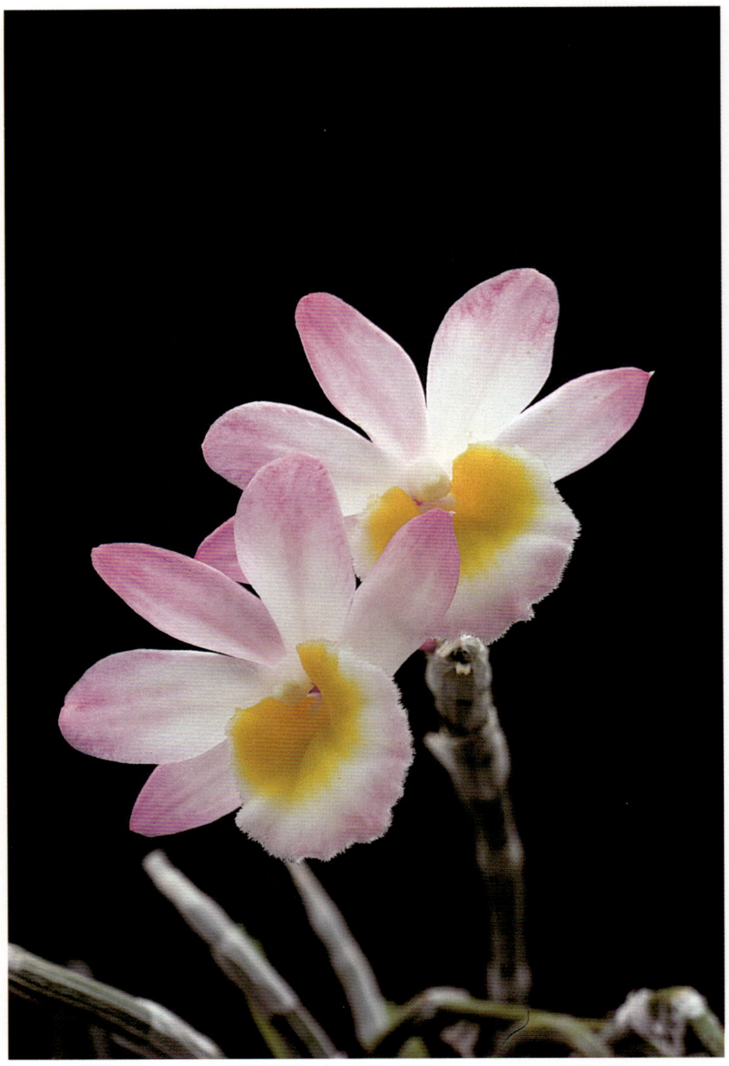

Dendrobium crepidatum

Dendrobium crepidatum occurs over a wide range, through the Himalayas to Burma and Thailand, Indochina and China. It usually grows as an epiphyte in open forest under monsoon conditions where a wet growing season is followed by a dry resting and flowering period. The beautiful flowers appear after the leaves have fallen, in clusters on the most recent stems.

Dendrobium harveyanum

Although first described in 1883, *Dendrobium harveyanum* has never been common, and for a long time, was not seen at all. In more recent years, plants have been found in northern Thailand and successfully flowered. The plants grows to about 25cm (10 inches) tall, with tough leaves on the upper parts of younger pseudobulbs, and the striking flowers appear, several at a time, from mainly leafless older stems. It is the fringed petals and lip which are notable features.

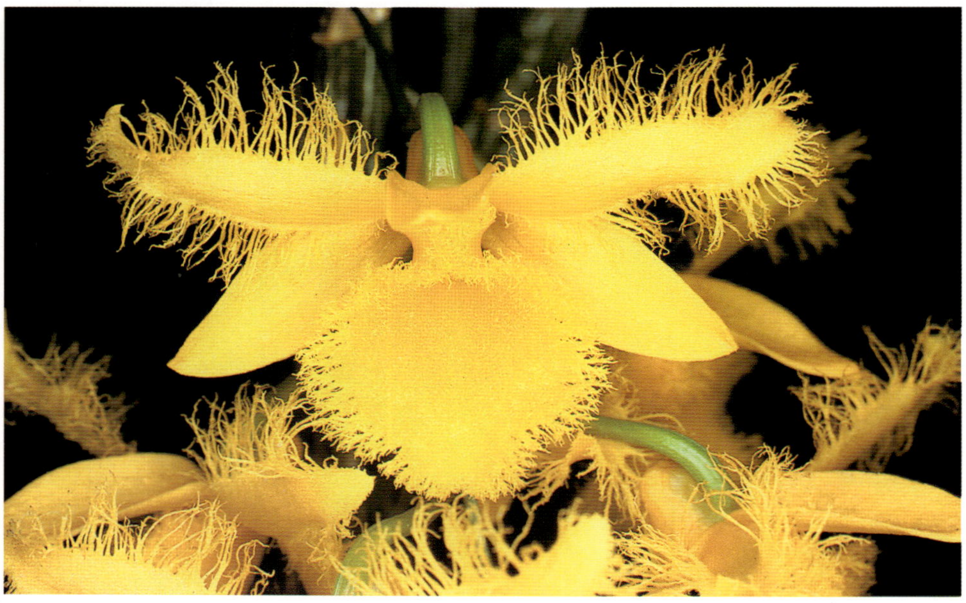

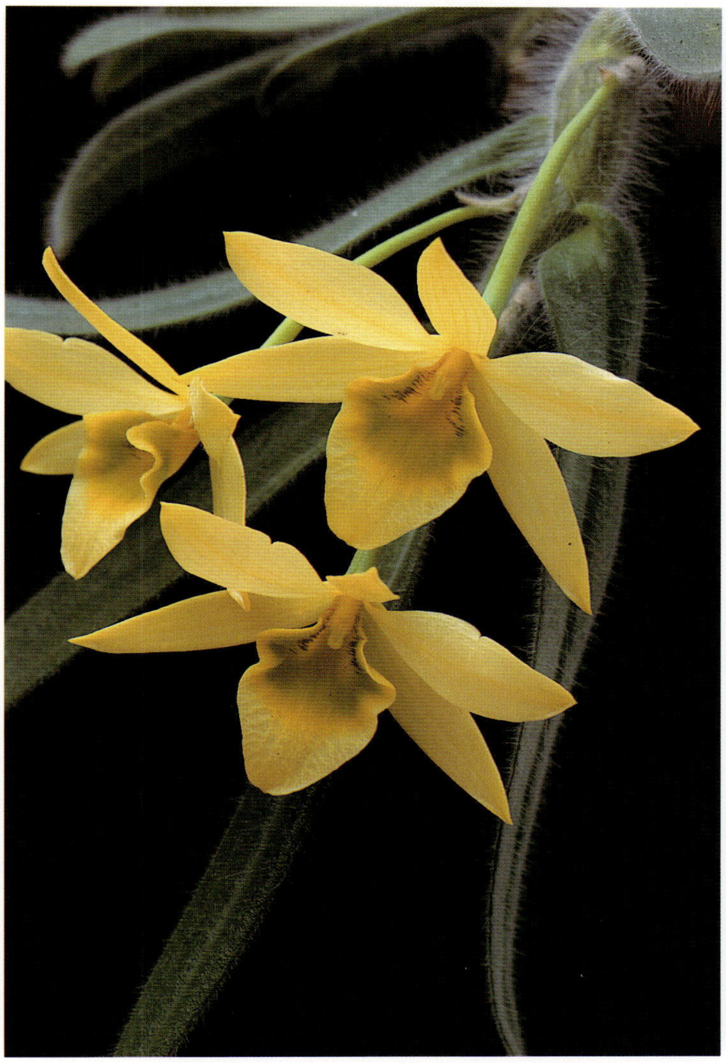

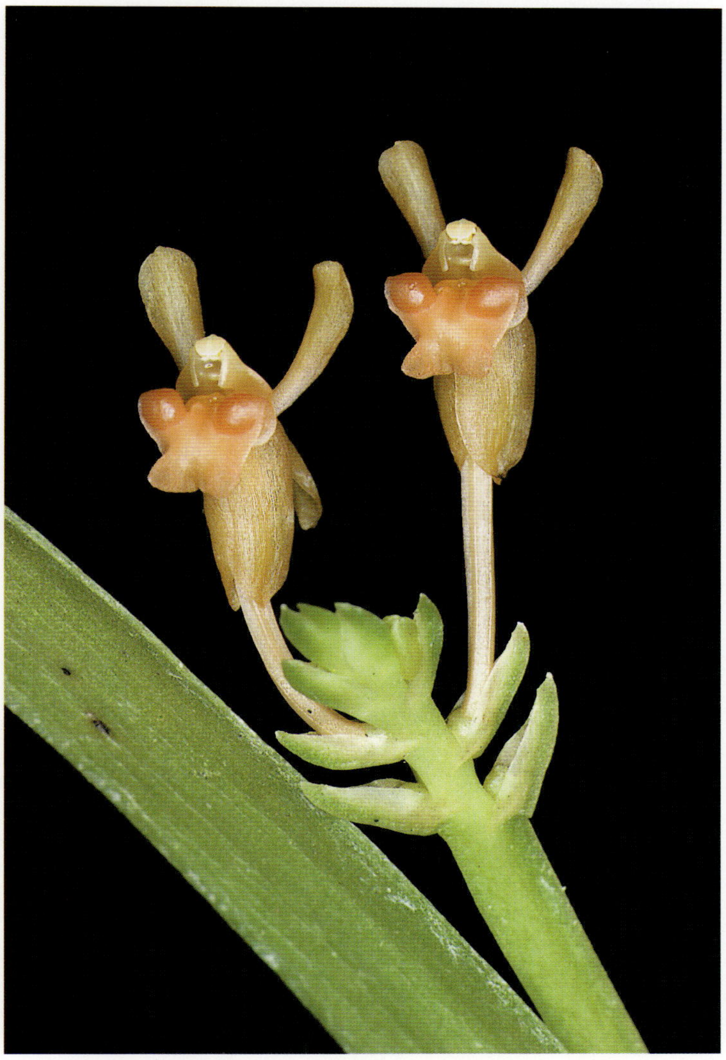

ABOVE: *Dendrobium senile*

The name 'senile' meaning hairy, aptly describes this species from Burma Thailand and Laos. The thin leaves and plump pseudobulbs are liberally covered with fine white hairs which persist for many years. *Dendrobium senile* grows as an epiphyte at moderate altitudes, and the fine flowers are produced on the leafy stems before summer growth begins.

ABOVE RIGHT: *Liparis gibbosa*

The genus *Liparis* contains about 250 species distributed world-wide, but concentrated in Asia. They are mostly small soft plants with small flowers, growing as either terrestrials or epiphytes. *Liparis gibbosa*, found from Thailand and Burma to Indonesia, is an epiphyte in evergreen forest. The flowers appear in succession from the apex of a slender stem and are about a centimeter long. The prominent parts are the two upright petals and the bumpy orange lip.

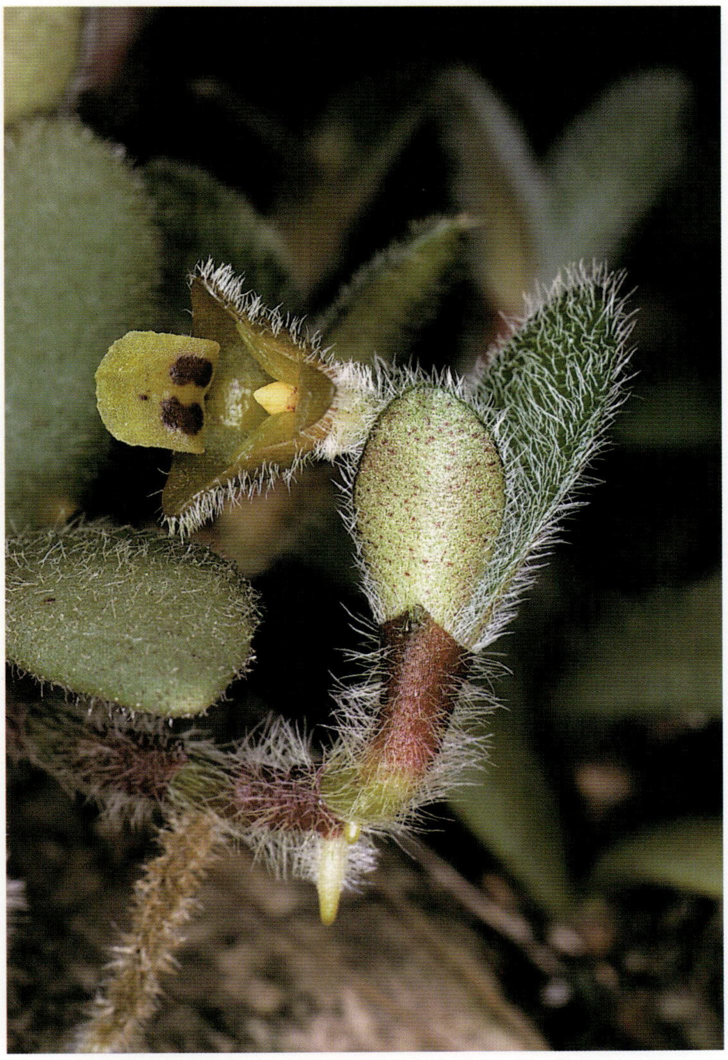

RIGHT: *Trichotosia dasyphylla*

Trichotosia dasyphylla is one of a group of small flowered Asian species which has fine hairs covering parts of the plants, and in this case, the whole of the plant including the flower, is hairy. It grows as an epiphyte, forming mats as the low creeping stems intertwine, and apart from being widespread in Thailand, is found also in the eastern Himalayas, Burma and Indochina. The solitary flowers appear at the center of new growths.

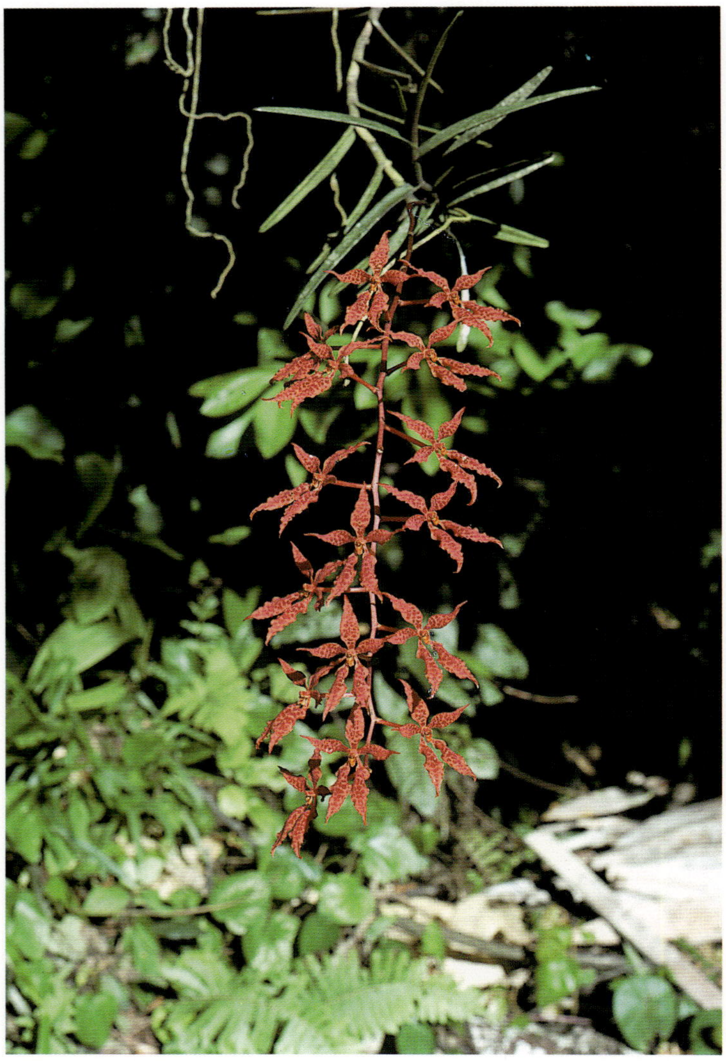

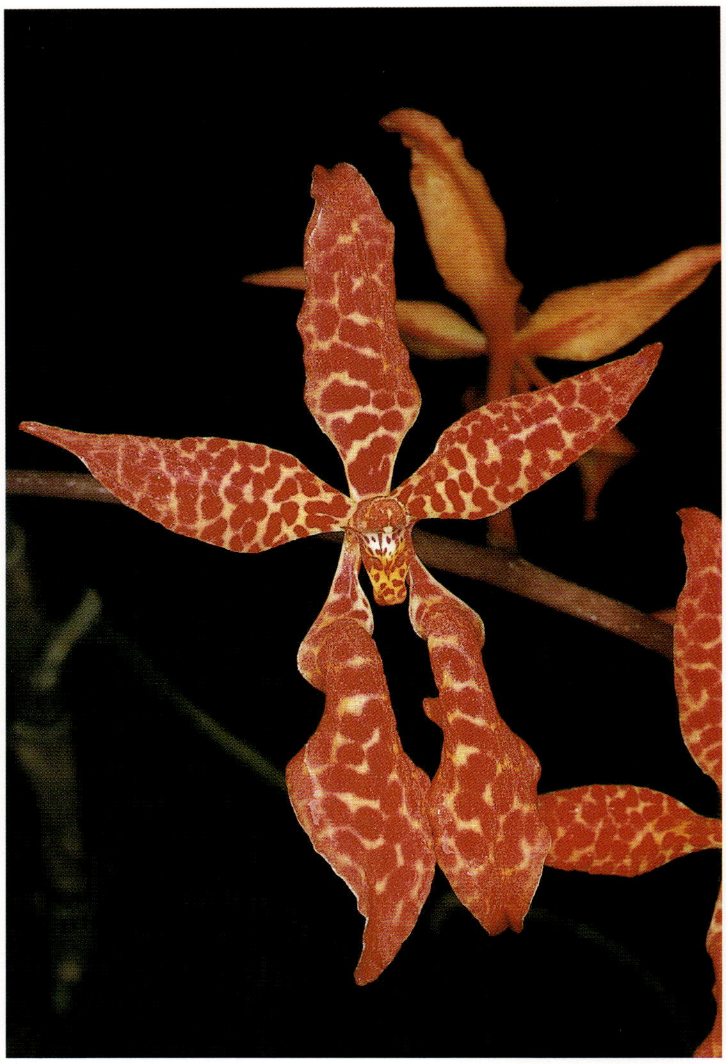

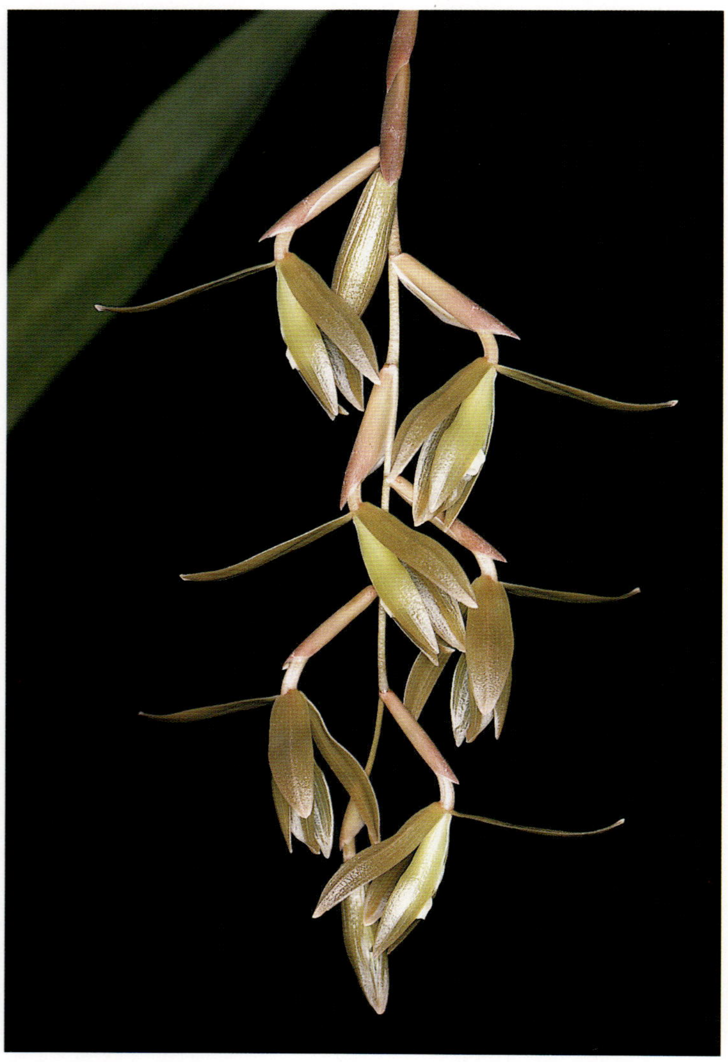

ABOVE LEFT: *Renanthera bella*

The Asian genus *Renanthera* contains about ten species, all of which have red or red-spotted yellow flowers. Some grow very tall, and are more suited to tropical cultivation, but several of the shorter stemmed ones, including *Renanthera monachica* from the Philippines, are suited to glasshouse growing. *Renanthera bella*, which is illustrated here, growing in its native Sabah, East Malaysia, grows as a forest epiphyte at altitudes between 400 and 1200m (1300-3940 feet).

ABOVE: *Renanthera bella*

Renanthera bella is quite new to science, being described only in 1981. The flower shape is distinct, with the lateral sepals being close together, and with the lip being much smaller than the other parts. Renanthera species hybridize readily with members of related genera, such as *Arachnis* and *Phalaenopsis*, and impart useful characters like color and spotting to their hybrids.

LEFT: *Coelogyne exalata*

Among the lesser known *Coelogyne* species is *Coelogyne exalata*, which comes from the Malaysian State of Sarawak, where it prefers to grow on tree trunks in primary forest. The elegant inflorescence hangs down to display the flowers, of which the most obvious parts are the extended dorsal sepals.

Vanda tricolor var suavis

Plants of *Vanda tricolor* show a characteristic mode of growth which is common to many tropical Asian orchids. The monopodial habit is one in which the stem grows indefinitely from the apex so that it becomes taller each year by the addition of two or three new leaves. Aerial roots grow from the stem at intervals, and the inflorescences appear from between the leaves towards the top. *Vanda tricolor var suavis* is native to Java, where it grows as an epiphyte at medium elevations. It has always been a favorite in cultivation as it grows and flowers readily even in Europe, and the large blooms are strongly scented.

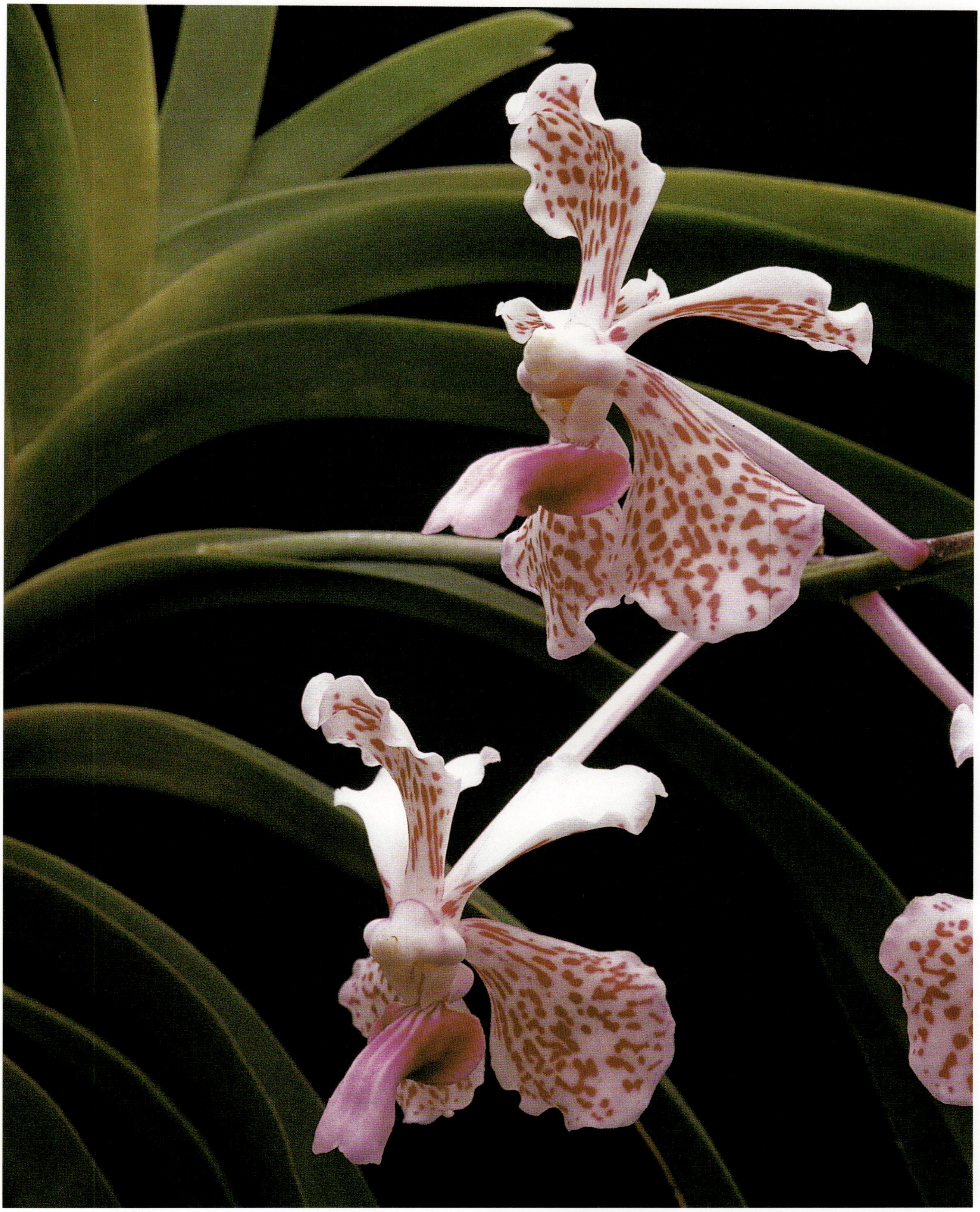

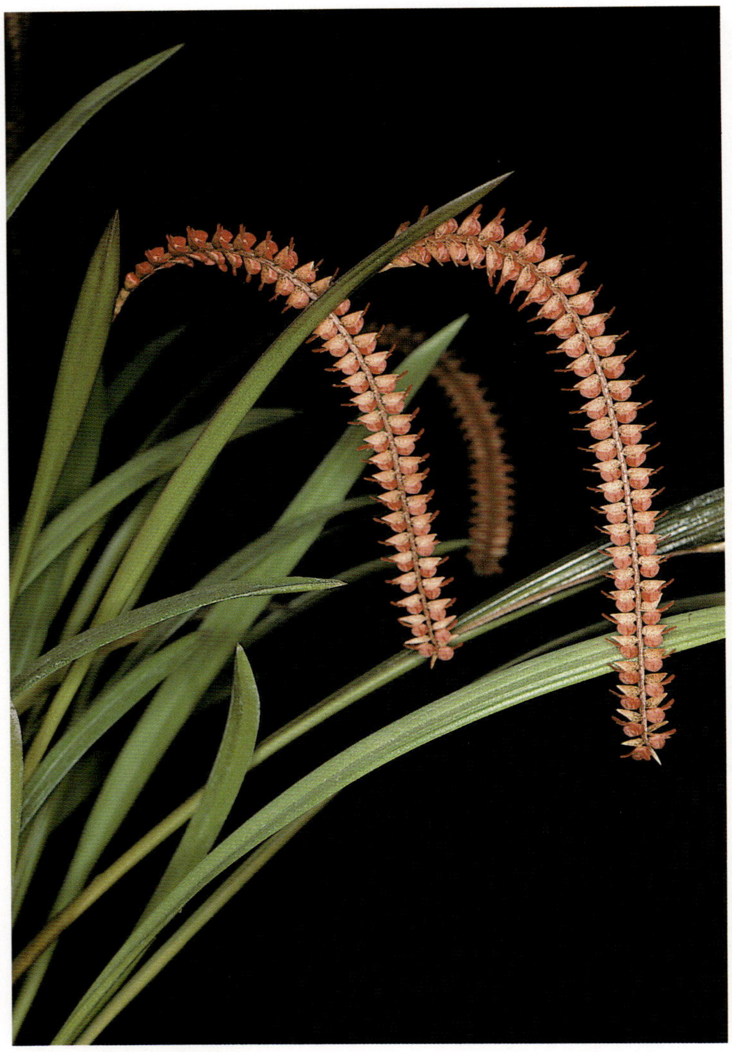

Acoridium saccolabium

Among the orchid flora of the Philippines, are a number of smaller species which are not well known. *Acoridium saccolabium* is rare in cultivation, but related to several popular species, blooming mainly in the spring and summer months. Although the brick red flowers of this plant are just visible, it is the prominent bracts beside each one which stand out. The dainty inflorescences appear inside the new leaf growths.

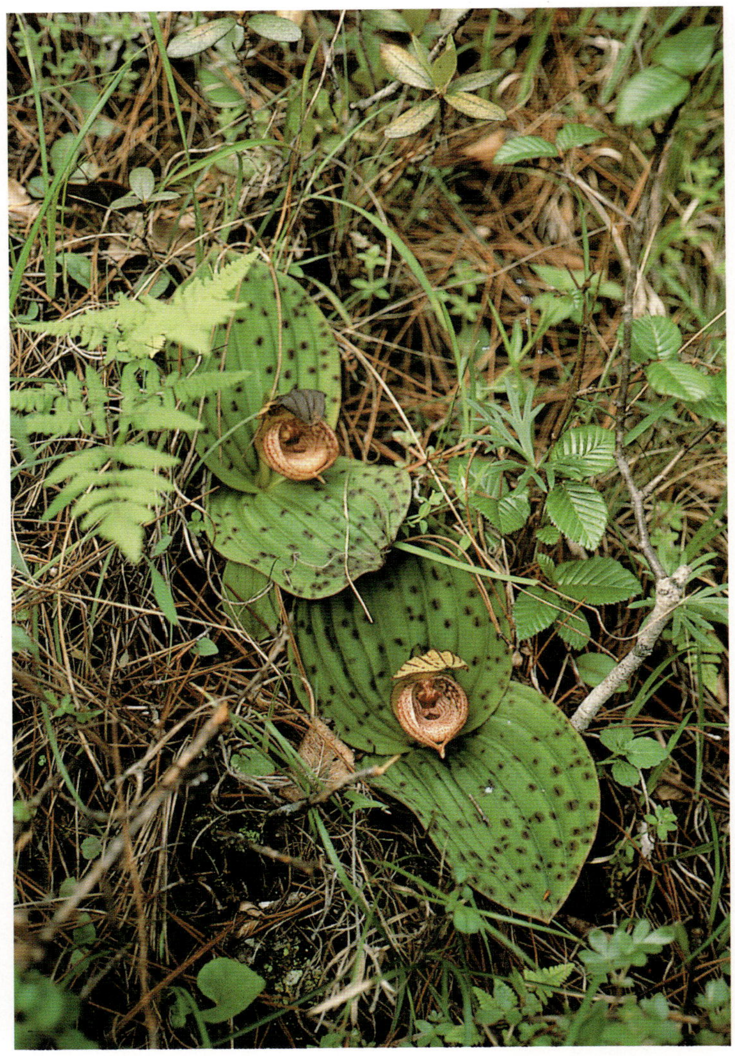

Cypripedium margaritaceum

Most of the fifty or so species of *Cypripedium* are found in North America and China. *C. margaritaceum* is confined to Yunnan Province in the south of China, and it has an unusual appearance due to its spotted leaves. Its natural habitat is on limestone or moraine slopes in open woodland, at altitudes between 2800 and 3400m (2200-11155 feet). Associated vegetation here includes conifers, poplars and rhododendrons.

Phalaenopsis amboinensis

Apart from those *Phalaenopsis* species which have flat flowers on long arching stems, there is another group which produces more colorful flowers on short stems. *Phalaenopsis amboinensis* occurs on islands in the south of Indonesia. Its flowers appear in succession over a long season and their coloring is important to breeders seeking to create strong yellow shades in the large hybrids.

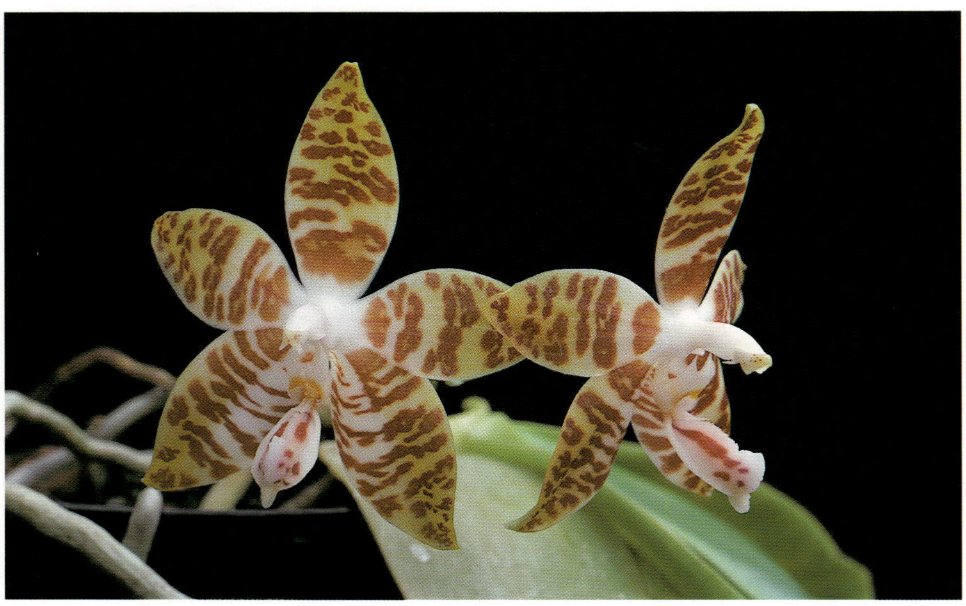

Cypripedium henryi

Although growing in similar habitats to the preceding species, *Cypripedium henryi* is more northerly and widespread in its distribution within China, coming from Sichuan Province at slightly lower elevations. It is closely related to the European *Cypripedium calceolus*, but tends to have two or three flowers on a stem, and greenish sepals and petals. Like many Chinese plants, it is named in honor of the great Irish plant collector, Augustine Henry, who traveled widely in China during the latter part of the nineteenth century.

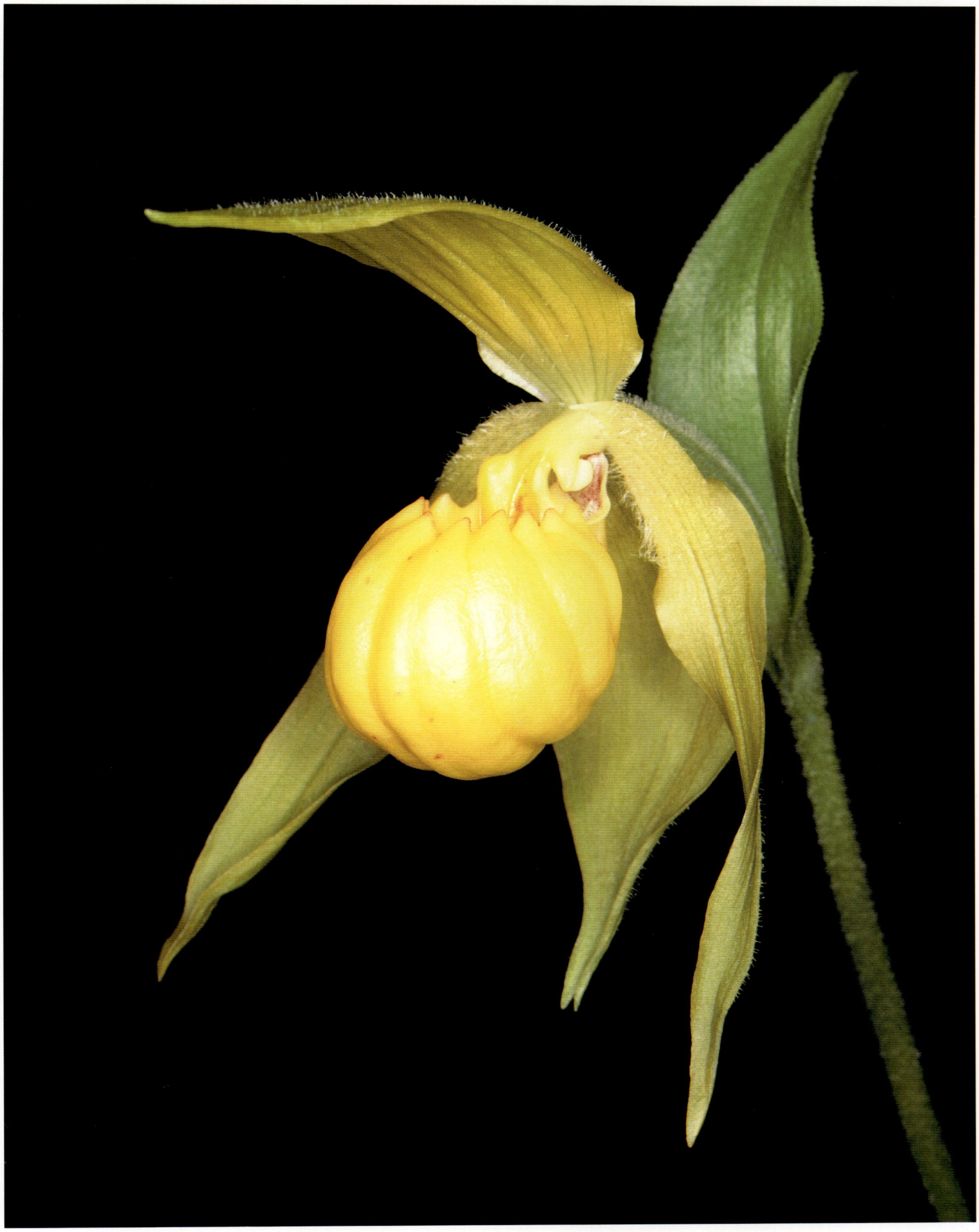

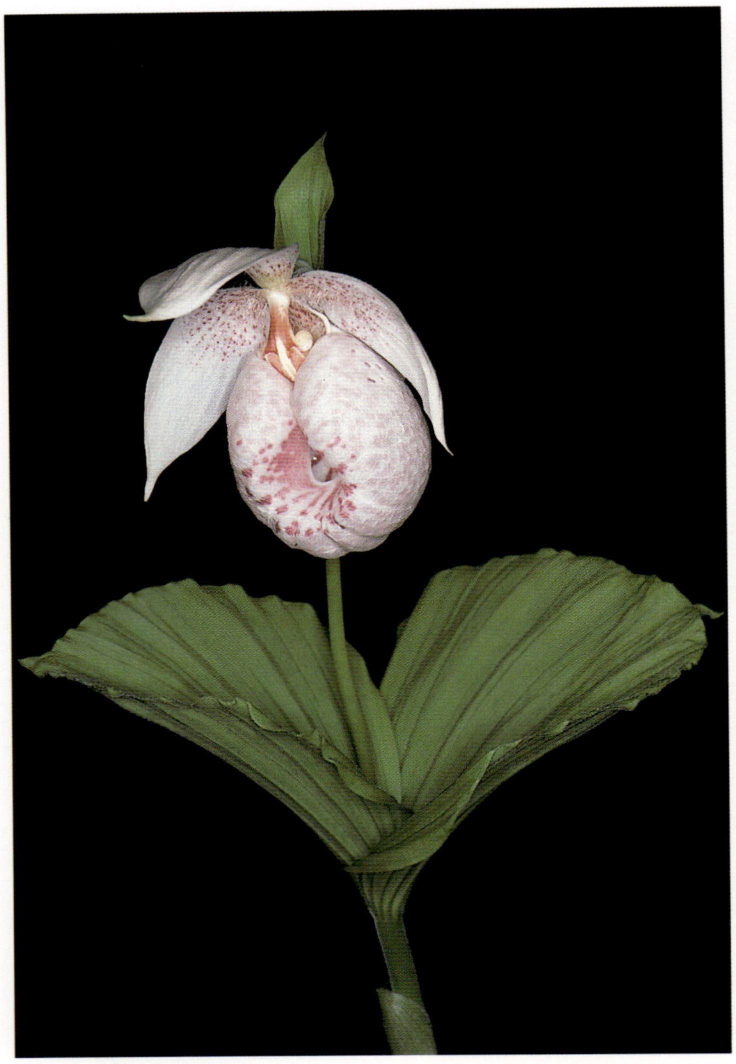

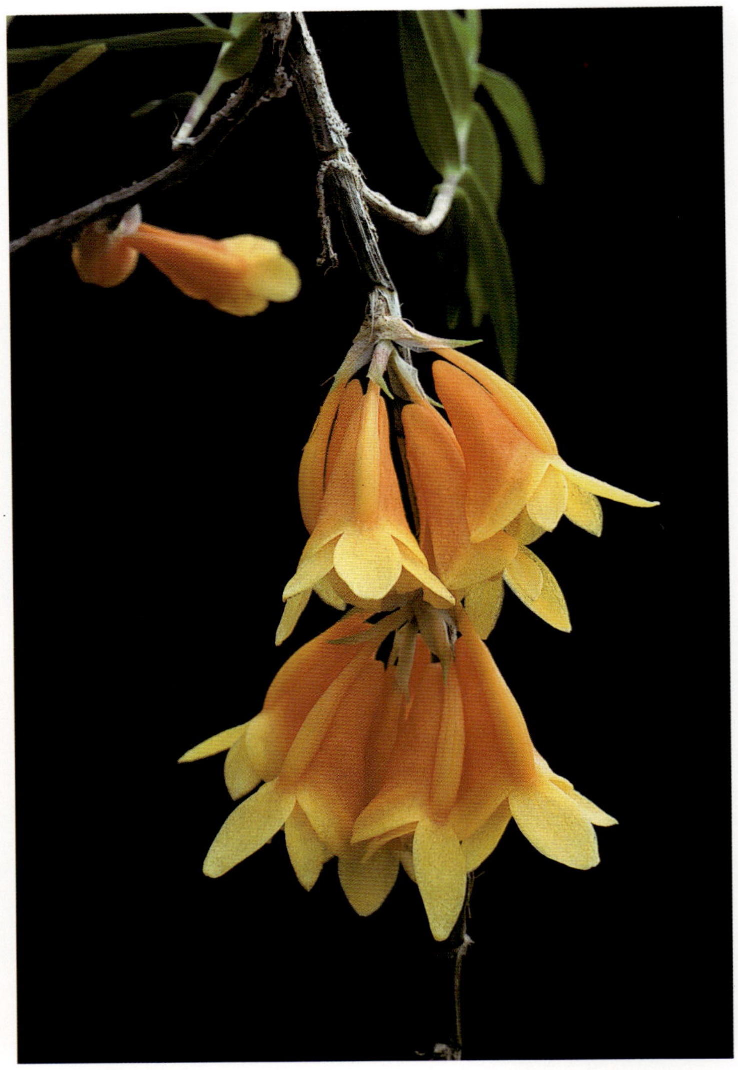

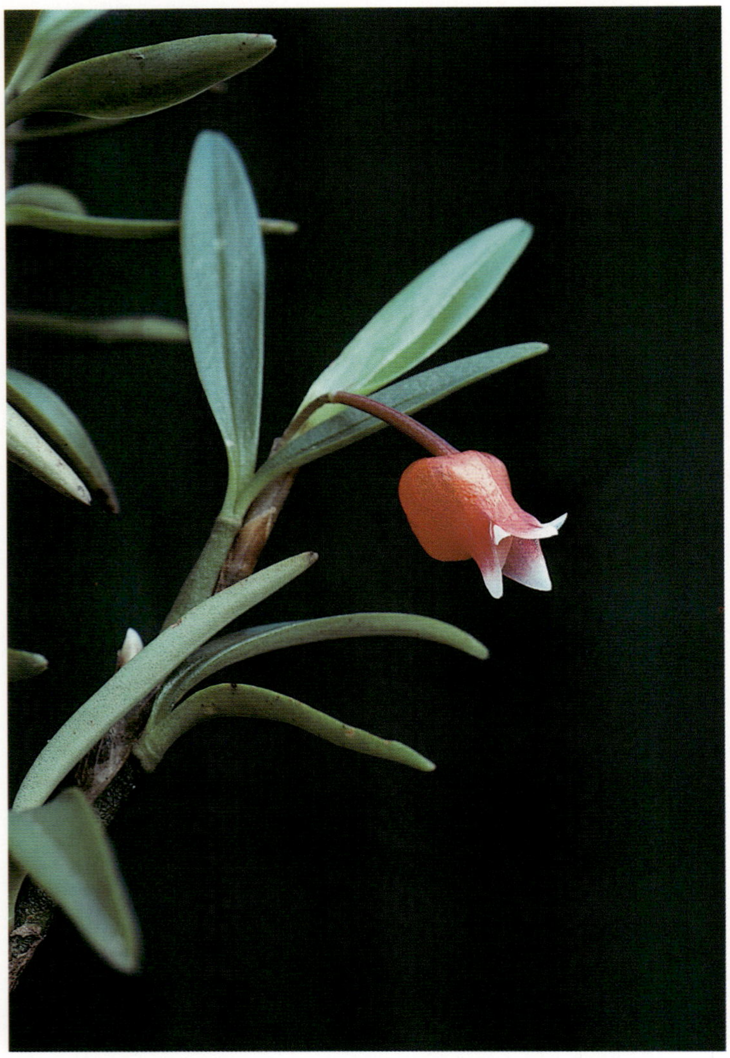

ABOVE LEFT: *Cypripedium japonicum var formosanum*

The unusual pleated leaves, which look as though they had been trimmed with scissors, immediately separate this species from the other two found on the island of Taiwan. Occurring high on the northern and eastern parts of the central mountain ranges, it prefers to grow in leaf litter on the forest floor, or in suitably damp open places.

ABOVE: *Dendrobium subclausum*

The bird-pollinated dendrobiums of Papua New Guinea are a colorful lot, with shades of yellow, orange and red predominating. *Dendrobium subclausum* is a common and variable species in rainforest, growing as an epiphyte at medium altitudes, and sometimes on rocks higher up. The slender branching stems may be up to 60cm (24 inches) long, and the clusters of tubular flowers appear at random from leafless parts of stems, even quite old ones.

LEFT: *Mediocalcar species*

The highlands of New Guinea are home to a great many fascinating orchids. Most of the fifty or so *Mediocalcar* species are found here, growing as creeping epiphytes in montane forest. Although the flowers are small, they are brightly colored in combinations of red, yellow and white, and are often produced in large numbers. The sepals are joined to form a globular shape with the tip of the lip appearing at the entrance, while the petals are hidden within.

Dendrobium cuthbertsonii

Small plants bearing relatively large and colorful flowers have always been popular in cultivation, and this little charmer is no exception. Fortunately it responds well in captivity, and is available as commercial seedlings. A more common color for the long lasting flowers is a bright orange-red but yellow or bicolored forms are also known. Widespread on the mountains of Papua New Guinea, at altitudes of up to 3000m (9840 feet), *Dendrobium cuthbertsonii* usually grows as an epiphyte, but has been known to colonize wet road cuttings.

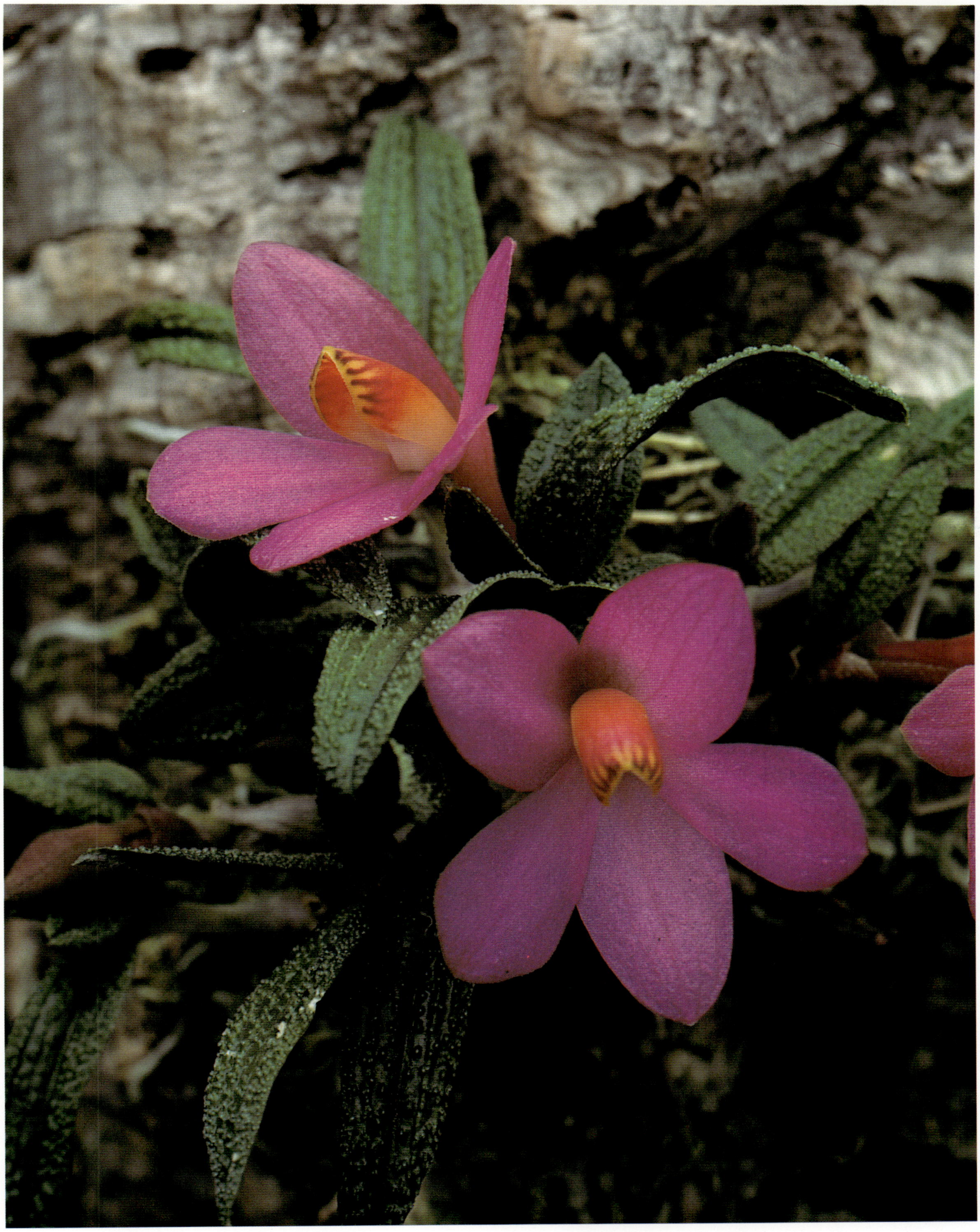

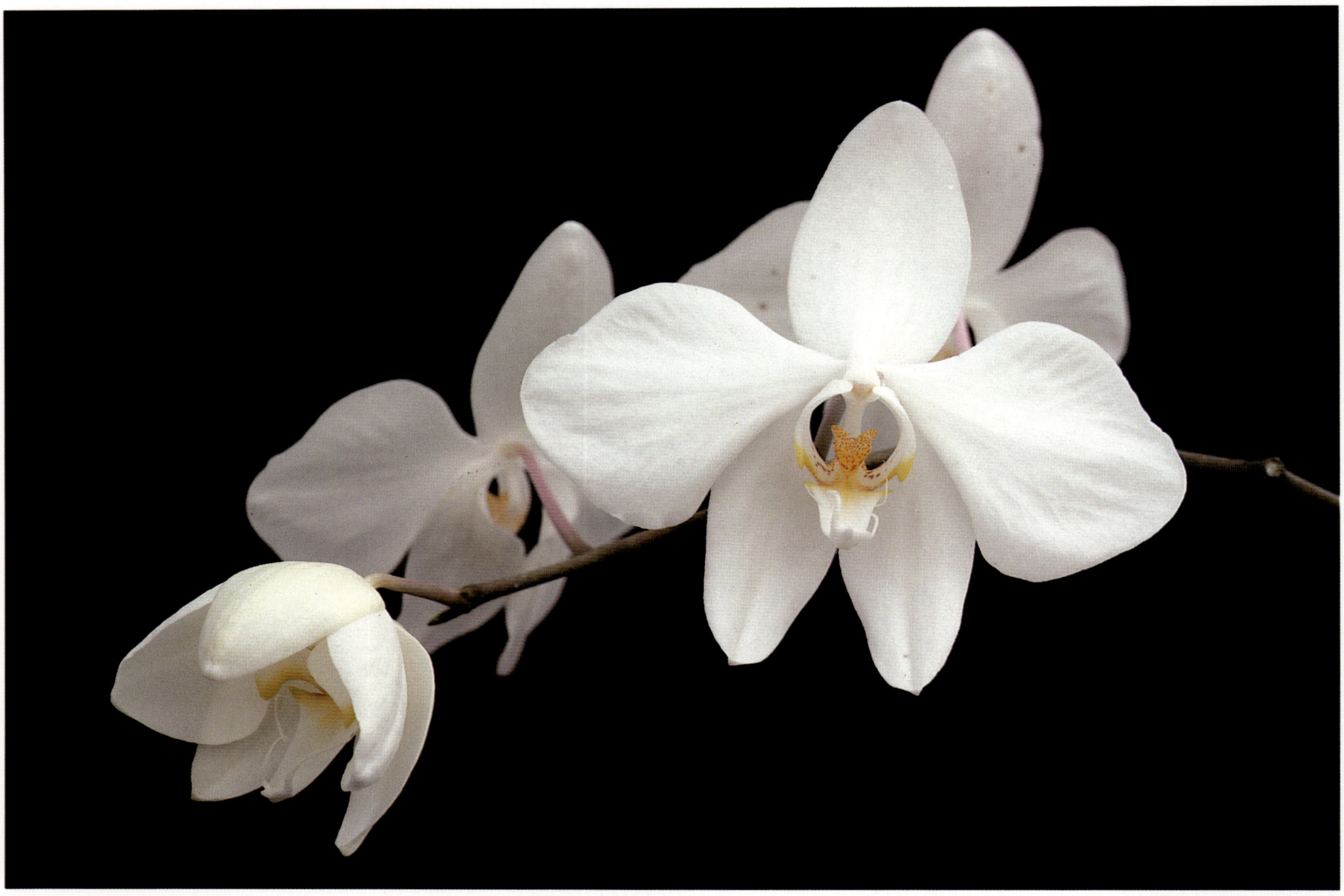

Phalaenopsis amabilis var papuana

The classic white *Phalaenopsis* hybrids originated from wild forms such as this one, collected in Papua NewGuinea, but found also in tropical Queensland, Australia. A very similar variety occurs in Indonesia. *Phalaenopsis amabilis*, with its thick fleshy leaves, needs warm humid conditions, so it usually grows as an epiphyte in sheltered lowland areas. The large flowers are long lasting and are displayed on an arching inflorescence.

Dendrobium macrophyllum

Whereas some orchids are notable for their hairiness, this one belongs to a small group with bristles on the ovary and sepals. *Dendrobium macrophyllum* grows as a forest epiphyte over a very wide range, from the Philippines to Java and Papua New Guinea, the Solomon Islands, and as far as Samoa in the east. The plants have broad evergreen leaves on top of stout pseudobulbs, and the heads of flowers are very long lasting.

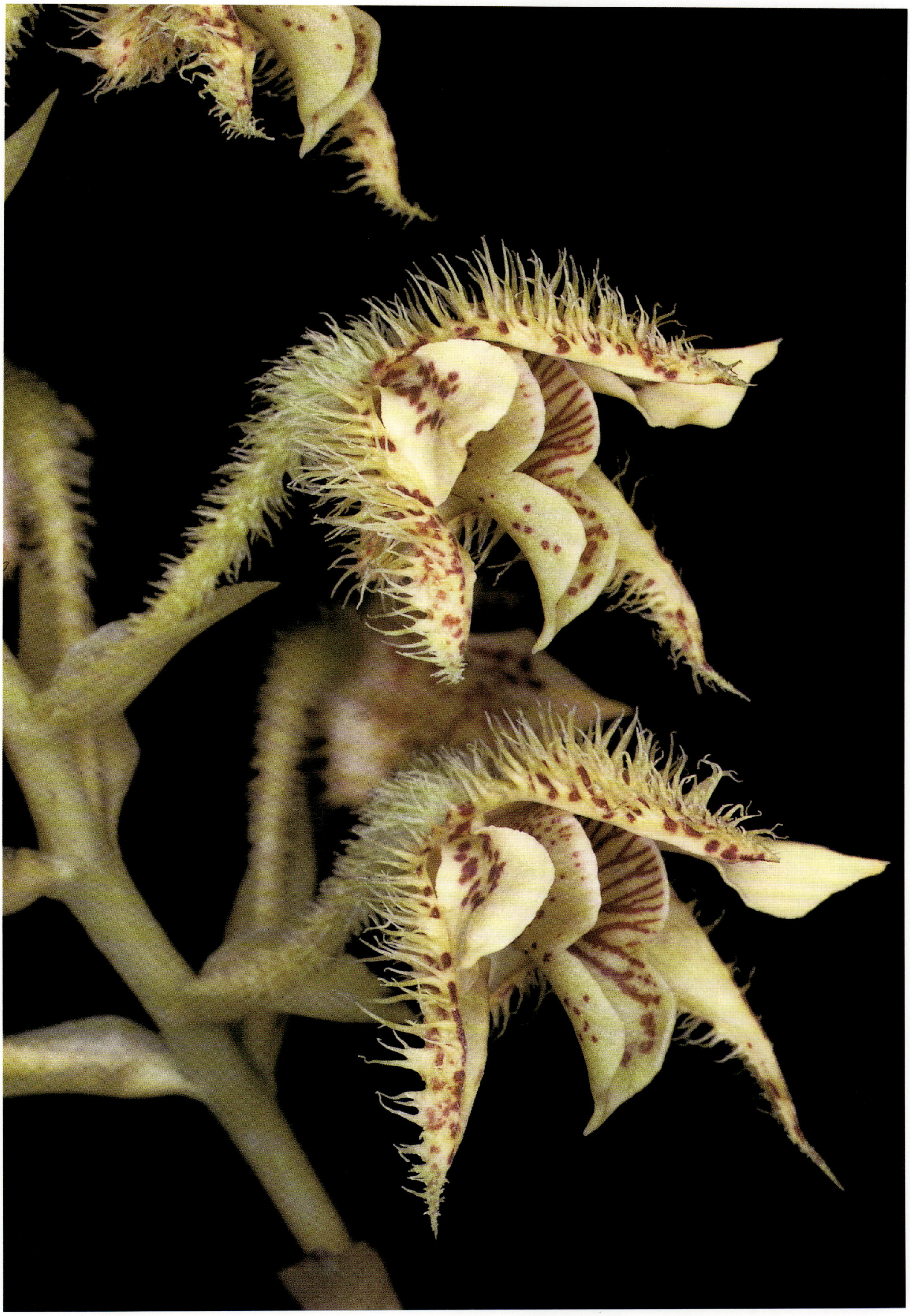

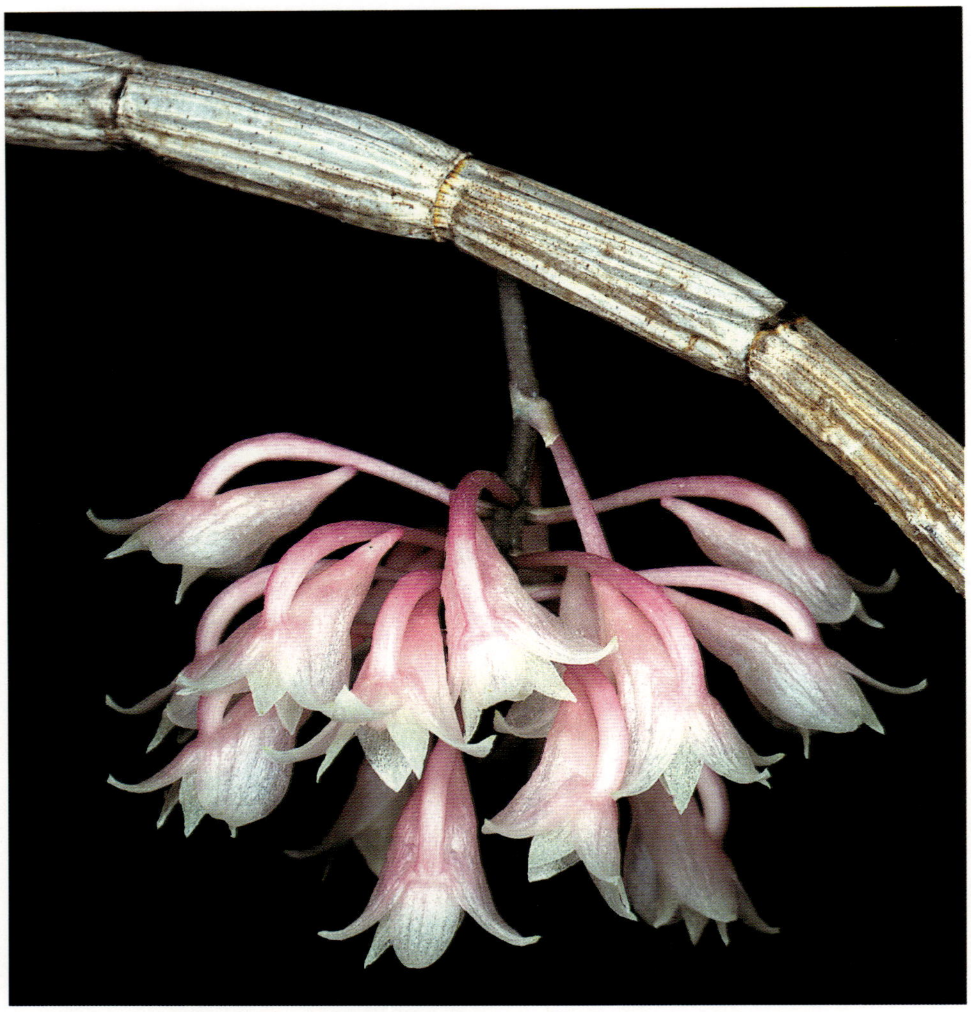

Dendrobium rarum

Many dendrobiums are not grown for their elegance and beauty as plants, as it is the flowers which are their saving grace. Such a species is this one from the rain forests of Papua New Guinea and Vanuatu. The slender stems may be a meter long and it is only after the narrow leaves have fallen that clusters of flowers appear. These are examples, with their tubular form, of adaptation to bird pollination.

Diuris purdiei

The terrestrial orchids of Australia are both numerous and intriguing in their colorful diversity. Common names are also colorful, and in Western Australia, where this one is found, *Diuris* species are known as donkey orchids, a reference to their prominent upright petals. *Diuris purdiei* is known only from localities within Perth city limits, and its main site is destined for development. It is seen here growing in open sandy soil, but other species prefer more shade and moisture.

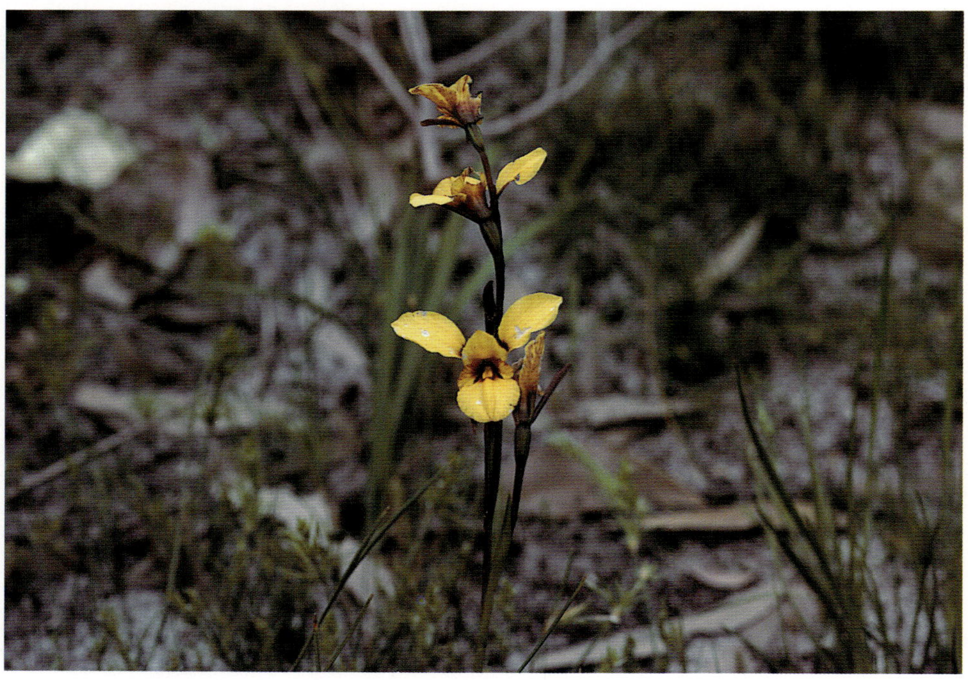

Thelymitra nuda

Commonly known as 'Sun Orchids', from their habit of widely opening their flowers only in bright sunshine, thelymitras occur mainly in Australia, with a few to the north and in New Zealand. Underground tubers protect them from summer heat and drought after the single leaf has died down. The flowers of this species may be blue, pink or mauve, and unusually the three petals are almost identical.

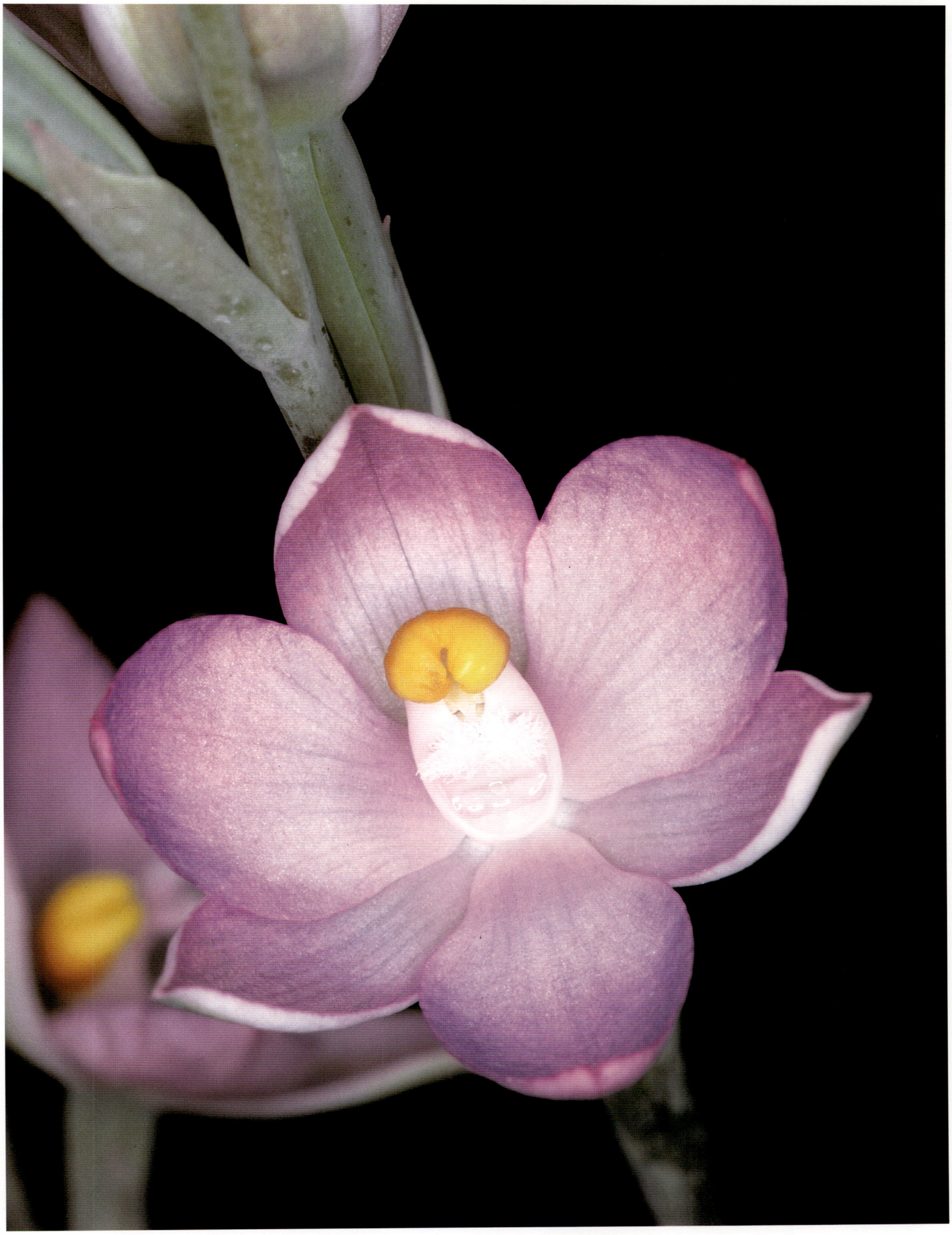

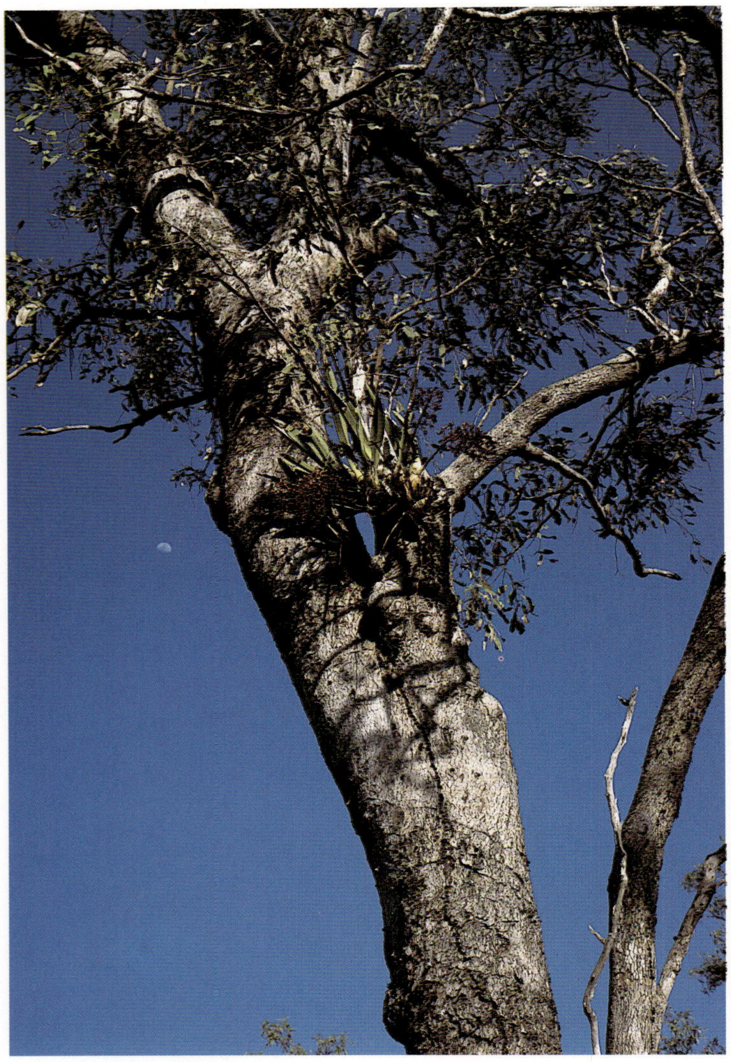

Cymbidium canaliculatum

There are three *Cymbidium* species found in the Australian tropics, and they are all adapted to living under conditons which are often harsh. *Cymbidium canaliculatum* prefers drier areas, and occurs in the east from northern New South Wales to Cape York Peninsula, and across the north as far as Western Australia. It grows as an epiphyte in open forest, often in the hollows of dead limbs, where the roots can penetrate the rotting wood. It experiences extremes of temperature, strong light and limited water supply.

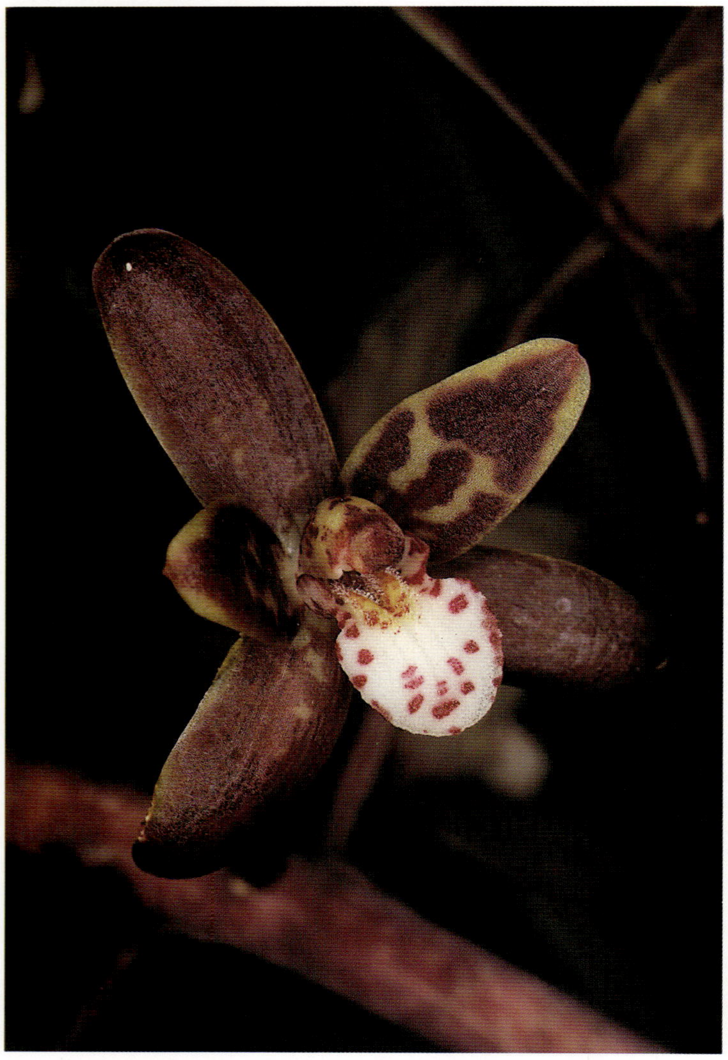

Cymbidium canaliculatum

For a large plant, *Cymbidium canaliculatum* produces quite small flowers up to 5cm (2 inches) in diameter, and varying in color from light green to purple or dull red. This is an example of one of the darker forms. Each of the inflorescences carries up to fifty flowers, and this has encouraged hybridizers to use the species even though the resulting plants may take up a lot of space.

Caladenia barbarossa

Another mainly Australian genus of terrestrial orchids is *Caladenia* containing at least 70 species, over half of which are confined to Western Australia. The plants have a single, usually hairy, leaf, a hairy stem and an underground tuber. *Caladenia barbarossa* comes from Western Australia, and is found growing in open areas. Pollination is by a wasp species which lands on the hairy lip, and is thrown by its tilting on to the column where pollen is stuck to the insect's back.

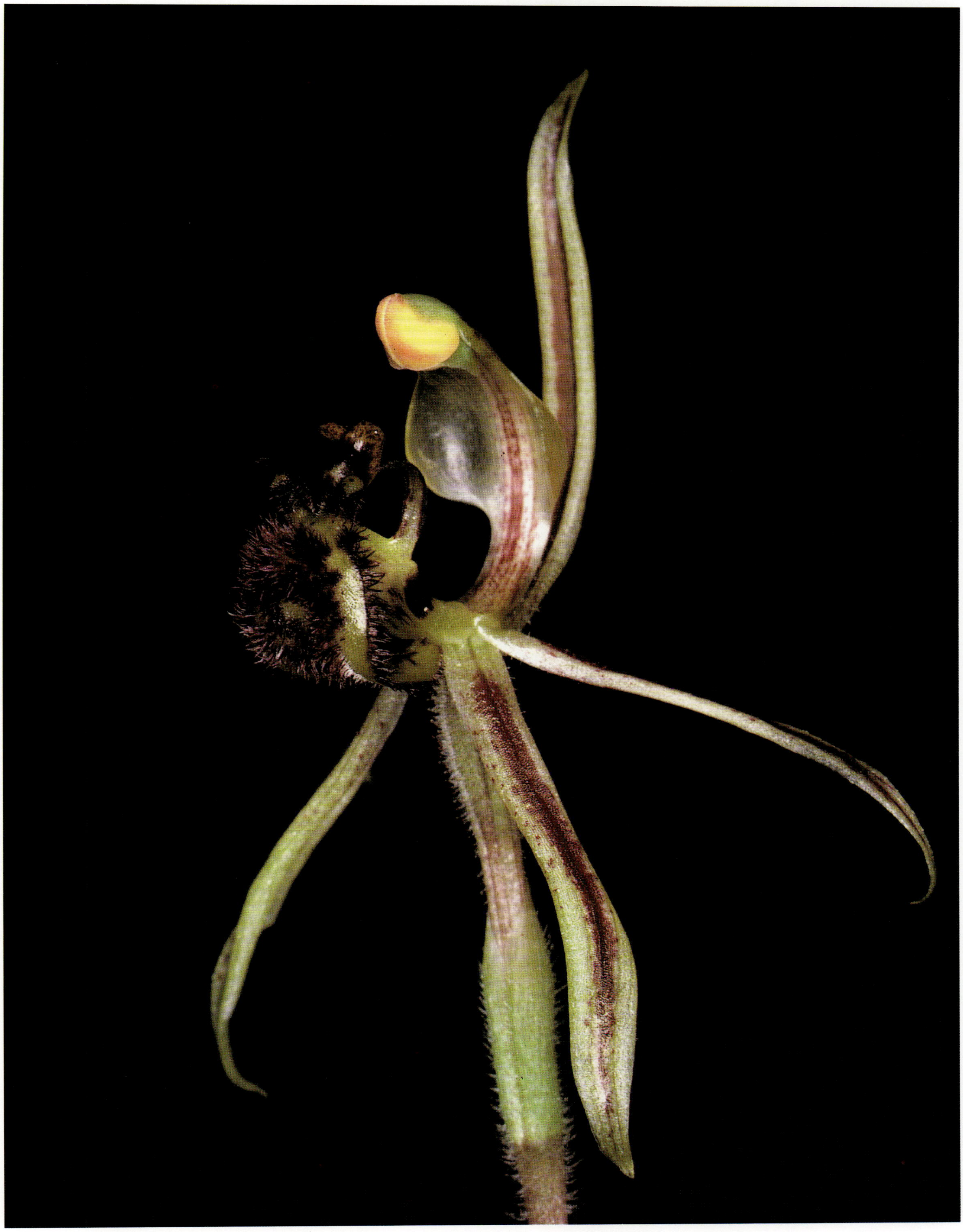

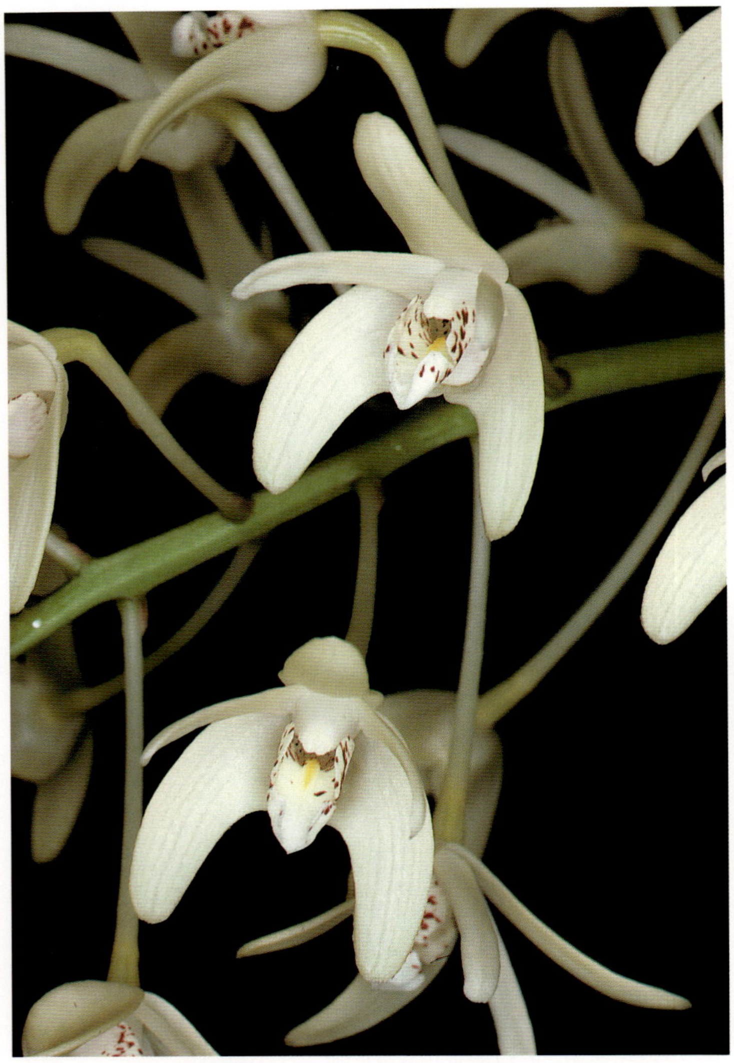

LEFT: *Dendrobium speciosum*

A large specimen in full flower is a magnificent sight, as it may involve thousands of individual blooms. Each inflorescence is up to 70cm (28 inches) long, but usually shorter, and carrying up to 100 flowers. These vary in color from white through cream to yellow, with the lip having red or purple markings. They have a strong sweet fragrance in sunlight, but nothing in dull weather or at night. This is obviously connected to pollination by bees.

BELOW: *Dendrobium smillieae*

A lowland tropical species of North Queensland in Australia, and in Papua New Guinea, this is sometimes known as the 'Bottlebrush Orchid'. The fine plant seen here was growing on rocks in open forest on Cape York Peninsula, but it equally grows as an epiphyte on a variety of trees or even treeferns. The tubular flowers have no scent, but are adapted to pollination by birds.

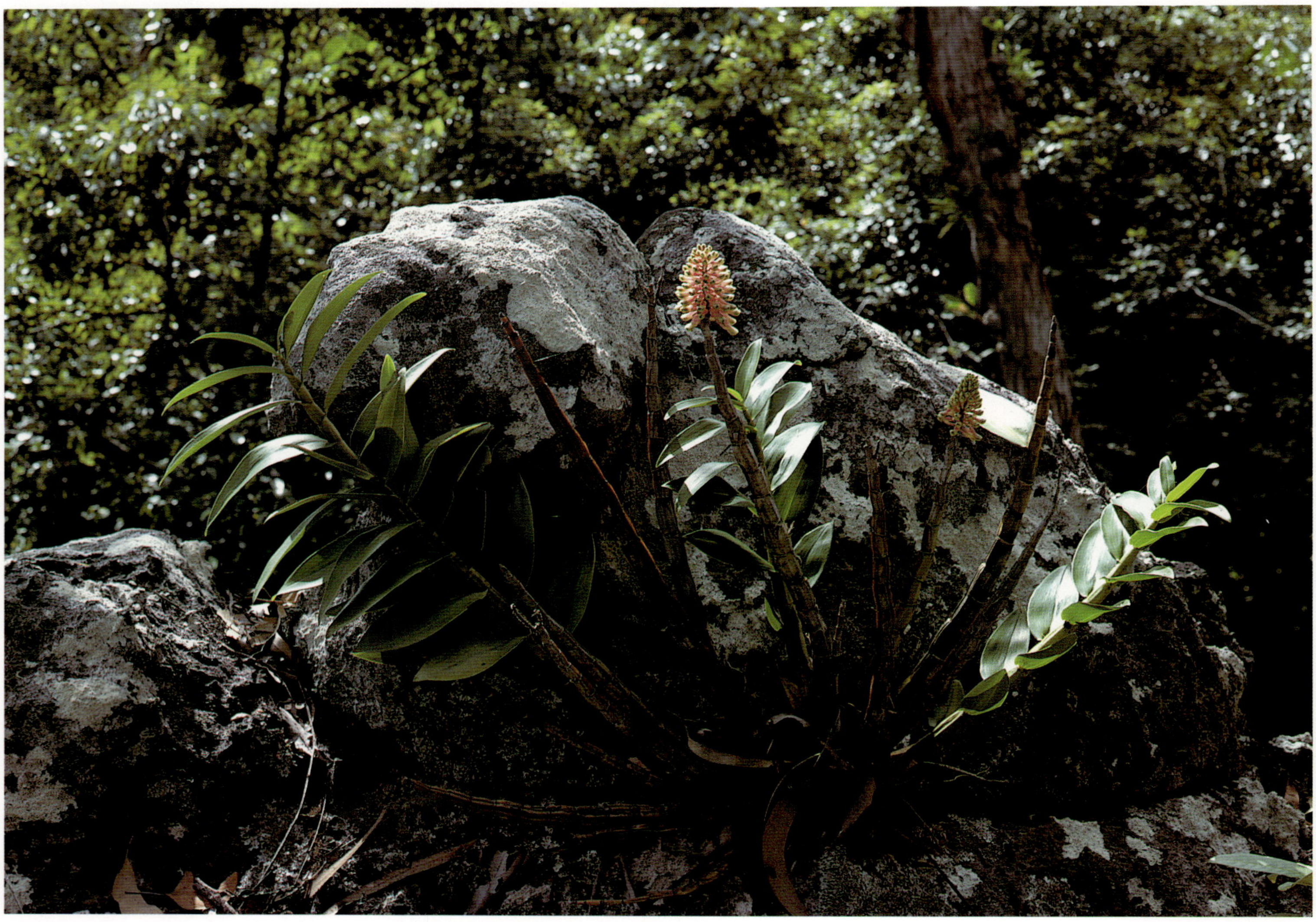

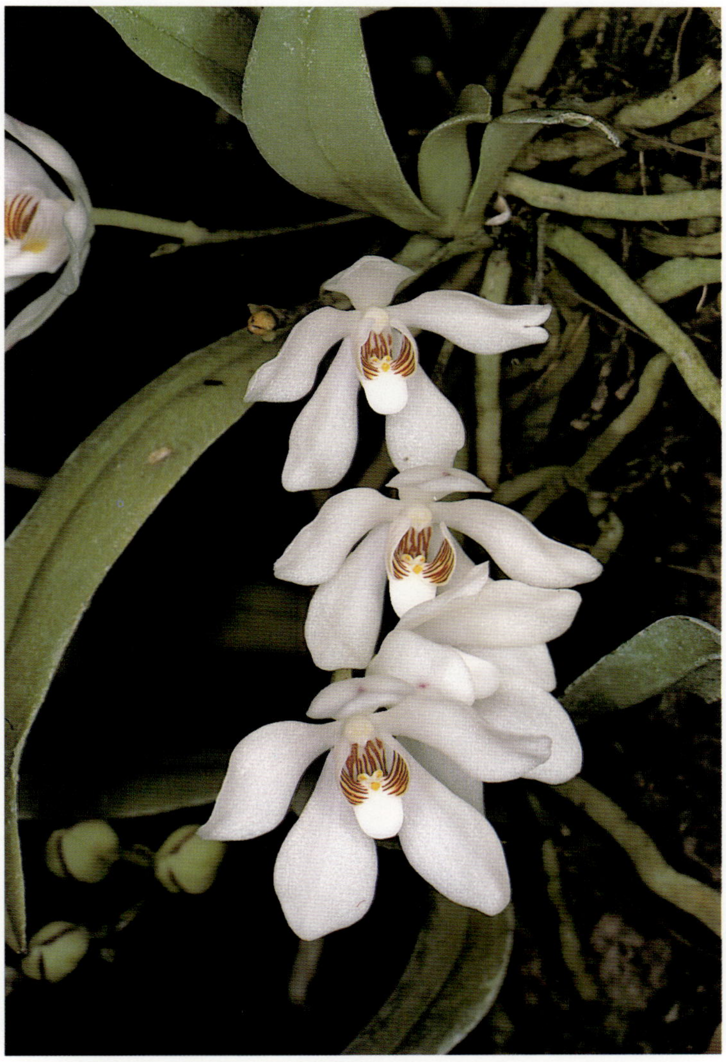

RIGHT: *Sarcochilus falcatus*

The 'Orange Blossom Orchid' of the eastern Australian coastal area, is aptly named for its appearance, if not for its pleasant scent. The beautiful flowers are up to 4cm (2 inches) in diameter, and last about a week. *Sarcochilus falcatus* is very much a plant of cool damp habitats, so that in Queensland, it is confined to high rainfall forest areas where it may grow with mosses on smaller branches. The plant itself has a short stem with several fleshy leaves, rather like a small phalaenopsis.

BELOW: *Dendrobium speciosum*

With popular names like 'Rock Lily' and 'King Orchid', in its native Australia, *Dendrobium speciosum* is one of the best known and most widespread orchids there. It seems equally at home growing as an epiphyte on rainforest trees, or as seen here, thriving on sandstone. The pseudobulbs vary in length from 8cm (3 inches) to more than a meter (3 feet), while the leathery leaves last for several years.

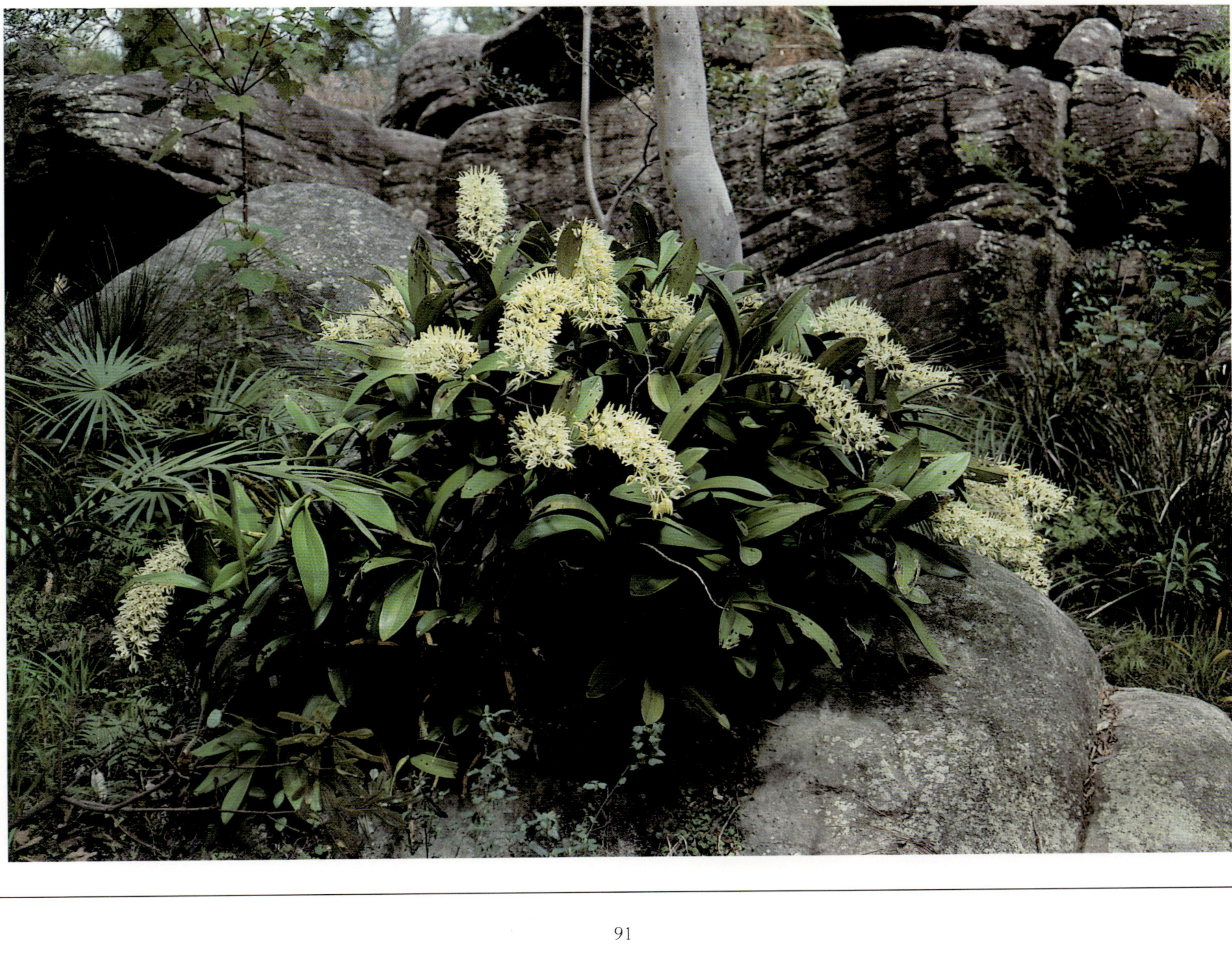

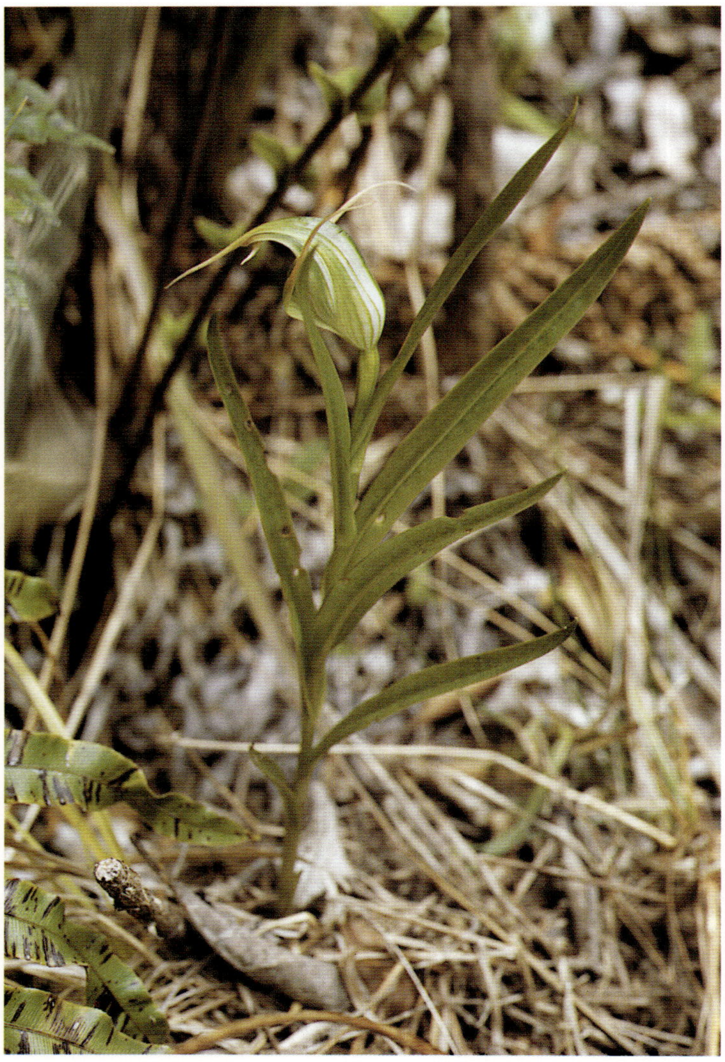

LEFT: *Pterostylis banksii*

The genus *Pterostylis* is another of those groups of terrestrial plants which are found mainly in Australia and New Zealand. *Pterostylis banksii* is the largest species in New Zealand, and this example was growing beside a path in open evergreen forest. The pollination mechanism is interesting, as the lip is irritable, so that flies which enter the flower, are pressed on to the pollen, before being released.

BELOW: *Earina mucronata*

At first sight, this is a clump of grass on a tree branch but in fact it is one of New Zealand's six species of epiphytic orchids, *Earina mucronata* which flowers in the spring and is found throughout the country. Although usually growing as an epiphyte, it is also found on rocks. The flowers are small and orange, and appear on the ends of the leafy stems.

RIGHT: *Earina autumnalis*

Another species found only in New Zealand, this one blooms around Easter, hence the name. The flowers are larger than those of *E. mucronata* and have a strong fragrance which often reveals the presence of the plants before they are seen. It generally prefers shadier and moister habitats than its relative, and under ideal conditions, the stems may be a meter (3 feet) or more long but in more exposed places, only 20cm (8 inches).

BELOW RIGHT: *Dendrobium cunninghamii*

The only *Dendrobium* in New Zealand, this is also the most southerly representative of a largely tropical genus. The flowers, which appear in the summer, are large compared to those of the other N.Z. epiphytes but still only 2cm (1 inch) across. The plants grow best in fairly light situations on tree trunks or sometimes rocks where there is plenty of moisture.

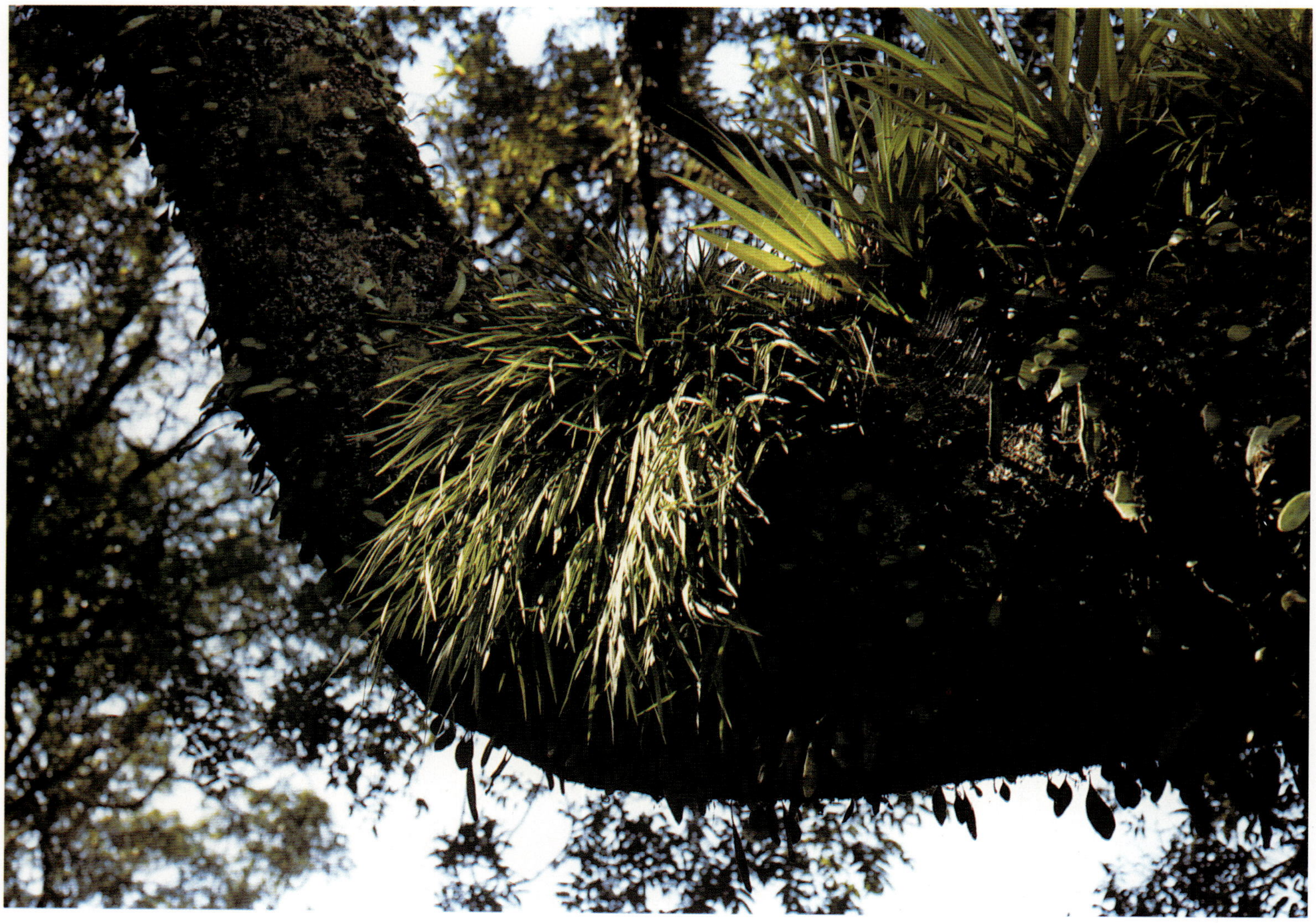

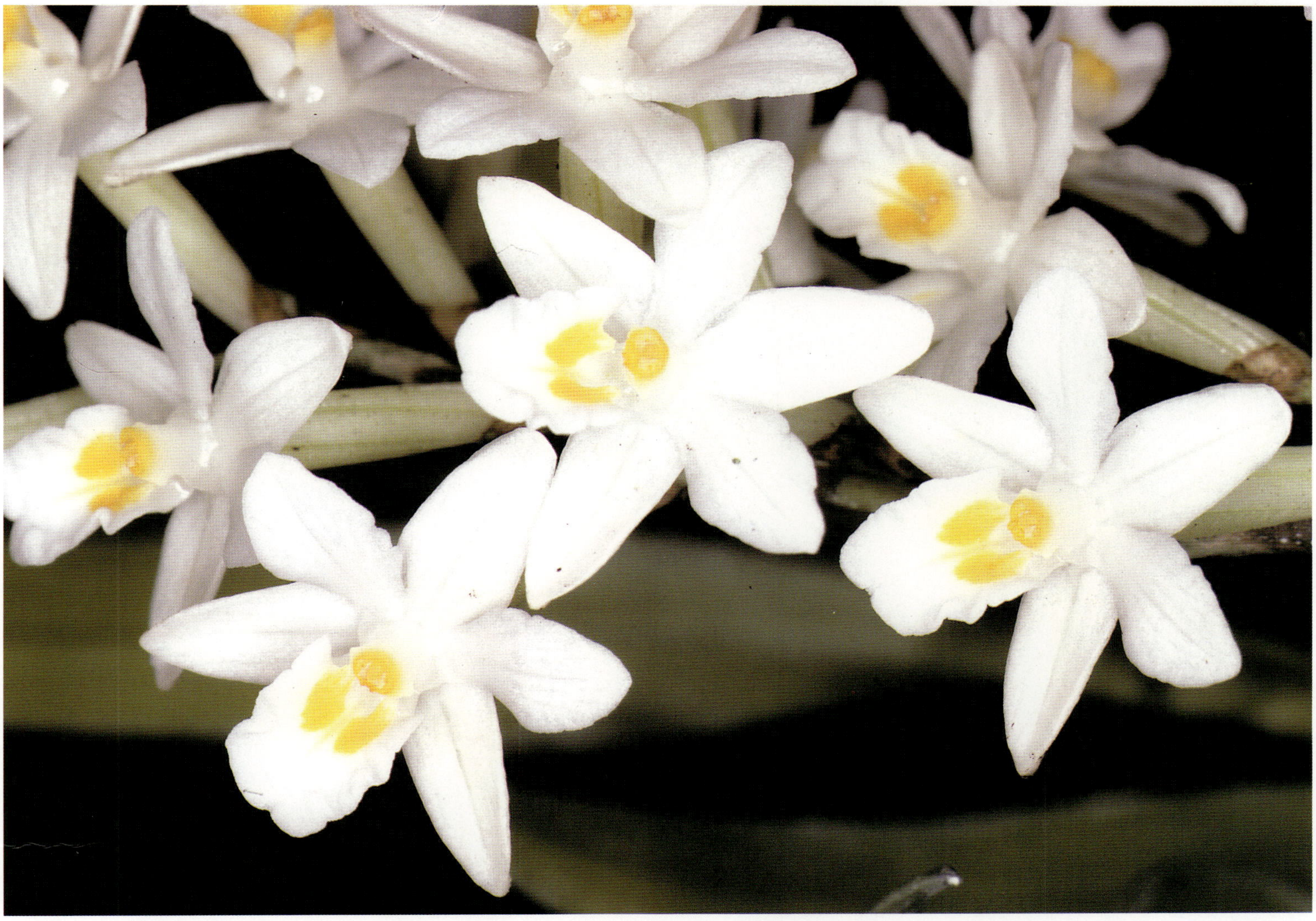

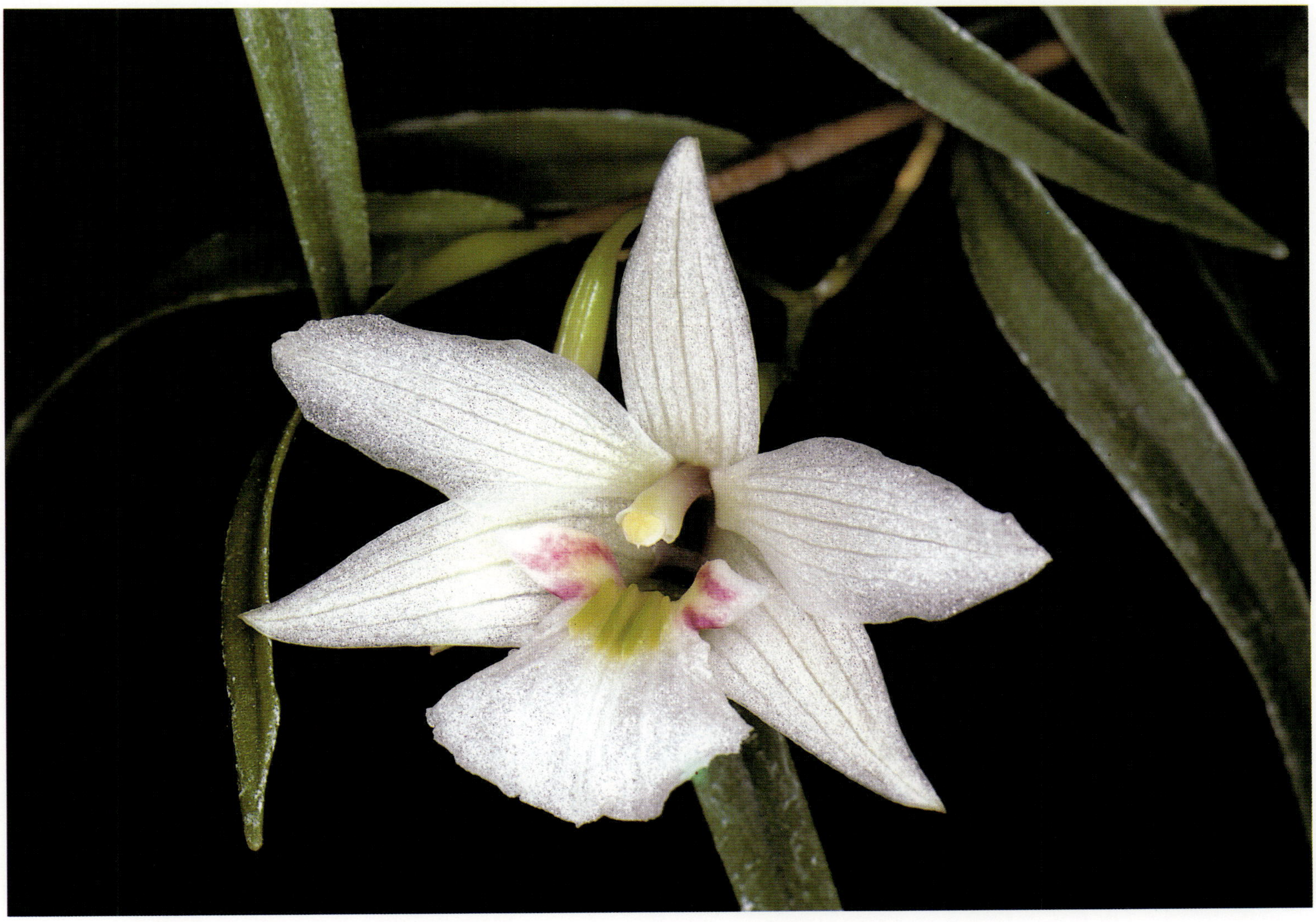

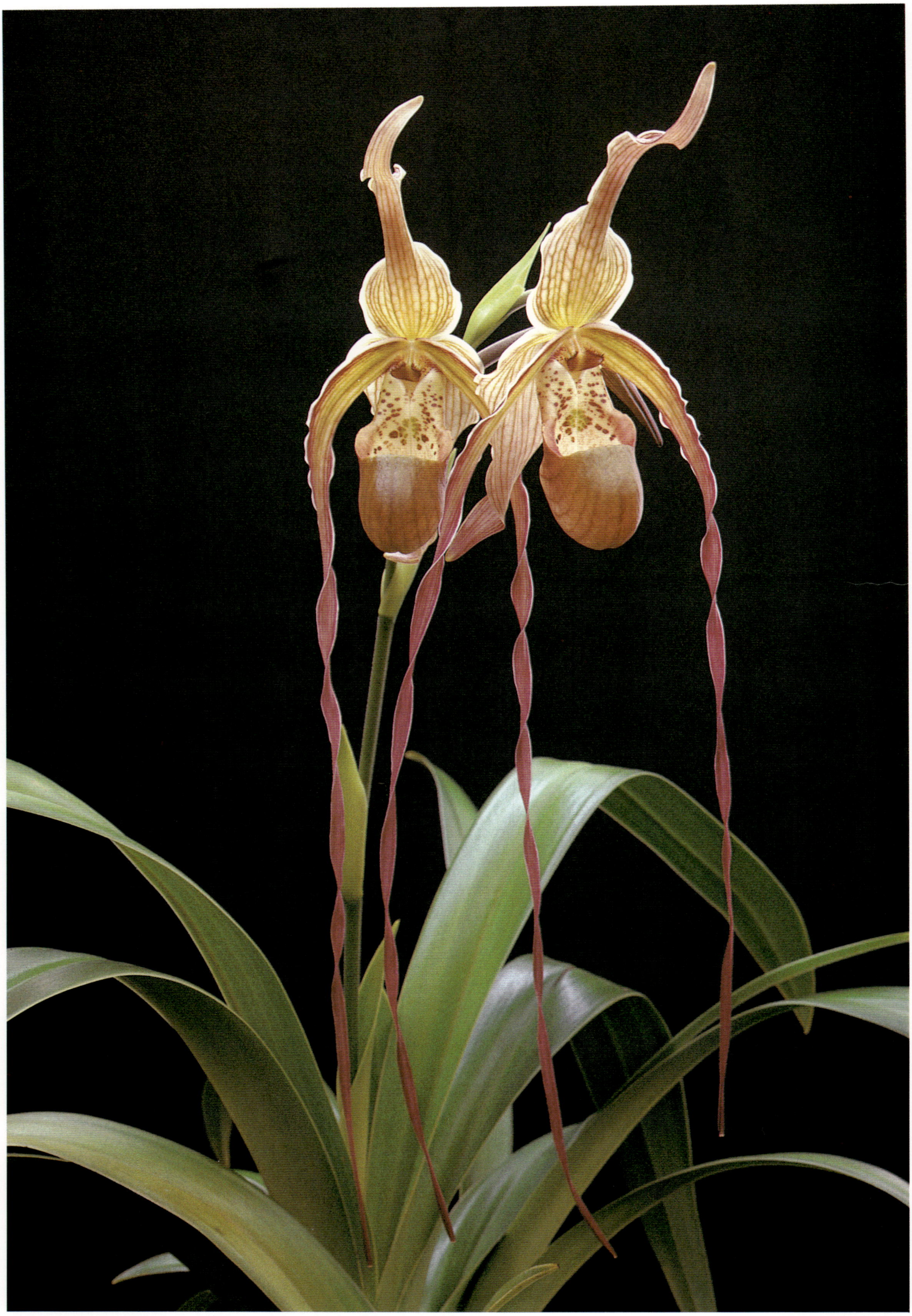

— 5 —
Hybrids

Phragmipedium Grande

One of the oldest orchid hybrids still in cultivation, having been registered in 1881, this remains a most desirable plant and is a vigorous grower. The most obvious features however, are the long petals which are over 30cm (12 inches) long. These are derived from one of the parents, *Phragmipedium caudatum*, native to the mountains of Tropical America, from Guatemala to Peru. The other parent, from similar areas, is *Phragmipedium longifolium* which has much shorter petals.

If the total of 20,000 species of wild orchids found in the world seems a lot, then the number of man-made hybrids created since the first one flowered in 1856 is truly staggering. Around 80,000 different hybrid grexes have been registered to date, and this number is increasing by over 2,000 each year. The orchid family is unusual in having an international hybrid register, maintained almost from the beginning and this provides an invaluable source of reference for growers and breeders. It was the Sander family, perhaps the greatest orchid nurserymen in Victorian Europe, and in particular, Fred K. Sander, son of the founder, who began compiling and publishing the original lists in 1895. His work was continued until 1960 by his nephew, David F. Sander but by then the numbers were increasing so rapidly that the Royal Horticultural Society agreed to take over, and remains the International Registration Authority to this day. The last five year Addendum, covering the years 1981-85 is an 800 page volume containing details of nearly 12,000 new hybrid crosses, but with the recent computerization of the records, future volumes will no doubt be more flexible in their presentation.

Creating hybrids is deceptively simple. Pollen from one flower is transferred to the stigma of the same flower or to another. If they are compatible

Dactylorhiza

Not all exotic hybrids come from tropical species. This *Dactylorhiza* or marsh orchid is a natural hybrid occurring in the west of Scotland. It has been cultivated as a garden perennial for many years, and thrives in a cool damp climate. The 60cm (24 inches) flowering stems provide an impressive summer display for several weeks before dying down to spend winter underground.

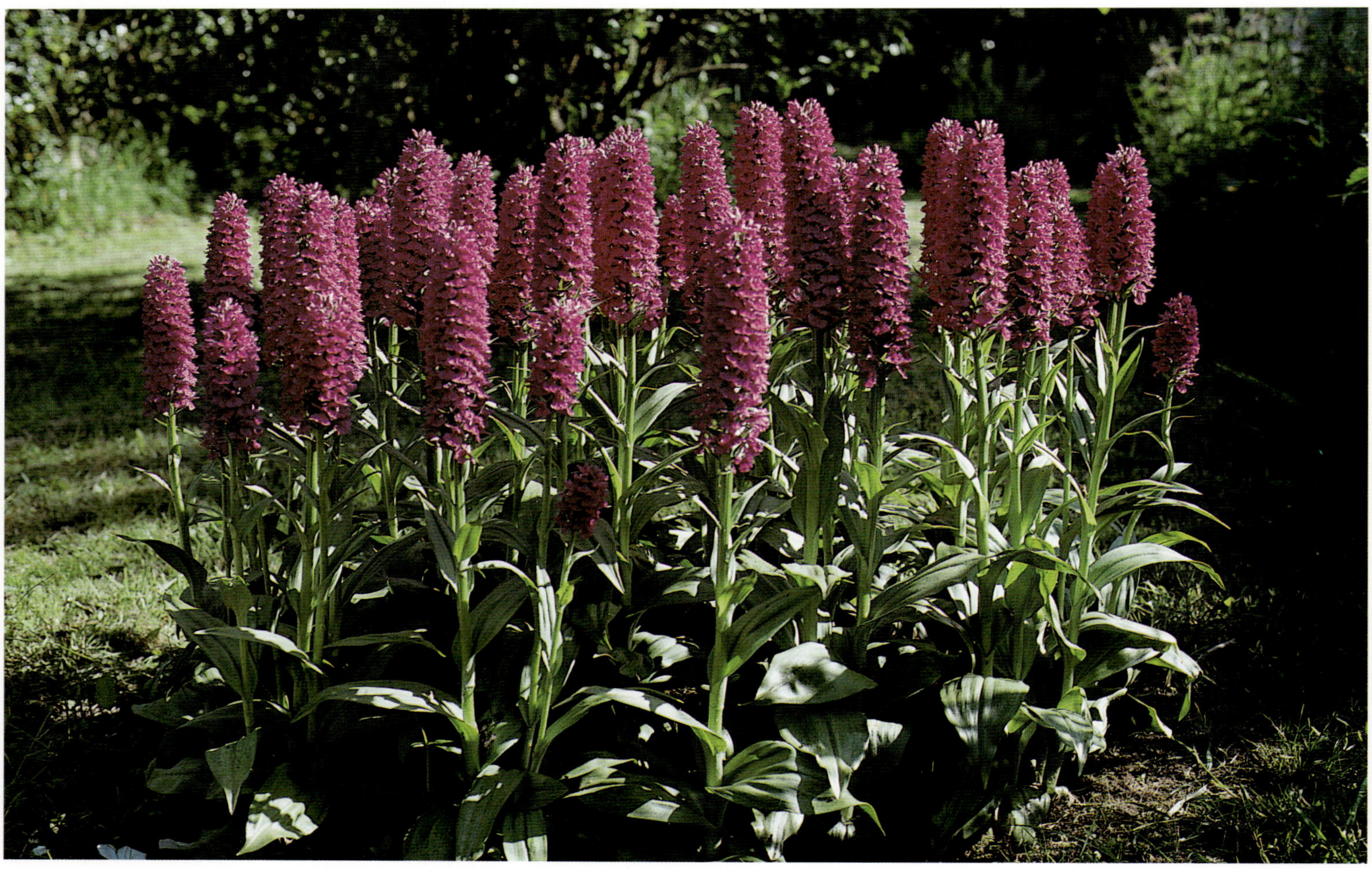

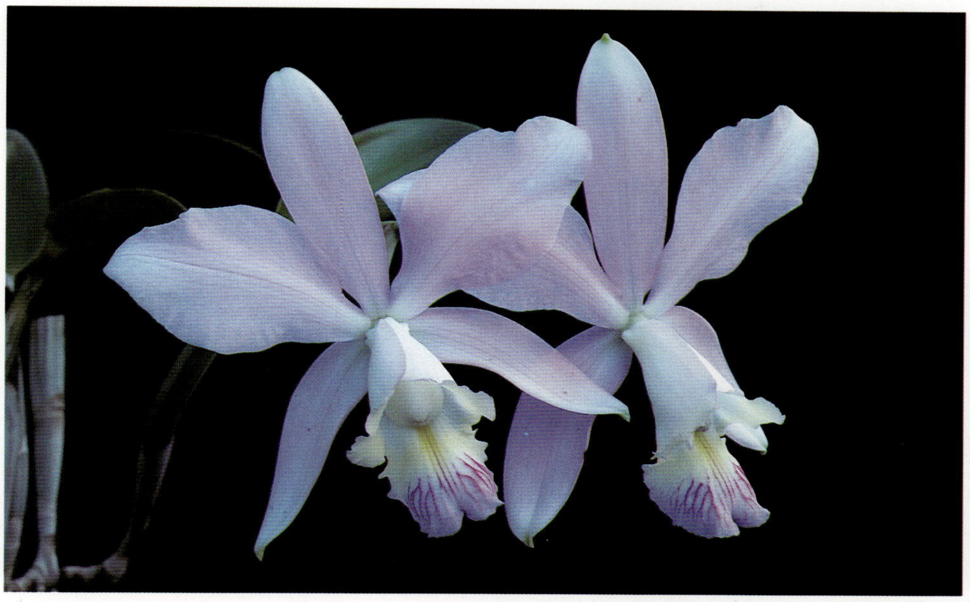

Cattleya Heathii

Another simple cross between two fine Brazilian species, *Cattleya loddigesii* and *Cattleya walkeriana*, it first flowered in 1907 but has been remade subsequently. The 12cm (5 inch) flowers are perfumed and last in perfection for at least a fortnight. More complex hybrid cattleyas are still important flowers for corsages in the United States.

in due course the ovary swells to form a capsule, and when it ripens, seed is released. There are pitfalls however. Many species are self-incompatible so that pollination needs to take place between different plants; timing of the operation can be critical, and many hybrids are themselves genetically sterile. Considering the number of orchid species, natural hybrids are quite uncommon as most species have specific pollinators. The first artificial hybrids were only carried out between closely related species but it was soon discovered that hybrid seed could readily be produced by crossing even distantly related species. It was also found that plants classified as being in different genera were compatible so that even greater variation was possible. With names like *Brassolaeliocattleya* arising from the resulting progeny of a cross between *Brassavola*, *Laelia* and *Cattleya*, the need for simplification led to the creation of hybrid generic names for the more complex combinations, so that *Potinara* is used instead of *Brassosophrolaeliocattleya*.

Hybrids between two species are known as primary hybrids and their characters are generally a mixture of those shown by the two parents. However when one or both parents are hybrids, the progeny become secondary hybrids and in the orchid family, such plants show great variation. Careful selection is necessary to provide the parents for future breeding. As was explained in the opening chapter, growing orchids from seed was a hit-and-miss affair until the 1920s, so that many early hybrids existed as only one or two plants. As sterile techniques improved, it became possible to grow thousands of seedlings from one capsule, and therefore to see the range of possible variation. Many of the oldest hybrids were vigorous however, and divisions of them may still be seen in collections today.

Cattleya Porcia

A magnificent spectacle with its head of a dozen or more 8cm (3 inch) flowers on top of 60cm (24 inch) pseudobulbs. Although a cross between a species and a complex hybrid, it is *Cattleya bowringiana* from Belize which is the dominant influence. First registered in 1927 by the great H.G. Alexander, the sheer size of the plant would rule it out for many people but such old hybrids never lose their decorative value.

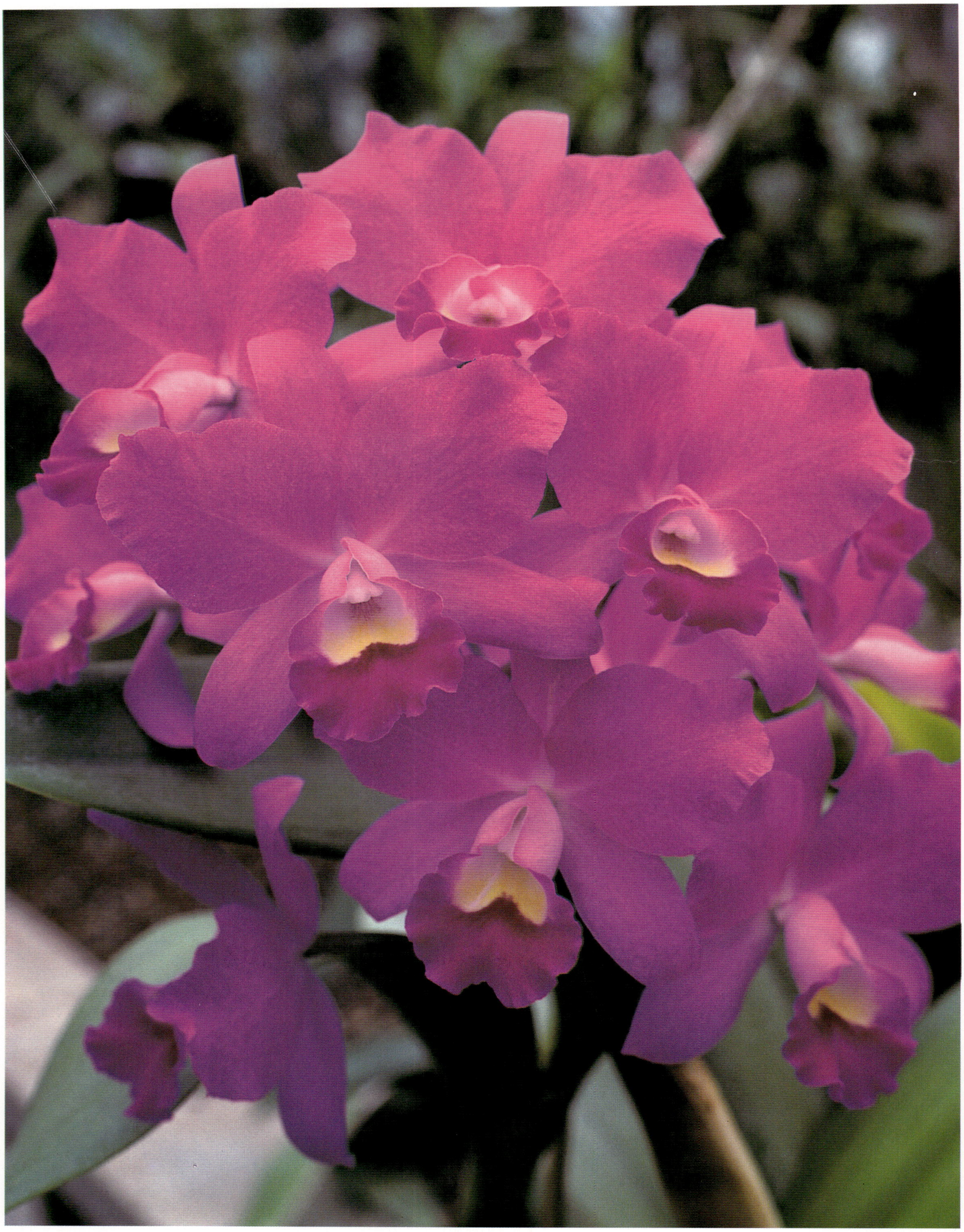

Hybrid plants are all around us, providing both color in our gardens and food on our tables. Orchid breeders work with similar decorative and functional results in mind. From the beginning there have always been those seeking novelty of form and color, and while some of the resulting hybrids are pleasing to the eye, others have been quickly forgotten. Orchid species tend to show a strong seasonal response to growth and flowering and for the important cut-flower and pot-plant industries, continuity of production is vital. In the past forty years in particular, the range of size and color in orchid hybrids has been greatly extended as has the flowering season. This is further enhanced by exports to the northern hemisphere from South Africa, Australia and New Zealand. With its rather unvarying climate near the equator, Singapore produces flowers throughout the year from locally bred hybrids which provide a good color range and long lasting qualities.

The characters which make a good pot-plant or cut-flower are very different from those required by breeders seeking coveted awards from such organizations as the Royal Horticultural Society or the American Orchid Society. In this case, flower shape and size are all important, almost regardless of whether the plant grows well or not. Many hundreds or even thousands of seedlings have to be grown to maturity in order to select the handful showing award potential. In many ways, fashions have come full circle, for as breeders have achieved the ideal form with its overlapping segments, so have different genera tended to look the same. The trend now is towards introducing new color combinations through a return to using species. This has the added advantage of making more vigorous plants, while the shapes are more varied and even reminiscent of older hybrids.

Laeliocattleya Recital

The genera *Laelia* and *Cattleya* are closely related and readily interbreed to give a wider range of color and shape than is possible with either one alone. This is a fine example of modern breeding with the 15cm (6 inch) flowers being well proportioned and deliciously scented. Laeliocattleyas come in many color combinations from pure white, through pinks and magentas, to striking yellows and golds.

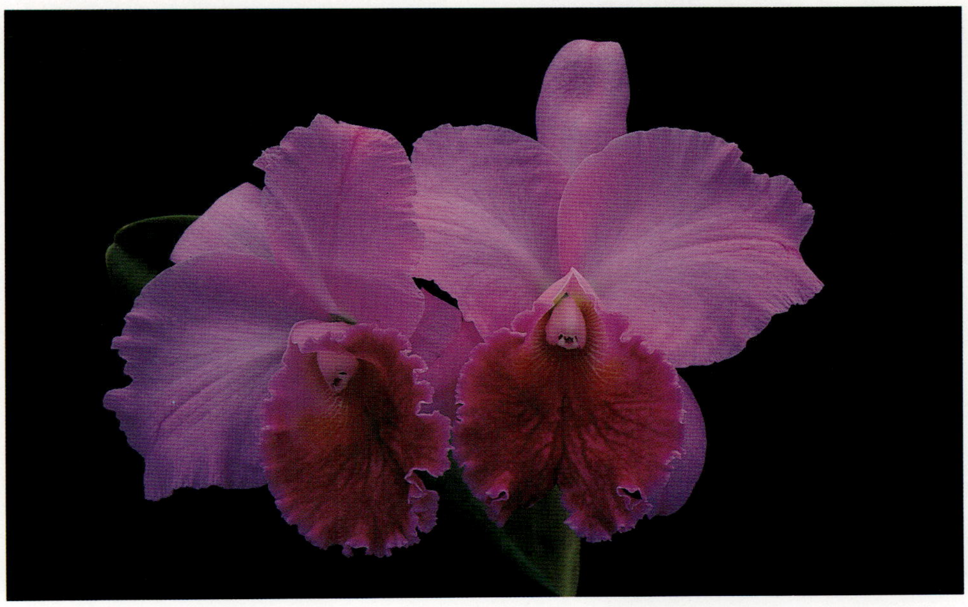

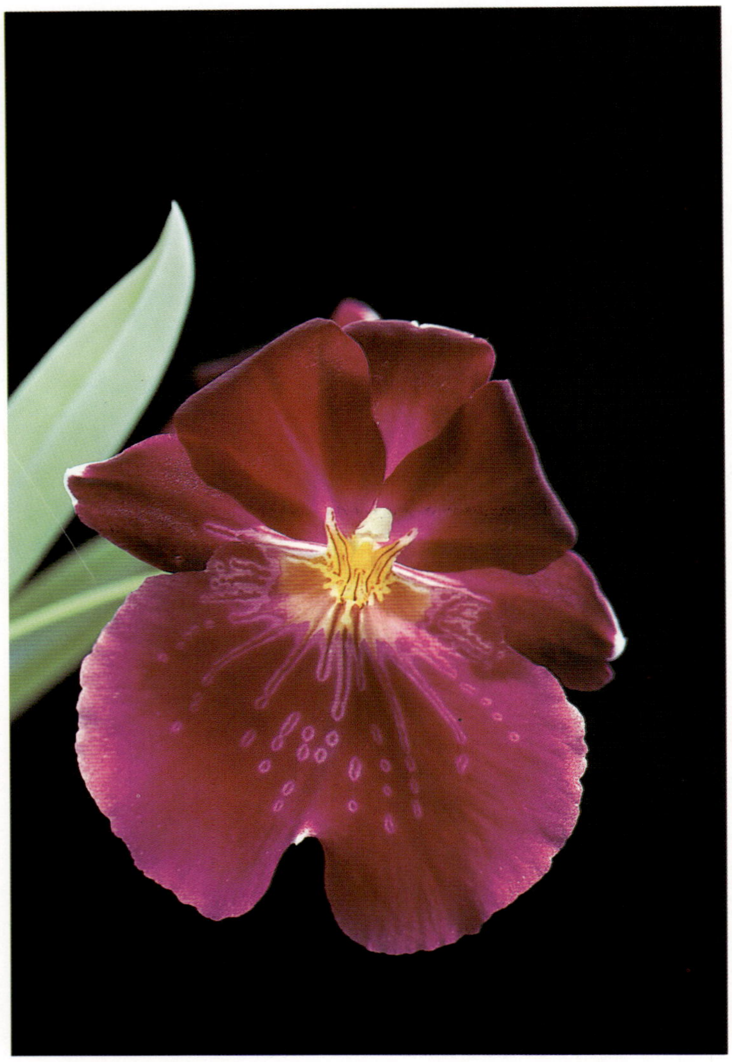

LEFT: *Miltonia* Celle 'Feuerwerk'

This aptly named plant received an award at the Third World Orchid Conference held in London in 1960. Unlike many other orchid hybrids, miltonias have hardly changed in shape over the years so that such flowers are as acceptable today as they were when introduced. Miltonias are grown to perfection in relatively cool climates where they are not exposed to extremes of temperature.

RIGHT: *Miltonia* Robert Strauss 'Snowfall'

The so-called 'pansy orchids' have been appreciated in cultivation for more than a century and although the flowers soon wither when cut, they last easily a month on the plant and are subtly scented as well. Modern hybrids such as this are derived mainly from only two species, both native to the Andes of Colombia. Many generations of crossing and selection have led to a wide range of colors and patterns.

BELOW LEFT: *Odontonia* Boussole 'Blanche'

The combination of *Odontoglossum* and *Miltonia* is far less popular now than it was in 1942 when it was registered. However it remains in cultivation, appreciated for its tall inflorescences of dazzling white flowers derived from the *Odontoglossum* parent and the broad lip contributed by the *Miltonia*.

BELOW: *Odontioda* Durham Miner

Odontoglossums were first crossed with the Peruvian species *Cochlioda noezliana* to utilize its brilliant orange-red colour. The resulting odontiodas now come in a wide range of colors, but the red ones are particularly striking and sought after. These Andean hybrid odontiodas thrive in cool humid conditions where there is good air circulation.

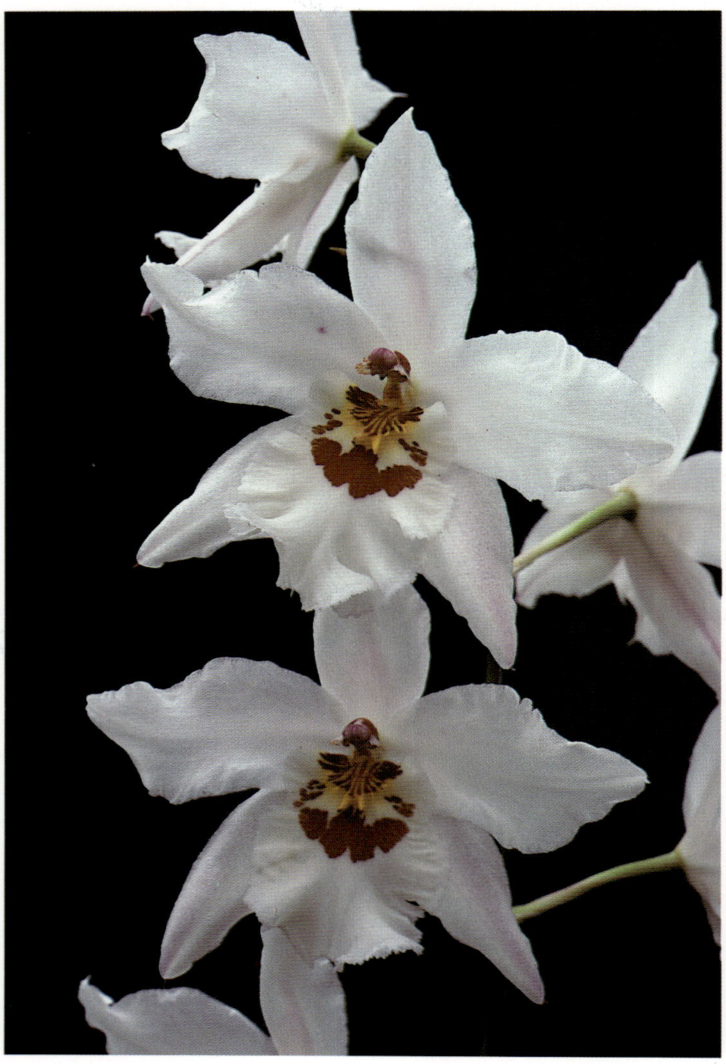

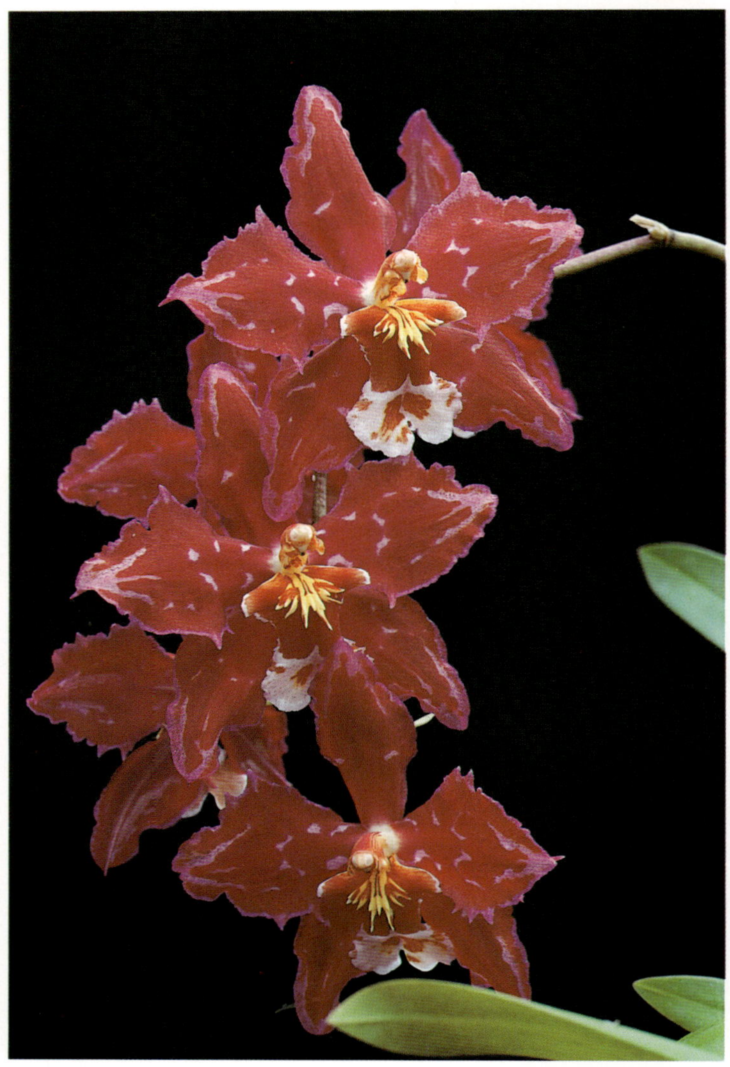

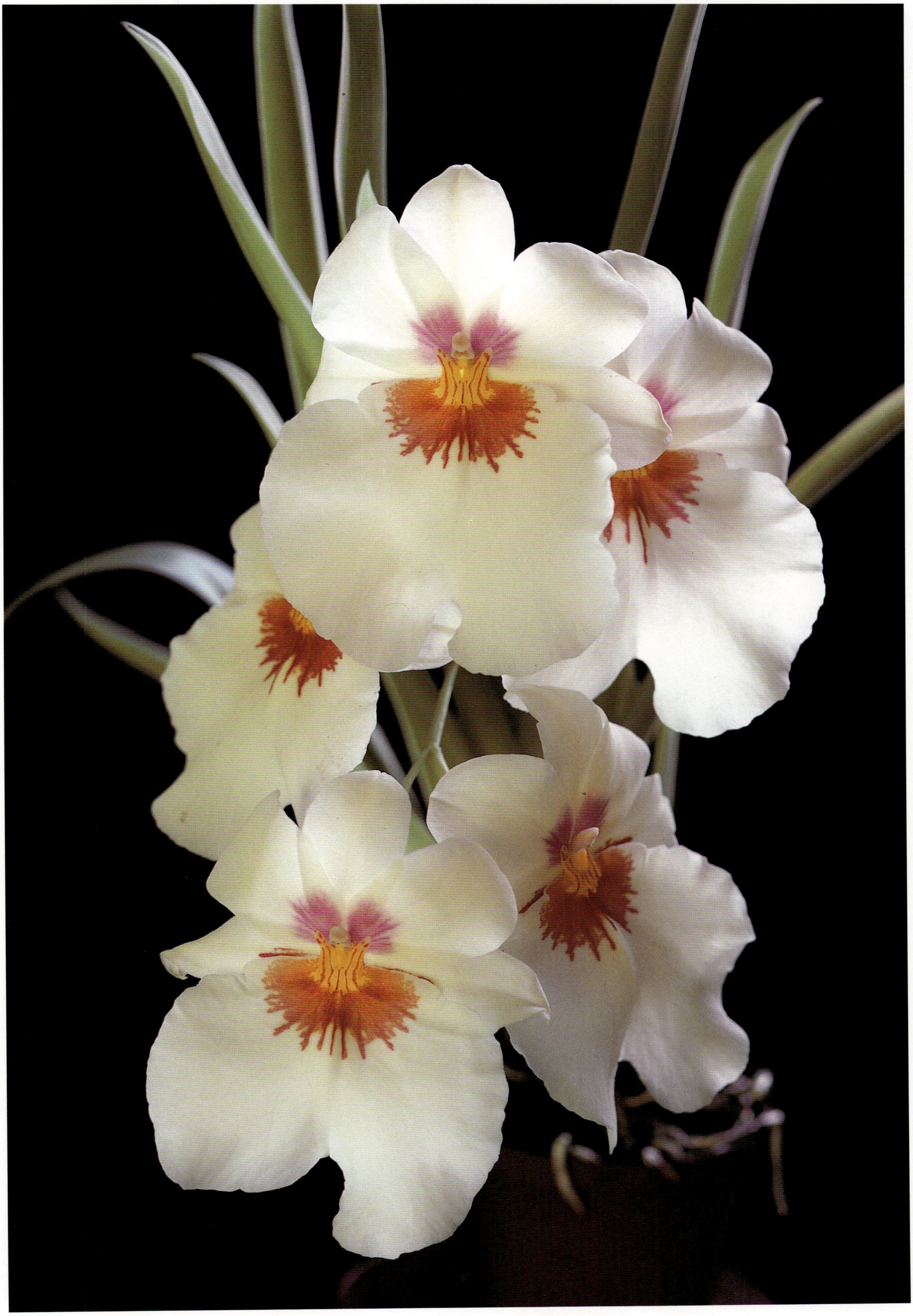

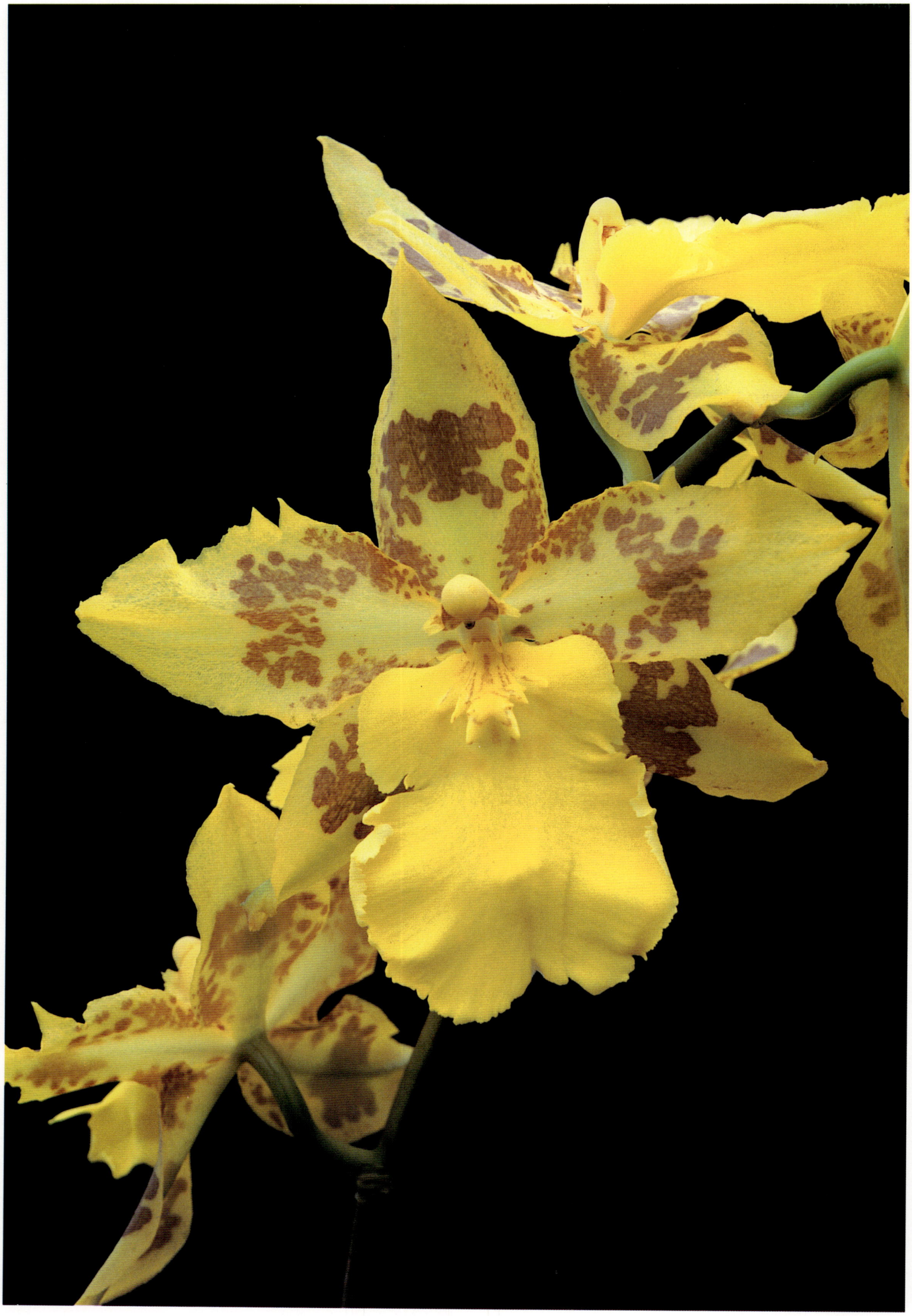

LEFT; *Odontocidium* Purbeck Gold

In same *Oncidium tigrinum* crossed with a complex yellow odontoglossum hybrid, has given a completely different result, increasing the lip size and intensifying the original yellow. Such unexpected qualities have made *Oncidium* species popular with hybridizers anxious to broaden the range of plants.

RIGHT: *Odontioda* Fremar × Luradea

A different type of *Odontioda*, in which the markings are more pronounced and the petals and sepals broader and therefore more overlapping. The flowers are usually well-displayed on arching stems and are long-lasting under cool conditions. Another advantage of these plants is their compact shape and small size compared to many *Cymbidium* hybrids.

BELOW: *Wilsonara* Nicola Jane

In an attempt to increase the heat tolerance of odontiodas, breeders have crossed them with *Oncidium* species from Central and South America, in this case *Oncidium tigrinum* from Mexico. This has tall inflorescences of yellow and brown flowers. While these colors have been lost in the resulting *Wilsonara*, the result is pleasing and the plants grow strongly.

BELOW RIGHT: *Disa* Kirstenbosch Pride

The beautiful disas of South Africa were cultivated and hybridized in Europe around the turn of the century, but only three species were involved. In the last ten years they have been taken up again in their native country and many fine hybrids have appeared, using different forms of well-known species, or in this example, a new one, *Disa cardinalis*. The National Botanic Gardens, Kirstenbosch registered the cross between *Disa uniflora* and *Disa cardinalis* in 1981.

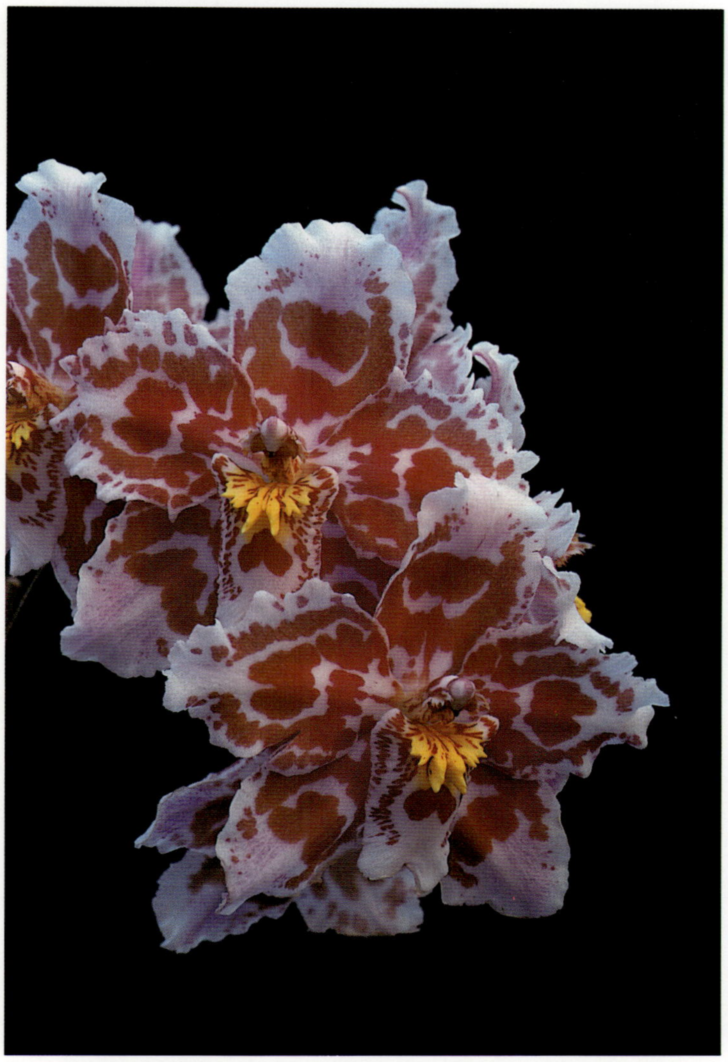

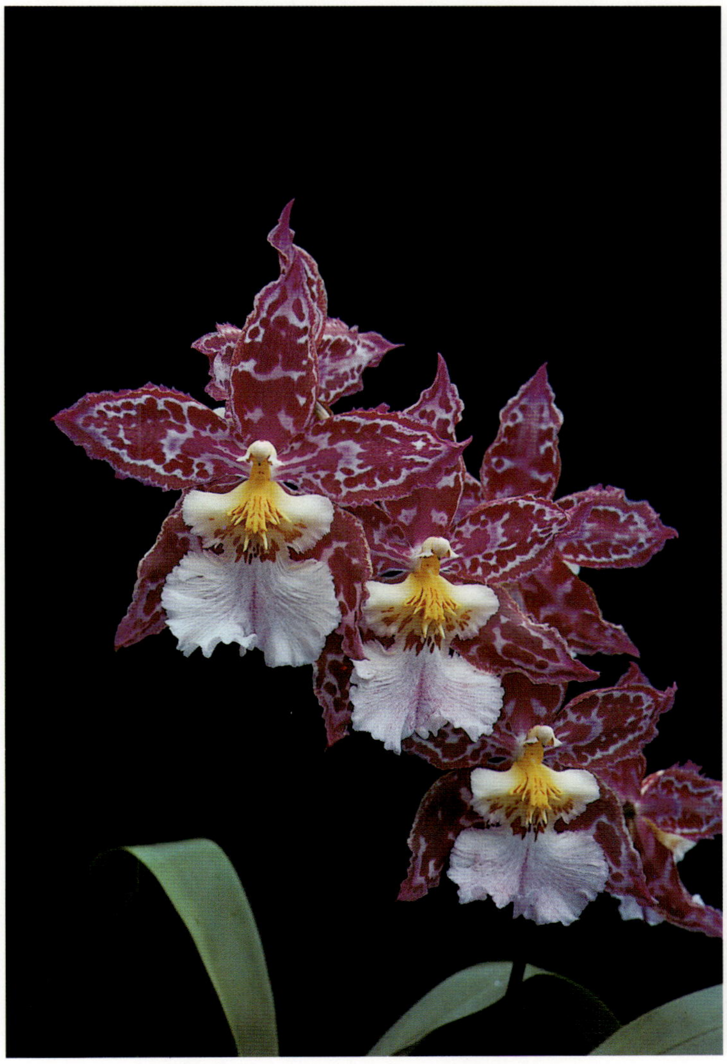

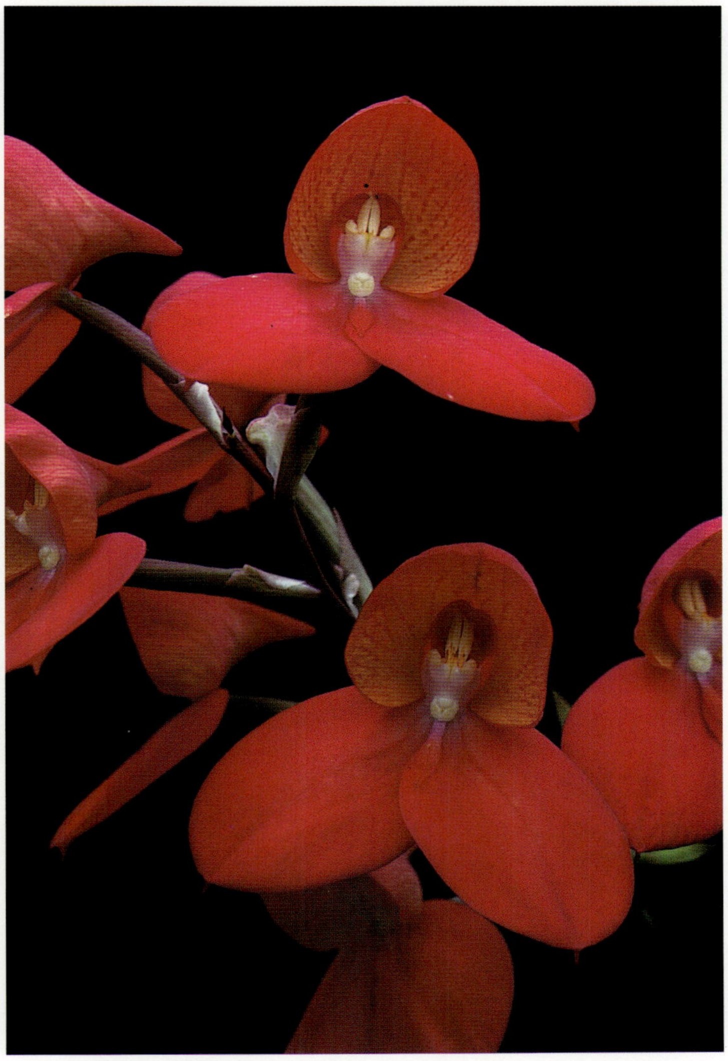

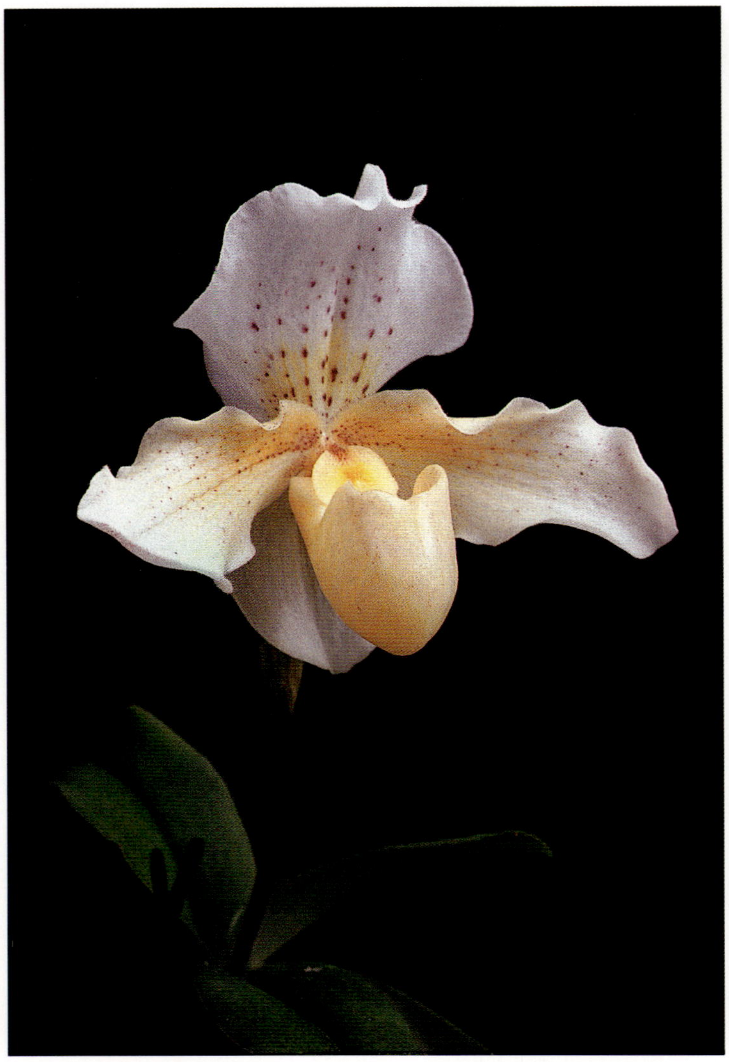

Paphiopedilum Rosy Dawn

The first Asian slipper orchid hybrid, *Paphiopedilum* Harrisianum, flowered in 1869. By the time Rosy Dawn flowered in 1935, there were many generations of hybrids behind it. Six different species were involved which explains why hybrid paphiopedilum seedlings are so variable. There is now a strong interest in primary crosses using more unusual species as parents.

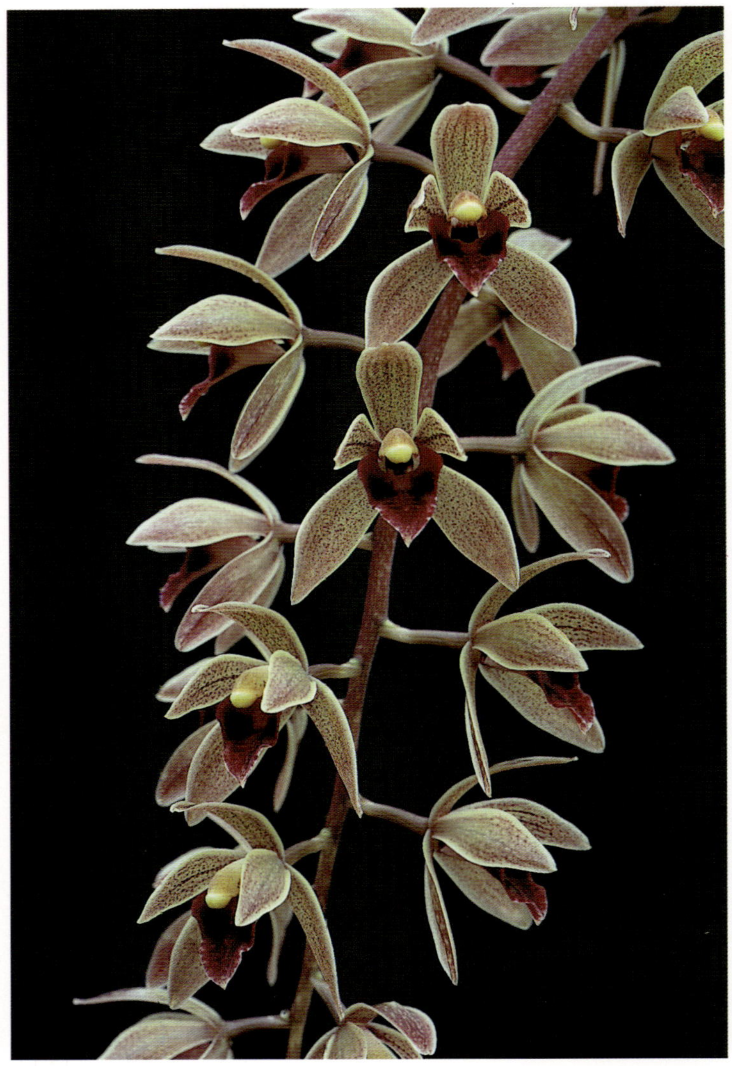

Cymbidium Sweet Devon

Unlike the case of paphiopedilums, modern *Cymbidium* breeding is dominated by the complex hybrids bred for the cut-flower and pot-plant trades as well as for exhibition. This example of a primary cross between *Cymbidium suave* of Australia, and *Cymbidium devonianum* of India and Thailand fits into none of these categories, but has great charm with its long pendent sprays of small flowers.

Cymbidium Moyglare

Cymbidium tigrinum from India and Burma is something of a dwarf in a land of giants, and its hybrids are dominated both by it small stature and the shape of its lip. Here crossed with a complex hybrid involving five other species, the result is a small plant bearing moderately sized flowers of a compelling freshness. Future breeding might well increase their size and number without losing their appeal.

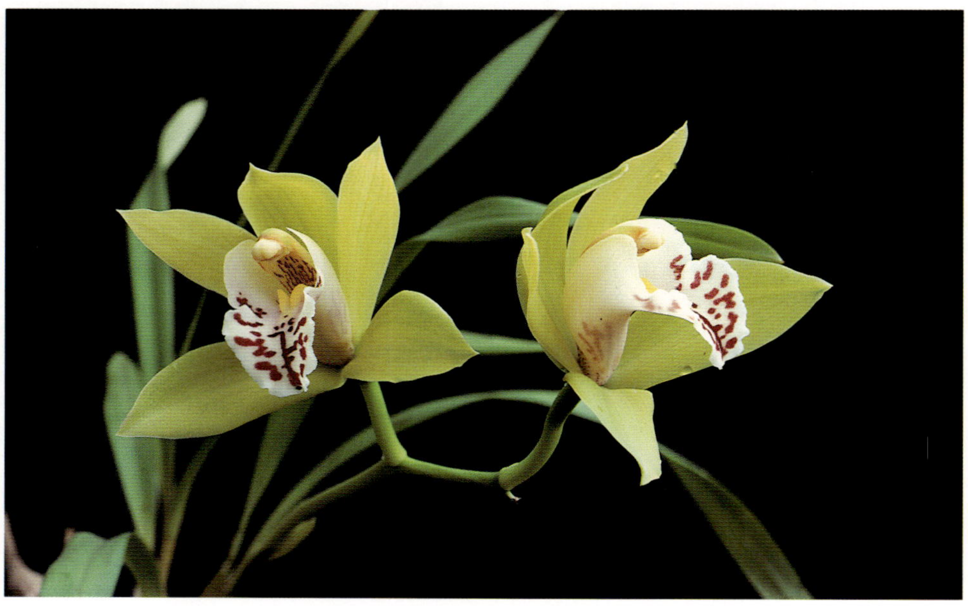

Cymbidium Tarzan

Although cymbidium breeding has come a long way since this hybrid was registered in 1952, it still grows well and provides a fine display during the winter months. So-called standard cymbidiums tend to be big plants with flowers between 10 and 15cm (4-6 inches) across. With their wide color range and long lasting qualities, they are successfully grown in the southern hemisphere for export out of season to the north and in Europe for the winter cut-flower market.

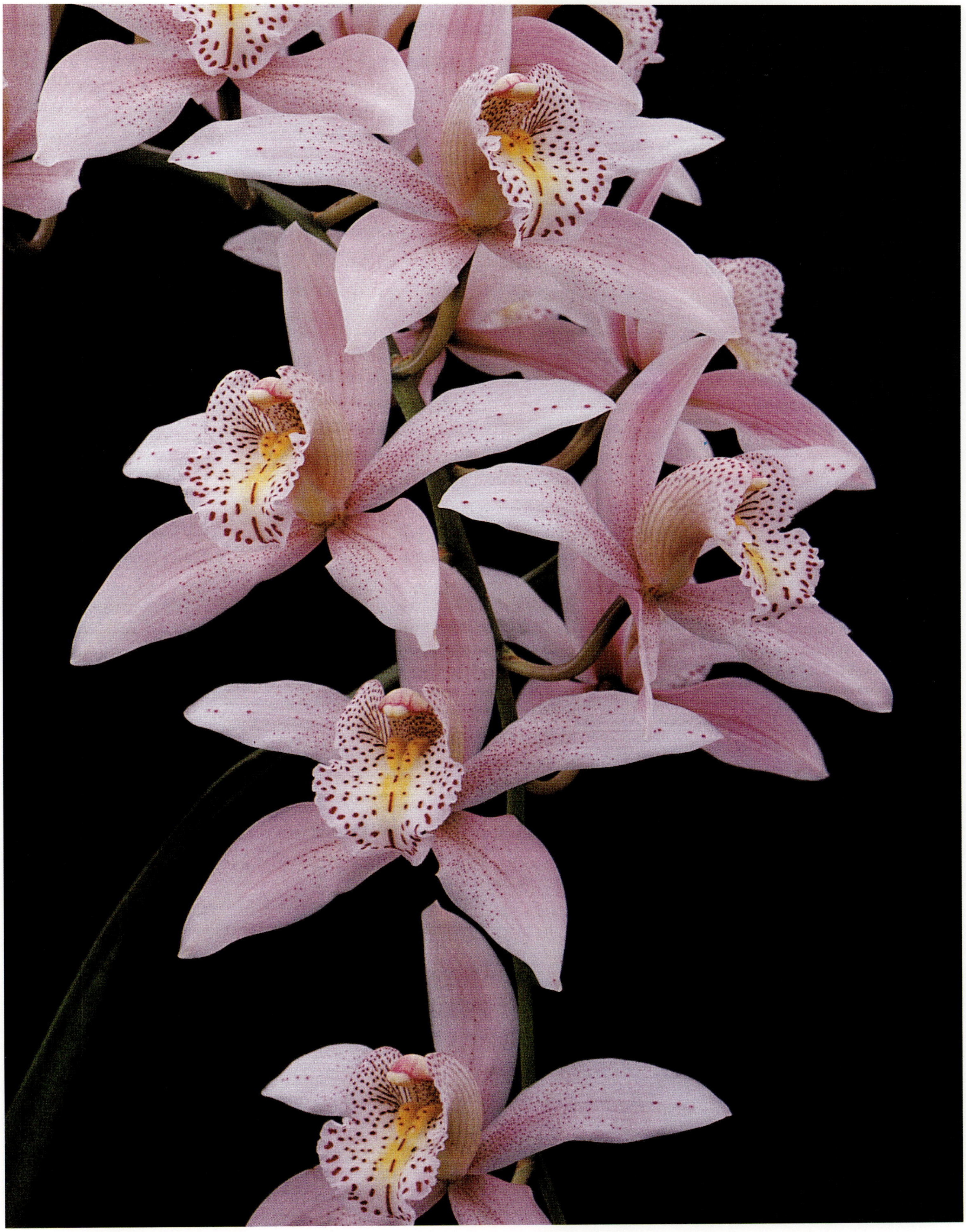

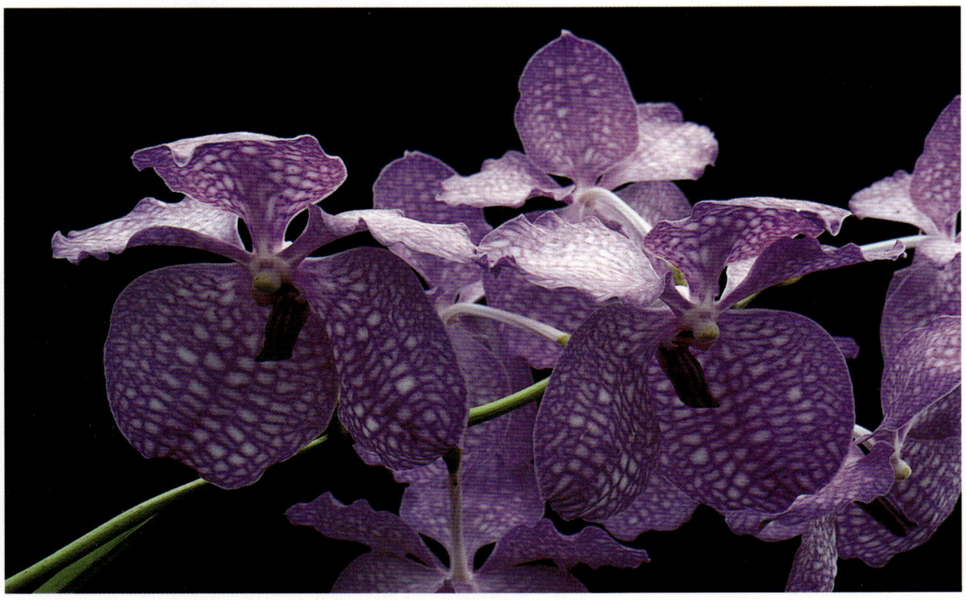

Vanda Rothschildiana

Tropical orchids with blue flowers are very uncommon so that one such as this which not only has large flowers but also grows well in places as far apart as Northern Europe, Thailand and Hawaii, must be very special. The blue *Vanda coerulea* from the Himalayas and Thailand was crossed with the magnificent *Vanda* or *Euanthe sanderiana* from the Philippines and registered in 1931. The hybrid has been remade many times using superior forms of the parent species, and as a result is freely available.

Phalaenopsis Barbara Moler × *amabilis*

The gracefully arching flowering stems of Phalaenopsis with their rows of large flat blooms are known wherever sufficient warmth and humidity are available for their growth. While the first hybrids to be grown on a large scale were the pure whites, later developments included pinks, yellows, stripes and contrasting combinations such as this one. Hybridizers have plenty of species to work on and new crosses are a feature at orchid shows throughout the world.

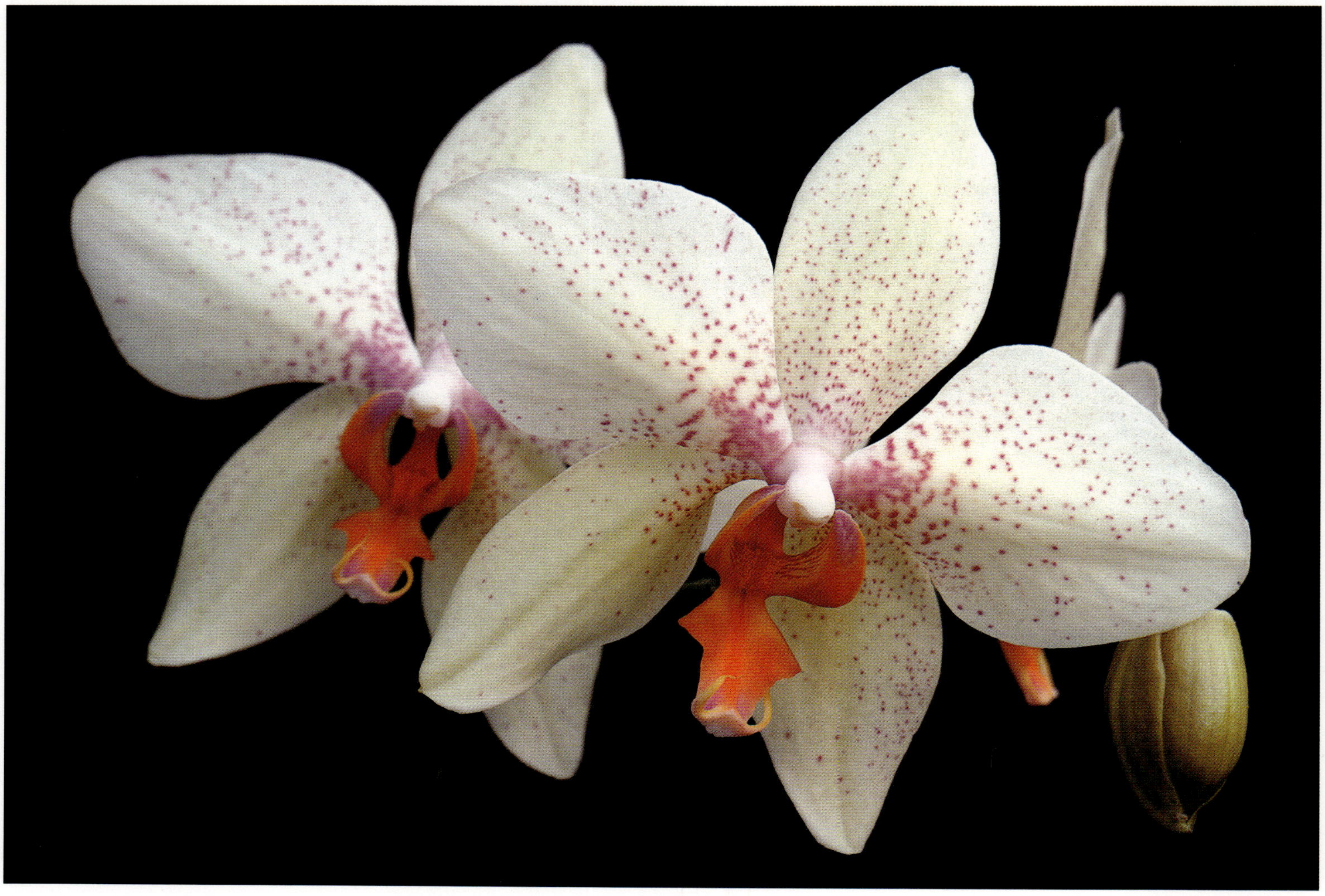

Cirrhopetalum Elizabeth Ann 'Bucklebury'

Hybrids of this kind do not usually attract much attention in the orchid world, but here is one which not only received an award from the Royal Horticultural Society, but has also been propagated and widely distributed. A cross between two similar tropical Asian species, the flowers are 18cm (7 inches) long and a well-grown plant will produce many such heads.

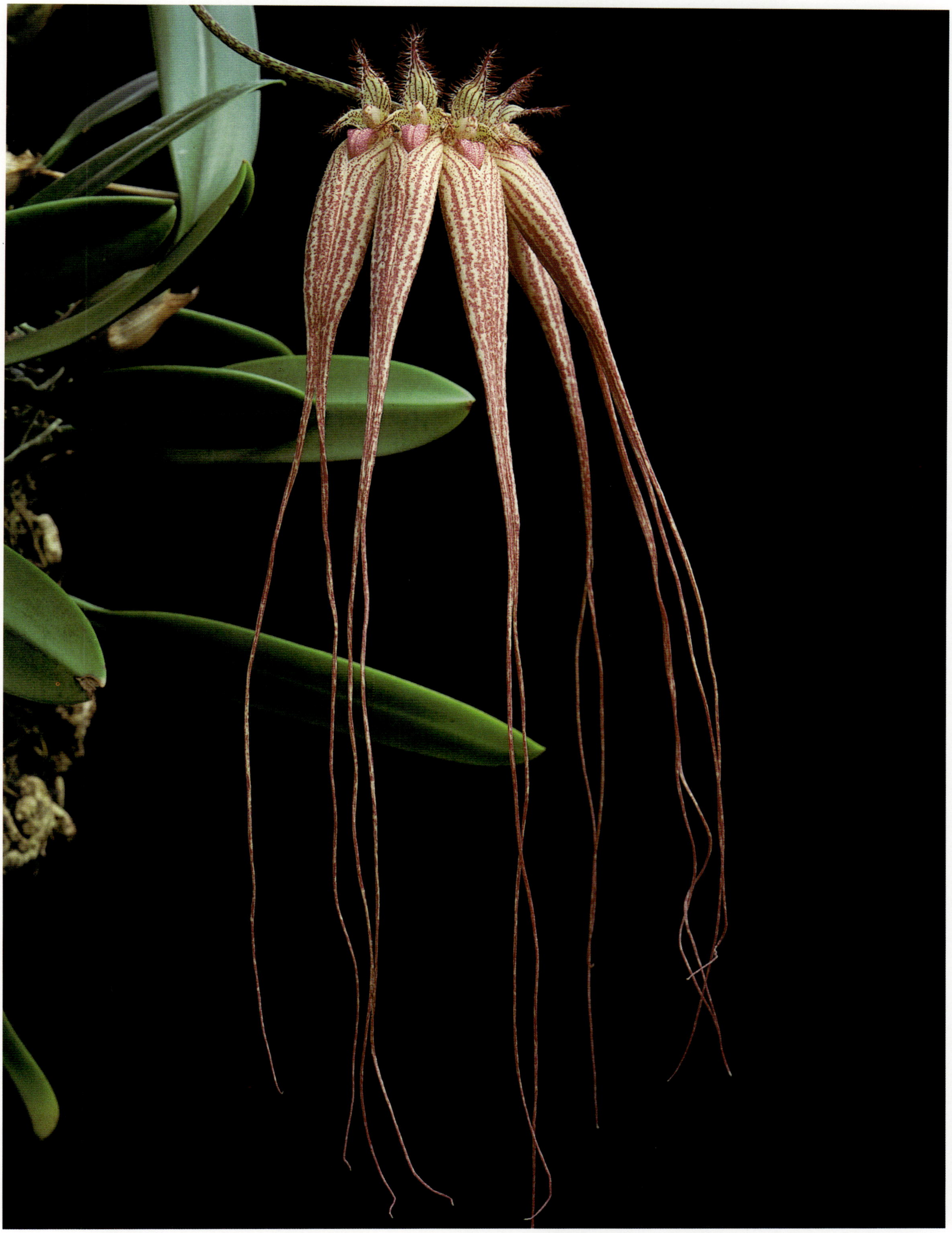

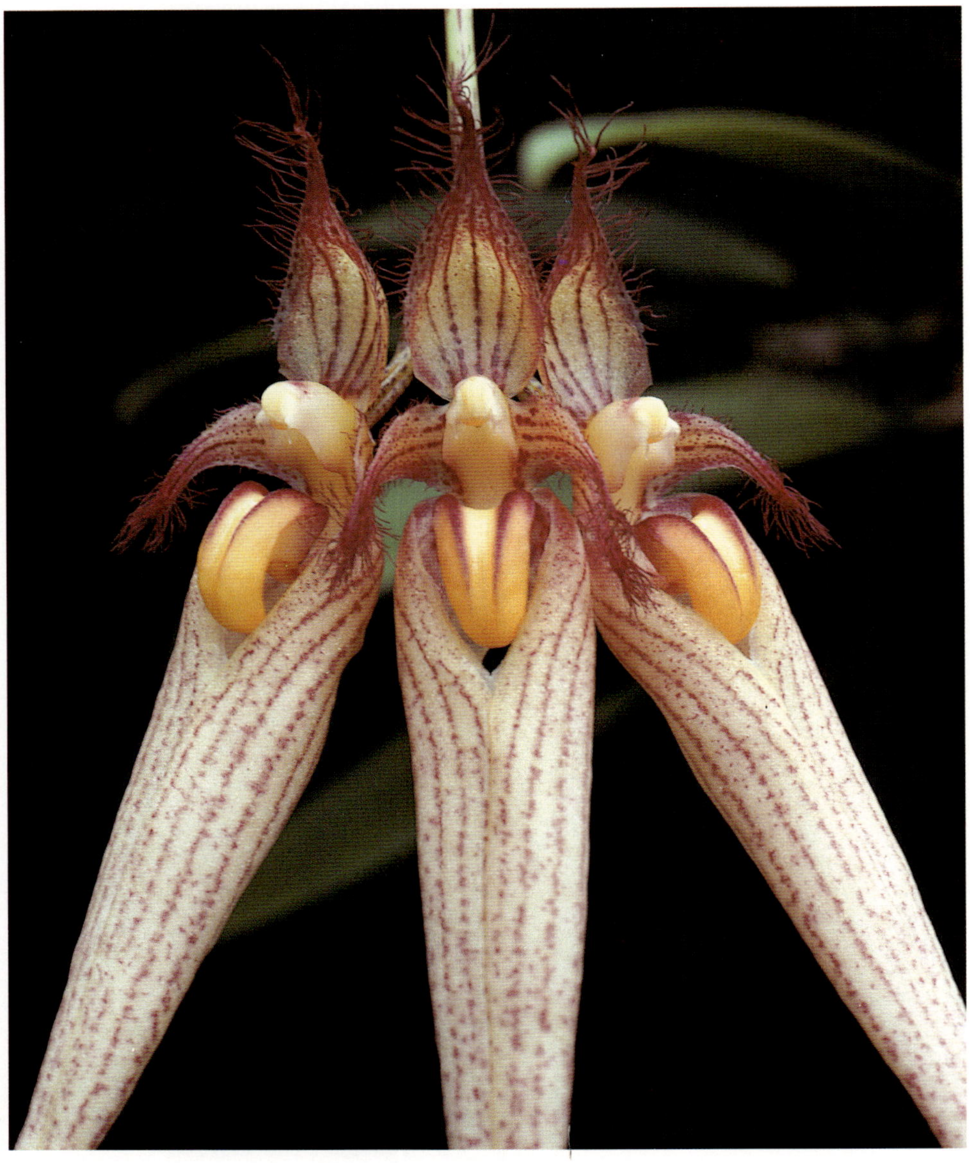

Cirrhopetalum Louis Sander

A forerunner of Elizabeth Ann, with one parent in common, the name honors one of the brothers of Fred Sander, already mentioned in connection with the hybrid register. It dates from 1936 and is still well-known in cultivation. The two lateral sepals are the prominent parts of the flower, while the petals and dorsal sepal are quite small. The yellow lip in the center is very finely hinged so that it moves freely, probably to attract pollinating flies.

Dendrobium Barbara Gittens

As one of the largest genera, containing numerous beautiful species, *Dendrobium* has attracted breeders from the earliest days of hybridizing. While the colorful tropical hybrids provide cut-flowers in Asia and Hawaii, plants such as this are likely to be found only in botanic gardens, where they enrich mixed displays. A cross between two species from Thailand and the Himalayas, *Dendrobium moschatum* and *Dendrobium chryseum*, Barbara Gittens was registered in 1953.

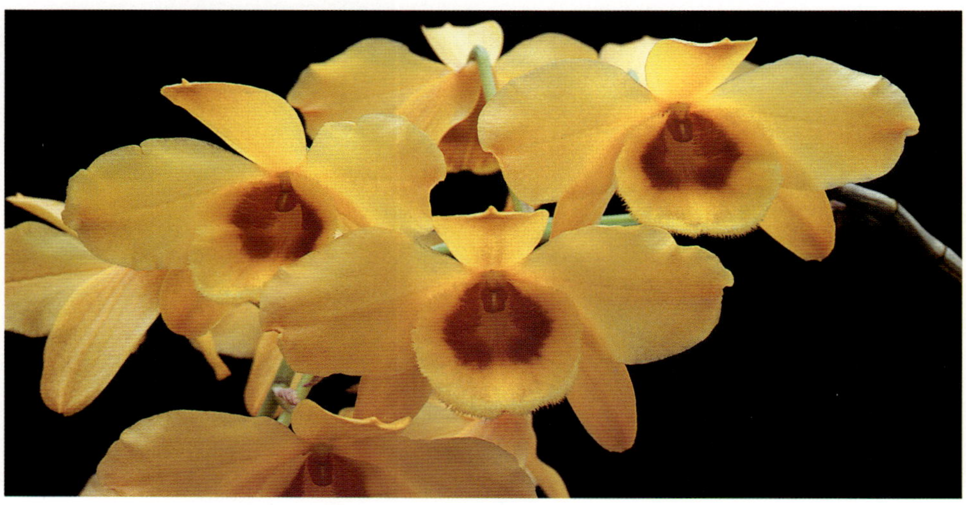

Dendrobium Malones 'Silvia'

Dendrobium nobile, from the foothills of the Himalayas, is a fine spring-flowering species which gives its name to a race of hybrids involving related species, known as nobile-type or soft-cane dendrobiums. These had been widely grown in the past but they really attracted attention through the efforts of Jiro Yamamoto in Japan, who raised a rainbow of new colors. His hybrid, Malones, was registered in 1973 and shows the typical brilliant colors and firm substance of the flowers.

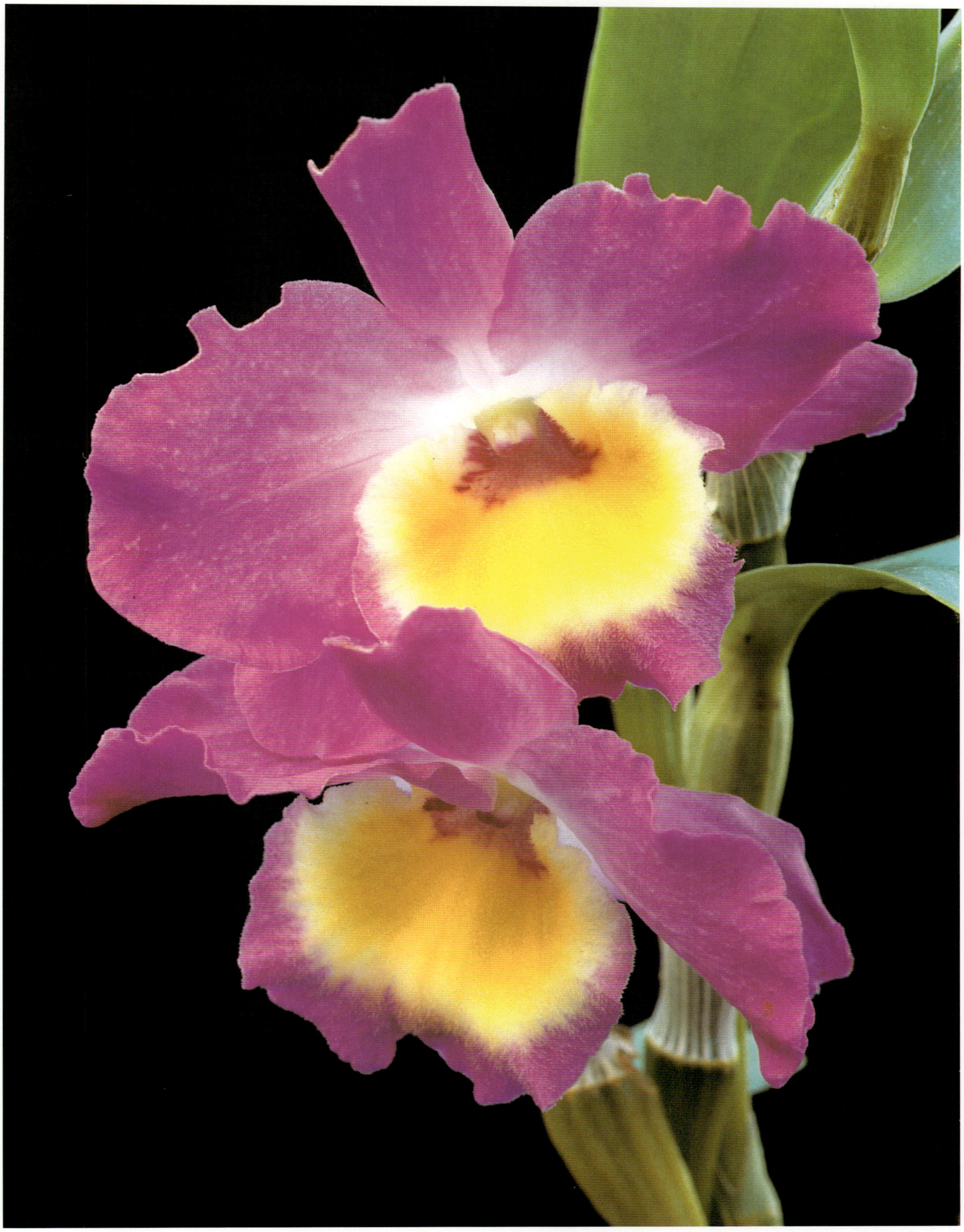

Glossary

anthers – the male parts of a flower in which the pollen is formed.
asymbiotic – germination and growth of seedlings without the use of fungi.
calcareous – associated with calcium, usually in the form of calcium carbonate as limestone or chalk.
capsule – a fruit which opens as it dries to release the seeds.
chlorophyll – the green pigment, found in most plants, which is involved in the conversion of sunlight energy into sugars.
corms – underground swollen stems found in some orchids and in plants like *Gladiolus*.
cultivar – a selected variety of a species or hybrid which in the case of orchids, has to be increased by division or tissue culture rather than from seed.
deciduous – losing all leaves for part of the year.
epiphyte – a plant which grows naturally on another plant without gaining direct nutrition from it.
inflorescence – the part of a plant which bears the flowers.
labellum – a modified petal, sometimes called the lip, and often used as a landing platform or attraction for pollinators.
lithophyte – a plant which grows naturally on rock.
monocotyledons – one of the two major divisions of flowering plants, including palms, grasses, lilies and orchids, which produce seeds with one cotyledon and have an endogenous manner of growth.
monopodial – a growth habit in which the stem may grow indefinitely over many years.
mycorrhiza – literally, fungus root. An essential relationship between a plant and fungus which works to their mutual benefit.
nectar – a sugary liquid secreted by plants, usually to attract pollinating insects.
nodes – those parts of a stem from which leaves arise.
ovary – the part of a flower which develops into the fruit, containing the seeds.
pseudobulbs – swollen stems which are above ground, as distinct from corms which are below ground.
resupinate – a situation in which the flower has the labellum or lip on the lower side, thus appearing to be upside down.
rhizome – a horizontal stem; in orchids, made up from the successive bases of shoots.
saprophyte – a plant which does not manufacture its own food, but obtains it from the soil. In the case of flowering plants, it is always with fungal aid.
sepals – the outer parts of a flower which enclose the bud. Tough and green in many plants, but colored in orchids.
sphagnum – mosses which grow in wet areas and found especially in temperate regions of the world. Such sphagnum bogs provide habitats for many kinds of plants, including some orchids and carnivorous plants.
staminode – a sterile stamen, or pollen bearing part of a flower; prominent in slipper orchids.
stigma – the female part of a flower which receives the pollen.
succulent – parts of plants, especially stems and leaves, which are thickened to store sap in dry environments.
terete – circular in cross-section, usually tapering.

Books for Further Reading

The Orchid Growers Handbook, I D James. 1988
Orchids as Houseplants, Rebecca T Northen. 1976
Home Orchid Growing, 4th Edition. Rebecca T Northen. 1990
Growing Orchids, Books 1, 2, 3, 4, J N Rentoul. 1980-85
Orchid Growing Illustrated, Brian and Wilma Rittershausen. 1985
Orchids as Houseplants, Brian and Wilma Rittershausen. 1989
Golden Guide to Orchids, Zim and Dillon Shuttleworth. 1989
Orchids for Everyone, Brian Williams and others. 1980

Index

Acknowledgments

The author would like to thank Dr Phillip Cribb and his assistant, Sarah Robbins for their invaluable assistance.

The publisher would like to thank Martin Bristow, the designer; Eleanor Stillwell, the editor and Helen Dawson for compiling the index. All illustrations are from the author's private collection except for the following:

Dr Phillip Cribb (private collection) Pages 61(both), 78(top left), 80(top right), 86(bottom), 88(top), 90(bottom), 91(bottom).